About the a̶u̶t̶h̶o̶r̶

David Whitburn studied both law and science at The University of Auckland. He worked for big-four chartered accountancy practice Deloitte, and then as a solicitor for Russell McVeagh, before immersing himself full-time in property investment. He started investing in property in 2002, and over the years has built up a successful property portfolio and also runs a popular education service for property investors. His corporate clients include two of New Zealand's largest banks.

David has been speaking at investment seminars and events since 2003, ranging from small local meetings to large conferences with many hundreds of attendees, and he has spoken to audiences in Australia, the United Kingdom and Malaysia, as well as many in New Zealand. He was elected to the board of the Auckland Property Investors' Association in 2004, and has held the offices of secretary and vice president, before being elected president in 2010.

David is sought after for his opinions and comments on the New Zealand property market. He appears frequently on national television, on radio, leading property and financial websites, in *New Zealand Property Investor* magazine, and in major New Zealand and international newspapers such as the *New Zealand Herald*, *Sunday Star-Times*, *Herald on Sunday* and the *Telegraph* (UK).

INVEST & PROSPER
WITH PROPERTY
HOW KIWIS CAN PROFIT FROM PROPERTY INVESTMENT

DAVID WHITBURN

RANDOM HOUSE
NEW ZEALAND

A RANDOM HOUSE BOOK
published by Random House New Zealand
18 Poland Road, Glenfield, Auckland, New Zealand

For more information about our titles go to www.randomhouse.co.nz

A catalogue record for this book is available from
the National Library of New Zealand

Random House New Zealand is part of the Random House Group
New York   London   Sydney   Auckland   Delhi   Johannesburg

First published 2011
© 2011 David Whitburn

The moral rights of the author have been asserted

ISBN 978 1 86979 753 9

Cover design: Carla Sy
Cover photo: Aaron Kirby
Text design: Graeme Leather
Printed in New Zealand by Printlink

This publication is printed on paper pulp sourced from sustainably grown and managed forests, using Elemental Chlorine Free (EFC) bleaching, and printed with 100% vegetable based inks.

Contents

Foreword by Kevin Green 7

Foreword by Sandy Richardson 9

Introduction 11

1   Why should I invest? 15

2   Why should I invest in property? 32

3   What do I need to know to get started? 37

4   Could I really become seriously rich? 48

5   Should I buy commercial or residential property? 51

6   What do I need to know to be a great investor? 57

7   What kind of goals should I set for my success? 65

8   What investment strategy is best for me? 73

9   How to get a great deal 94

10 How to find great properties 105

11 How do I check out a property? 113

12 How do I structure my property ownership? 116

13 What do I do about paying tax or getting tax rebates? 123

14 How can I find the money to invest in property? 132

15 What is a revolving-credit or offset account? 144

16 Fixed vs floating interest rates 148

17 How can I save money on my mortgage? 153

18   What type of loan is right for me?   159

19   How to structure your loan   167

20   What do I need to know about accounting and taxation?   172

21   Depreciation: making it as simple as possible   182

22   Renovate, redecorate and revalue   192

23   What do I need to know about valuations?   197

24   Keeping your investment safe   204

25   Managing your property   211

26   How to minimise the risks   239

27   Don't derail your own success   245

28   How to prepare an offer   248

29   Due diligence   258

30   Education   270

31   Useful websites   272

Glossary   273

Index   279

Acknowledgements   287

Foreword

by Kevin Green

It is a privilege to write this foreword for leading New Zealand property educator David Whitburn. I am proud to see him publish this book, and I have no doubt that David's intellect, investment experience and fine teaching skills will ensure it is successful.

I started my own journey as a struggling dairy farmer in Burry Port, near Llanelli in Southern Wales, in 1998. After winning the Nuffield Scholarship in Agriculture I interviewed and studied the likes of Sir Richard Branson and Bill Gates. This opened my eyes to the simple secrets of success as I saw who I wanted to be and knew I needed to change. I realised I had some knowledge gaps so I enrolled in an intensive property-mentoring programme as well as a number of advanced courses similar to those offered by David. This gave me the toolkit I needed for safety, certainty and speed in the growth of my portfolio.

I know this book will help to fill in some gaps in your knowledge, and will hopefully serve as the catalyst for your property-investment journey too. After buying my first property (I put the deposit on my credit card), I quickly renovated it and sold it at a profit, and bought another. The rest is history as I then went out and bought 80 properties in my first year, and now I hold hundreds of properties across the United Kingdom, with a portfolio value of over NZ$80 million. I now have my own bank in the United Kingdom, and serve the community as an ambassador to the Make-A-Wish Foundation and patron of the Hunger Project.

David shares my passion for property education. His book gives an excellent overview of property investment in New Zealand, including why you must invest, where you should invest, and an amazing chapter on strategies for investing in property. It also contains a lot of high-quality technical and general information. The glossary and references near the very end of this book have proved extremely useful resources for me as I sought to familiarise myself with New Zealand market conditions when I spoke at two large property investment seminars there.

I love New Zealand and have visited seven times now. It's much like Wales, just with better weather! After spending some quality time with David and his business partner David Leon, whom I have known for around a decade, I took up their invitation to join the advisory board of NZ Wealth Mentor Limited. Their teachings, professionalism, integrity and events are of a quality many educators aspire to, but so few reach. The feedback and results from David's clients has been nothing short of fantastic. I have seen David's insights, great client service and presentation skills in action, and we have shared the stage together at large events.

This book is an invaluable resource and is a must-have for the library of all New Zealand property investors. It will serve as a very useful manual for investors for many years to come.

Kevin Green
www.kevingreen.co.uk

Kevin is one of the United Kingdom's largest private social housing providers and a leading global property educator.
He has also starred in BBC's *Secret Millionaire*.

Foreword

by Sandy Richardson

Kicking off a brand new residential property investment team early in 2010 was an exciting time and I was looking for experts with whom to surround myself. A suggestion was made that I chat with David Whitburn, someone who had been investing in property himself from an early age. Not only had he trained as a tax accountant, he was also a solicitor, the vice-president, and soon to be president, of the Auckland Property Investors' Association and owner of a successful property investment mentoring company.

While working with David, I've found him to be a passionate individual who loves sharing his knowledge on property investment, so when he approached me regarding his book, I was very excited. It has been some time since a book focusing on property investment in New Zealand was released.

Having had the opportunity to sneak an early read of the book, I was amazed at the breadth of content David covers; it's going to be a great resource for people to refer to time and time again. Whether you are considering buying your very first investment property, or you already have several, there is something in here for every investor.

Of course, there is more to being a good property investor than just buying a good property — although this is a great start! Whether it be how you structure the ownership of your property, how you maintain and develop it or even manage the tenants who live in it, David covers all these topics and a whole lot more in this book.

Here in New Zealand we have many different investment options available to us, but for one reason or another, Kiwis have a love affair with investment property that won't go away. Perhaps it's the solidity of bricks and mortar, the fact a property is a tangible investment that can be seen, or is it something else?

David is the first to acknowledge that there's more to investing than property alone. However, in this book, through his respectful, expert approach, he proves that for many New Zealanders it's hard to go past bricks and mortar.

Sandy Richardson

Sandy Richardson is a sales manager at Bank of New Zealand and heads a team of property investment managers who specialise in residential property investment.

Introduction

How can you become wealthier? What are the right steps to take to grow your net worth and secure your financial future? I have asked myself these questions, and the answer was simple: invest in property correctly. My love of property doesn't stem from sentiment or nostalgia. It's the result of years of trial and error in the field of investing.

I began investing when I was very young, when we still had just two TV channels, the New Zealand cricket team regularly thrashed the Australians and one- and two-cent coins were legal tender. I started with savings accounts and loved seeing the interest grow each month. Next I moved on to term deposits. The returns were fine; I didn't lose anything, but I wasn't making much, and I felt disappointed with the amount of money eroded by inflation and tax. Then in the mid- and late-1990s at university, I started an event-management business with a friend. For a few good months we made plenty of money organising balls for university faculties before branching out to large corporate social clubs. However we virtually lost the lot on a disastrous event called 'A Night in Hawaii' — frankly, losing $18,000 was enough to put me off Hawaii forever.

By the time I was working in my first full-time job, at big-four chartered accountancy and consulting practice Deloitte, I was keen — probably too keen — to invest in a more exciting field. What could be more exciting than biotech shares in the dot-com boom of the late nineties? I was encouraged by my workplace share-club buddies, who seemed much older and wiser than me at the time. The New Zealand dollar was at 45c against the greenback and we all took a bath in the dot-bomb crash in 2000. I lost $25,000, which was just a fraction of what some of my colleagues were stung for, but I was only making a fraction of their salaries, so I guess it was all relative.

Then I read a few books about property investing, and I began to wonder if I'd found an investment where I could really succeed. But I wanted to be certain; I'd been burned too often to throw my money into the ring without any training. So I invested in myself by attending seminars to learn the rules (I'll admit that I'm a bit of a stickler for rules), and I continued to go to those seminars for nearly a year before I put any money into a house. In hindsight, I should have paid for a decent mentor, but I couldn't have known that at the time.

When I finally decided to put my money where my training was, I spent two months learning about my 'specialist suburb'. I chose to invest in Manurewa, in South Auckland, as I thought there was a good likelihood of making a positive cash flow. I spent all my weekends at open homes. At the time there were no real-estate websites, no Google Maps with Street View or Google Earth, no council GIS viewers, no Android and iPhone real estate apps, and none of the other useful and time-saving technology that we take for granted today. I had to physically visit properties all over my chosen region, spending hours driving around with agents in their cars. I looked at 45 properties in that area, and around a dozen in neighbouring suburbs. I made offers on a few, went to a few auctions, and finally arrived at an auction where I was the only bidder. In hindsight, it wasn't a brilliant buy. Nor was another of my early properties, a straight-off-the-plan development that turned into a minor headache.

But over time, I made money on these properties. I also learned that full-time employment wasn't for me. Despite a tidy salary rise I was earning far more from the capital appreciation of my property portfolio, so I left to immerse myself in the wonderful world of property investment. I needed to develop my 'street smarts'.

This was a key turning point in my life, as I learned the importance of growing my assets. I knew I would thrive if I totally immersed myself in the property market, and I've never yet lost any money on property to this day. That's why I am so passionate about investing in property. Even when I've made less-than-perfect (and sometimes regrettable) decisions, by changing my strategy and using my common sense I've been able to salvage a profit. I managed to survive the global financial crisis (GFC) without taking a loss on any of my properties, even though I sold one at what appeared to be the bottom of the market. 2008 was a near-impossible year — one of my companies owed double what it had due to it at one point. The company survived, everyone got paid, and I had grey hairs appear for the first time. Yet my long-term property investments keep humming along. In my opinion property investment is a fantastic way to multiply your money.

Not convinced? Historically, property prices just keep rising. Looking back, you can see that while your mortgage stayed the same or your repayments reduced it over time, your property became more and more valuable every decade so your equity kept increasing. There's no reason to believe that's going to change: provided you can meet your loan repayments, over time you'll make money. It does depend on taking a long-term view — a property's value doesn't track evenly along in an upward direction. Instead, it hops and jumps for a few years, then flattens out for a few more. Sometimes it might be three years of rapid gains, followed by seven years of flat prices.

Still not convinced? If you want to make money and have control over your finances, property investment is my top choice. Unlike passive investments, *you* get to call the shots. If things aren't going well, *you* can find a solution that will solve the problem or minimise the damage. The risks, though always present, can be managed.

Investor, trader, developer

Every homeowner has money invested in property, but that doesn't make every homeowner a property investor in the strict sense of the term:

○ A *property investor* buys property to keep for the long term, normally using tenants to generate cash flow.

○ A *property trader* buys a property to sell quickly for a profit. Some traders manage to sell property at a profit without doing any additional work to it (occasionally they on-sell on the day they settle), but most do some renovations to increase the value of the home.

○ A *property developer* buys a property and develops it to sell for a profit. The development can range from subdividing a plot and selling the sections to building an entire shopping complex and leasing the shops.

Property investors like me traditionally like to 'buy and hold'. That's a way of explaining that I buy houses but I don't often sell them. Instead, I hold onto them for the long term to take advantage of capital gain (the increasing value of properties over time). The ideal scenario is to retire with a portfolio where the cash flow from rent pays me enough to support my lifestyle. In fact, I know that this will happen for me a lot sooner than retirement age, so I can stop working. Wouldn't that be nice for you too?

'Yes,' you're thinking, 'nice for you. Never going to happen to me, though.' But it could. If you can:

○ sacrifice a chunk of your disposable income — invest it instead of spending it

○ learn everything you can about your new industry — and keep up-to-date

○ have a long-term view — and hang in there through the tough times

○ get a skilled property mentor to assist you with forming your investment strategy and to teach you 'how to fish'

○ manage your debt — and always make your repayments on time

○ get the right advice from a team of property professionals to assist you (your lawyer, accountant, banker, mortgage broker, property manager and so on).

Why have you picked up this book?

Do you want to grow your money and increase your financial know-how?

Financial success is the main motivator for most of the students I help train in property investing. For some, it's the desire to get out of the stressful cycle of being both cash-poor and time-poor; either one of those circumstances is enough to keep many students motivated. For others it may be the desire for an early retirement or a beach house. They may want enough passive cash flow to be able to educate their children at private schools or to take six-monthly overseas holidays. Some people want to be in a financial position to give back to their communities (churches, community groups, sporting clubs).

Whatever reasons and goals you have, it is critical that you have a plan for your own life: how you want to live it, when you will retire, and what your retirement will look like. Start with big long-term dreams and keep reading. You're on your way.

1 | Why should I invest?

What is your money doing for you? And more importantly, what are you doing with your money? It doesn't matter whether you're making $30,000 per year or $300,000, you probably spend most of your time working hard. Then when you get a break, you spend a good chunk of your disposable income on the activities that help you relax and forget about work — until Monday morning rolls around again.

If you spend all your disposable income on gadgets, toys and holidays, you're going to suffer a serious drop in lifestyle when you retire. (The same applies if you spend your money servicing giant credit-card or store debts at giddying rates of interest.) At present, when you hit retirement in New Zealand aged 65, you receive government superannuation of $17,676 after tax per year as a single person living alone, or $13,597 after tax per person if you are married, in a civil union or part of a de facto couple (where both partners qualify).

However, no matter what you earn, you can begin to control your financial situation by owning assets which both create an income and increase in value. Investing is where you put your money out to work for you.

Let's assume you still plan to retire at 65. You need to save to provide the income you want for around 20 years, because current statistics indicate that by 2031, 65-year-old men will be expected to live until they are 84 and women until they are 87. Statistics also indicate that at the current retirement age of 65, the average person has less than $6,000 income from other sources to supplement national superannuation.

Selling the family home and going out renting is not top of most retirees' wish lists! In order to have a steady cash flow in our retirement years, we have to own assets other than our family home. We don't want to have to cut back on eating, drinking, clothing, and visiting family and friends, so we need to plan for these expenses and have the right mix of assets to meet our living costs, which will rise over time because of inflation.

I love investing, and I share a lot of my passion for it in this book. Investing is absolutely fantastic; there are few sweeter phrases in the English language than 'passive income'. This means that you do not have to put in any personal exertion to make more money, so you're no longer on the treadmill of work–spend–work. When you invest, your money makes you more money.

Saving: not just for rich pricks

'Saving' is not a dirty word, although the average New Zealander seems to think that it is. I often encounter negative attitudes to saving — for instance, a nurse once told me that 'saving is for rich pricks'. Another stunning savings belief came from a tenant, who is unemployed and collects an invalid's benefit (although luckily his disability does not prevent him from pursuing his vocation as a PlayStation and Nintendo Wii gaming expert). He was complaining to me that he couldn't afford 22-inch chrome wheels for his lowered Subaru. I didn't bother to explain to him that his priorities needed examining, but I did ask him if he had any savings.

'Why should I save?' he replied incredulously. 'There's no point, the government will sort me out.' Unfortunately, with the amount of superannuation he's going to be getting from the government in retirement, he's not even going to be able to afford any new PlayStation games.

If you're reading this book, you probably have an inkling that saving some of your income is a good idea. I believe it's more than just a good idea, it's an essential lifelong habit. Savings should be as ingrained as brushing your teeth.

The simple rule is this: money makes money. It was true in the time of Shakespeare and it's just as true today. We can all make money; money doesn't evaluate its owner, it doesn't decide whether we are worthy. We control whether we have money or not — that is one of the beauties of capitalism. Those with capital (assets) such as bank accounts, equities or property are entitled to receive income from that capital. You receive interest from the money you lend to the bank or finance company. You receive dividends from companies you hold shares in. You receive rents from property you own. In addition there is capital appreciation (although obviously term deposits and other cash investments in the same currency don't appreciate unless the interest is re-invested).

Compound: bad news in hospital, great news in finance

Compound interest is an example of the way that money makes money for you. If you have a term-deposit account, you are a lender of money. You are lending your money (the principal) to the bank in exchange for a payment of interest, as well as receiving the principal back at the end of the loan period. Interest is the money paid by the bank (the borrower) to you (the lender).

If you reinvested your principal plus the interest you earned at the end of the loan, this higher amount would become the new principal figure. You will have created a larger sum of money from which you can earn interest. The new amount of interest is called compound interest.

Here's an example of what I'm talking about. Let's say Frances puts $40,000 (principal) on term deposit with her bank at 5% for one year. Now for ease of calculation I have assumed interest rates stay the same (they don't for any significant period of time) and that the return is net of tax.

Return on a $40,000 investment at 5% p.a. over 10 years

Date	Interest	Principal
April 2011	$0	$40,000
April 2012	$2,000	$42,000
April 2013	$2,100	$44,100
April 2014	$2,205	$46,305
April 2015	$2,315	$48,620
April 2016	$2,431	$51,051
April 2017	$2,553	$53,604
April 2018	$2,680	$56,284
April 2019	$2,814	$59,098
April 2020	$2,955	$62,053
April 2021	$3,103	$65,156

After 10 years Frances's principal would have compounded to $65,156, a rise of $25,156 from her original investment.

However, if Frances had spent the interest earned on the term deposit instead of reinvesting it, then her principal would have remained at $40,000. She would also have earned less interest, as each year she would receive 5% of her $40,000 principal, which is $2,000. Her total interest would be 10 years of $2,000 interest, or $20,000. Reinvesting the interest every year would have given Frances $5,156 of compound interest as well — and don't forget the additional principal.

The difference is even more marked over a 30-year timeframe — by earning interest on interest as well as principal, Frances's $40,000 would turn into $172,878.

Here is a graph showing the effect of compound interest in this example.

Compound interest at work

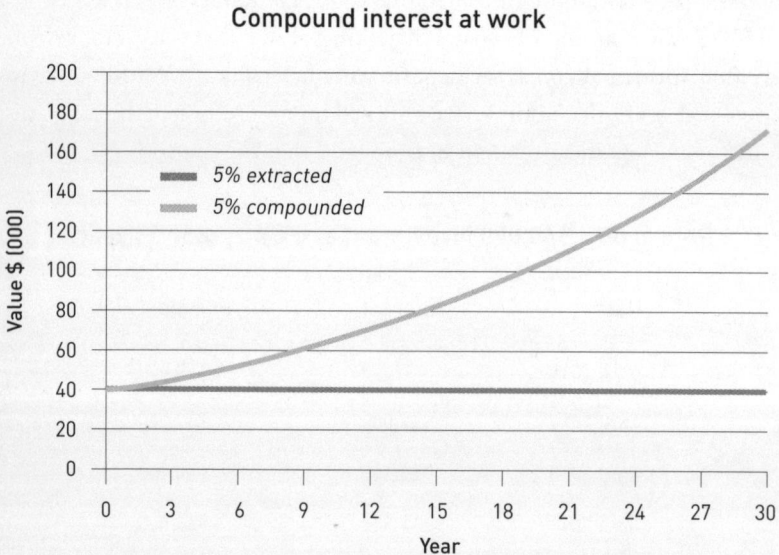

But my savings might get wiped out!

Gun-shy over disasters like Bridgecorp, Hanover Finance, Strategic Finance and Blue Chip? These finance companies, and numerous others, promised high returns but many investors (including many retired people) lost their savings. The promoters usually made some money though. These investments were simply too risky — I never did understand the logic of investing in these finance companies to potentially earn a 2.5% higher gross return, which after taxes is just over a 1.5% net return for most taxpayers.

I know that many are up in arms as their financial planners and advisors received good commissions for recommending these products. But at the end of the day, if you hand control of your money over to someone else, what can you really expect? The advisor wants to be well remunerated, and they often overlook the level of debt (or gearing) the finance companies carry, as well as the timing of the economic and property cycles. I think most financial planners do an outstanding job; the overwhelming majority are not to be blamed for the decimation of many of their clients' savings and retirement portfolios. Many Kiwis lost their nest eggs in 2008 and 2009, and part of that was down to a lack of financial knowledge.

I recommend that you buy an A-grade investment: direct ownership in New Zealand property. There are risks. The property market is cyclical. Property has gone down in New Zealand in some years (1990, 1998, 2000, 2008 and 2010 over the past 21 years). A property's price can drop (especially in small towns or rural areas), a house can burn down, tenants can trash your property, they can fail to pay the rent, and you might be unable to sell your property at the price you want. But property is something that has been around for a very long time, and I am going to explain to you how to greatly mitigate all of these risks.

This book goes through some of the safe ways to purchase property in New Zealand, and is not about being overly cute or clever. For example, you can, and should, insure the buildings on the land for total replacement value. But you don't have to insure the land. Over the medium and long term land goes up very nicely in New Zealand (except in small towns that depend on just one or two core industries, such as Moerewa in Northland — when the freezing works closed, land and property values plummeted). In cities (which I categorise as permanent populations over 50,000 people) land values don't plummet.

Why should I invest when the government can look after me?

Have you worked as a leading civil servant for many years, and are you just reaching retirement age? If the answer is yes, you can put this book down because the government genuinely will look after you well in retirement. Unfortunately, for everyone else, the government doesn't have enough money to look after you properly. (This is despite ever-increasing tax revenues over time.)

It's certainly not guaranteed that there will be a government pension available in 2050, and I believe that with our ageing population and the large number of baby boomers born between 1945 and 1964 starting to turn 65, the level of national superannuation will have to be reduced and the age of eligibility increased. So even if there is a pension in 2050, it is highly likely to be a pittance. If you don't want a retirement like this, you will need to save for yourself. This is the difference between existing and living. Invest and prosper.

Invest to become wealthy

There has to be a point to investing. Why not choose to become wealthy? Being wealthy means different things to different people. When I was on a boat travelling through western and central Laos along the Mekong River, being wealthy would mean having enough food and resources to provide for villagers' needs for a number of years. To me, being wealthy means having the financial freedom to choose whether to work or not. This also ties in with my goals of having enough time to do what I want, helping my children get started in life and having good health to enjoy a long and prosperous life.

Wouldn't you like to be able to choose where, when and for how long you go on holiday, or to have the clothes, car, house, bach and lifestyle of your dreams? By changing your financial habits, setting long-term goals and taking personal responsibility for achieving them, you can make a massive difference in your life, with a truly magnificent asset base and a passive income for you to enjoy.

What is your net worth?

It's important to know your net worth as it's the starting point for setting realistic goals. To measure your net worth we have a relatively simple equation:

$$Assets - Liabilities = Equity$$

There is a simple exercise I would like you to do at this stage, and that is to calculate your net worth. Here's a short summary table for you to complete.

Calculating your net worth

Assets	Value	Liabilities	Value
Own home		Home mortgage	
Investments		Investment loans	
Furniture and personal property		Furniture and personal property loans	
Car		Car finance	
Other		Other belongings	
Total assets		**Total liabilities**	

Your net worth can be regularly measured, and you can check that it is increasing over time, bringing you closer to achieving your financial goals.

But I need a new iPad! No, you don't

As I said earlier, the funny thing about money is that anyone can make it. Money doesn't discriminate or select its owners. Here's how:

○ You can't just be a sheep and follow the crowd. Do what you know is right and don't be swayed by the neighbours' new Subaru with 22-inch chrome wheels.

○ You have to get up early or go to bed late sometimes — because you need to hunt for deals when other people are sleeping.

○ You have to have self-discipline. That means not buying the latest phone, iPad, DVD or game. It means not going on expensive holidays, until you really can afford them.

○ You have to become a lifelong learner. It's essential to keep up to date with trends, new research and data. Reading about investing inspires even the most successful individuals.

Financial education in schools is very disappointing — most young people leave school sadly ignorant of even the most basic financial tenets. The number of 18- to 24-year-olds entering No Asset Procedure (low-value bankruptcy for debts under $40,000 that can't be repaid, excluding student loan balances), or becoming bankrupt has skyrocketed in recent years. Even a thorough explanation of how credit cards operate could have a major long-term impact on a 17-year-old's financial habits, let alone some understanding of the virtues of investing. But instead, the rapid proliferation of consumer finance to buy cars, furniture, computers, holidays — and the ease of getting personal loans for just about anything — has greatly assisted New Zealanders to spend more than we earn.

The main reason why so many Kiwis find it hard to save for their first house is ingrained bad spending habits. We need to separate needs from wants. Yes, we have to satisfy our needs: food, shelter and clothing, medical care and other essentials. That's not to say that we can't also have a few of our wants — in fact they can motivate us to achieve goals and also give us some quality of life. But instead of spending over $50 every Friday night at the pub, $1,000 a year on lottery tickets, $40 a week on coffee and $100 per week on 'stuff', you can indulge yourself slightly less and cut these costs by half, or eliminate them altogether, and put this money into debt reduction or savings.

We need to learn to distinguish our needs from our wants — and to focus on satisfying our needs, and prioritising our wants. If we don't, saving will continue to be a dying art.

What can I do to have more money?

I was lucky enough to come from a family where the financial basics were a way of life and a high value was placed on education. That allowed me to get a head start on success and wealth-building. But for many New Zealanders, their financial education consists of contradictory advice and old wives' tales.

Do any of these phrases sound familiar?

○ 'It's better to be poor because the government will look after me, so I don't have to look after myself.'

○ 'It's too hard to make money.'

○ 'I can't make money.'

○ 'Money is the root of all evil.'

○ 'You will lose all your friends if you become wealthy.'

I've heard all these statements from my tenants over the years. But I've never heard them said at a Property Investors' Association meeting. Wealth is a consequence of the actions you take — it's not just a prize.

Become an automatic investor

Here's the big challenge: put aside at least 15% of your gross income into debt reduction or savings. If you do this your savings will quickly build up. I know because I have been doing this each and every year since I was 10, when I started mowing my parents' lawns and vacuuming their cars, vacuuming my grandparents' house and selling Latin vocab lists to my classmates at school. I've had some other equally unenviable jobs, including turning ties inside out, pumping fuel at the petrol station and selling Christmas trinkets in a retail store.

Before I had my first full-time job as a tax consultant at Deloitte, my CV might have been unimpressive, but my savings account was nothing to sniff at. I'm not telling you this to brag, but to point out that you don't need to be earning loads of money in order to start squirreling away the kind of money that can one day turn into bricks and mortar.

Now I know that not everyone can just save 15% of their gross income straight away — however, I am certain that if most people drew up a budget and kept to it, 4% would be achievable, and given time at least 10%. Why don't you put your next pay rise directly into debt reduction or savings? Set yourself a goal to become an automatic investor or to save more.

Case study: Nicola (September 2011)

Nicola's income was $32,000 per annum. She was only able to save 2%, which she diligently put into her KiwiSaver account, and her employer contributed a further 2% as is compulsory. Nicola received a net amount of $2,174 per month. She then received a pay rise of $3,500 per annum, which meant she had a net income of $2,403 per month. Nicola put all of this extra money into savings — meaning that she was saving an extra $229 per month. She also received a further $8.75 per month in her KiwiSaver account (as her pay rise meant that her 2% contribution and her employer's 2% contribution were both higher, as well as the resulting increase in the government's Member Tax Credit of 50c per every $1 contributed up to $521.43 per year).

Debt reduction or savings?

When I get money should I reduce my debts or put it into savings? This depends on the rate of interest you are paying on your debts. I recommend drawing up a schedule of all your debts. To be a good financial manager, you have to always know your current financial position or be able to at least find this out quickly.

Take Chris, a tenant of mine, for example. I wanted him to pay his rent on time, and so I helped him to work out his debt schedule. He owed money to a finance company, which I'm not going to name, because despite being relatively skilled in the art of civil litigation, I don't want to be knee-capped by this particularly unscrupulous business. However, I must give my considered opinion: some personal finance companies are basically leeches preying on the strugglers in our community, wreaking financial havoc as they breach the Credit Contracts and Consumer Finance Act 2003 with their exorbitant 28.75% interest rates and all sorts of other unreasonable loan fees (random loan application, loan documentation, loan inspection, loan statement, and the 'We thought about your loan so charged you for it' fees).

This is what Chris's debts looked like:

Creditor and interest rate	Amount owed
American Express (standard 20.75% credit card)	$3,884
Visa (standard 19.5% credit card)	$2,372
MasterCard (low interest 11.99% credit card)	$1,220
Car finance (12.95%)	$12,700
Super Shady Personal Finance (28.75% interest)	$3,724
Total	$23,900

Where should he put his money first? The simple answer is to start with the highest interest rate and work your way down. In Chris's case, he should start with the Super Shady Personal Finance debt. If I were him, I would put all my effort into saving as much as I could and eliminating this debt. If

Chris leaves the Super Shady debt untouched, at 28.75% p.a. it would rise to $4,795, then balloon to $6,174 in two years' time. After three years, it would escalate up to a massive $7,949 mountain of debt, and there would be additional fees on top of this amount. So this debt must be paid first, and at an interest rate that high it must be paid as quickly as possible.

Next it is time to hit the American Express credit card as it has the second-highest interest rate at 20.75%, and then the Visa would be paid down third with its rate of 19.5%.

The car-finance company and low-interest MasterCard are a bit of a toss-up. It will depend on the terms of each agreement, including early repayment penalties (if any) on the car-finance loan agreement, and the cost of having the low-interest credit card (in terms of much higher than normal 'card fees').

Once you've made a list of your debts, in most circumstances you'll want to focus on one debt at a time, beginning with the highest interest rate and working your way down the list. Savings come second.

What about a balance transfer?

You might have spotted an offer for a balance transfer to a new credit card, which gets you 0% or very low interest on your credit card for six months. Is this a good deal?

Let's put it this way: do you think credit-card companies are charitable institutions? No. You know as well as I do that they are highly motivated controllers of money and debt. They have been around for an extremely long time, and I can assure you they are out to make as much money for themselves as possible. This is how it works:

1. You purchase an item during this special discount rate period using your new card, and you are charged interest at the standard rate, typically around 20% interest per annum.

2. If you try to repay the item you just purchased because you wanted to save interest, sorry you are out of luck. Your payment gets applied to the low-interest debt (the balance you transferred) first.

3. You're unable to pay all of the balance you transferred and, with tougher credit criteria, are unable to qualify for another card, or you transfer the debt to another supplier, or perhaps you've done your dash with all the credit-card companies. Then your six months is up and you get charged the full rate of interest, usually

around 20%. If you are really lucky you also get pinged with late-payment penalty fees, and in some cases administration fees, which also incur interest.

It's very easy to make money when you're charging interest rates of 20%. So control your credit card; don't let it control you. Don't let servicing your credit-card debt gobble up your ability to save.

What about my home loan?

Once your debts are paid off, is it better to put money into savings or paying more off your home loan? This comes down to a number of factors, including your personal risk tolerance. Some people I know hate having any debt, even a mortgage on their property, and they want it gone as soon as possible. Others want to save hard and don't care what level of lending they have on their home, or what the home-loan interest rates are, or the likely return on savings at the time.

I still currently have a loan on my own home, but I want to reduce its balance. However, I also want to save. What I do is pay down the principal on my home loan aggressively, and I save very hard too. Unlike a lot of people, I don't think a flash car is a boost to my ego, so I don't waste money on car repayments for a depreciating asset. (I notice that for many of my tenants, a car is their only asset, which is a pretty depressing idea — it's the only item they own of value and that value is dropping like a stone.)

KiwiSaver

What is KiwiSaver?

KiwiSaver is a government savings initiative administered by the Inland Revenue Department, to help provide for the retirement needs of New Zealanders. Approved providers are able to offer KiwiSaver products (managed funds) to New Zealanders. The choice is yours:

○ Some funds will be conservative, investing in cash and fixed-interest securities.

○ A little less conservative are the average-risk balanced funds, which invest in cash, fixed interest and some shares and property.

○ At the riskier end, aggressive or growth funds mainly invest in property and shares, particularly international shares (which historically have a higher return than shares in New Zealand).

KiwiSaver is designed to ease the retirement burden on our government, and to require some individual and employer responsibility for retirement funds. Employers have to contribute 2% (rising to 3% on 1 April 2013) of each employee's gross payment into their KiwiSaver scheme. As an employee, you can choose to contribute 2%, 4% or 8% of your gross income. You can make voluntary payments too. (If you're self-employed or a business owner you can also make voluntary payments.)

With over 1,000,000 New Zealanders holding KiwiSaver accounts, our government has put over $1 billion into KiwiSaver accounts in kick-starts alone. KiwiSaver is a very serious business; it's little wonder companies market so hard to get you to invest in their KiwiSaver funds.

Why should I have a KiwiSaver fund?

For a start, you get $1,000 given to you as a kick-start by the government. I enrolled my son in KiwiSaver when he was just five weeks old. He had $1,000 in his account three months later, and he didn't have to sign anything (I did as his parent and legal guardian). Two years on, with no additional contributions, it was worth nearly $1,200.

Even if you do absolutely nothing else to improve your financial position, why not open a KiwiSaver fund to get the initial $1,000 government contribution?

2011 Budget changes

In the May 2011 budget, the government halved the member tax credit (MTC), so it now contributes 50c for each $1 contributed by individual KiwiSaver members, up to a maximum of $521.43 per year (or $522.85 in a leap year). This means that the KiwiSaver year running from 1 July 2010 to 30 June 2011 was the last year the MTC was matched by the government up to $20 per week ($1,042.86 per year, or $1,045.71 in a leap year). Also, all employer contributions to employees' KiwiSaver accounts (and complying superannuation funds) will be subject to employer superannuation contribution tax (ESCT) from 1 April 2012. ESCT will be applied at a rate equivalent to each employee's marginal tax rate.

There will be legislation introduced shortly to raise the minimum employee contribution rate from 2% to 3% for all members from 1 April 2013 onwards. The default contribution rate for new employees who do not select a rate will also be 3% from that date. In addition compulsory employer contributions will rise from 2% to 3% from 1 April 2013.

Impact of the 2011 Budget changes

The scheme has gone from a gold-plated scheme to a silver-plated one. Essentially, you can contribute your own money up to $1,042 and get the government to give you a 50% return. Salaried and waged people have the bonus of employer contributions, currently 2% and rising to 3% from 1 April 2013. Despite the MTC change I will continue to put $1,050 per year into my KiwiSaver account, which means that I will receive the $521.43 MTC and have (at least) $1,571.43 invested annually. This is the level at which I intend to leave my own KiwiSaver investing.

However, you can contribute much more money than this if you wish. Currently you can elect to contribute 2%, 4% or 8% of your salary or wages to KiwiSaver. If you are self-employed or a business owner, then you will need to make contributions yourself, in which case you should consider contributing at least $1,042.86 by 30 June every year.

Personally, I don't like to invest more than the minimum amount, because you cannot withdraw all the funds until you hit the government-prescribed retirement age (currently 65) unless:

○ you move overseas for more than one year

○ you have a serious or terminal illness, or are permanently disabled from working

○ you suffer significant financial hardship (although you still can't withdraw the $1,000 kick-start government contribution or member tax credits), or

○ you buy your first home (although you can't withdraw the $1,000 kick-start government contribution or member tax credits).

First home subsidy

Another government department, Housing New Zealand, administers the first home deposit subsidy scheme. After three years of contributing at least 2% of your income to a KiwiSaver scheme, if you are buying your first home and are planning to live in it for at least six months, you can receive a subsidy of between $3,000 and $5,000 ($1,000 per year to a maximum of $5,000). There are price caps and technicalities covering situations where you have owned a home before. You can find out more at the Housing

New Zealand website, www.hnzc.govt.nz (search for 'first home subsidy'), or by calling the Housing New Zealand home ownership enquiry line on ph 0508 935 266.

KiwiSaver in action

Here's a real-life example of Dustin's investment in KiwiSaver. Dustin is a self-employed IT consultant in his early thirties. To make the table easier to follow I have treated his balanced fund as giving a constant net 4% investment return from the period after 30 June 2011. Check out Dustin's KiwiSaver account and the return on his investment:

Owner contribution	Government contribution	Total annual contribution	Investment returns	Closing balance	Date
$0	$1,000.00	$1,000.00	0	$1,000.00	30 June 2008
$1,050	$1,042.86	$2,092.86	$140.00	$2,952.86	30 June 2009
$1,050	$1,042.86	$2,092.86	$75.43	$5,121.15	30 June 2010
$1,050	$1,042.86	$2,092.86	$208.27	$7,422.28	30 June 2011
$1,050	$521.43	$1,571.43	$296.89	$9,290.60	30 June 2012
$1,050	$521.43	$1,571.43	$371.62	$11,233.66	30 June 2013
$1,050	$521.43	$1,571.43	$449.35	$13,254.43	30 June 2014
$1,050	$521.43	$1,571.43	$530.18	$15,256.04	30 June 2015
$7,350	$6,214.30	$13,564.30	$1,791.74	$15,356.04	30 June 2015

Dustin started in KiwiSaver in June 2008 (so no return was credited to him in that year). By 30 June 2011 he had invested just $3,150 of his own money, yet his KiwiSaver balance was now $7,422, an increase of $4,272 in just three years. Look at the return on investment (ROI) on Dustin's funds: a massive 45% per year from Dustin's start in June 2008 to June 2011. It's pretty hard to beat and maintain that, even with direct property investment, except on your first couple of properties in big boom years for property prices.

Dustin is projected to have a KiwiSaver balance of $15,356 in 2015. Not bad with only $7,350 contributed. However the changes to KiwiSaver and having more years in the scheme means that the ROI drops significantly for Dustin's KiwiSaver to 15.6%.

Dustin has the financial ability to put in considerably more than in previous years, but he has decided it is better for him to put the money toward reducing his home loan (a non tax-deductible debt). Also, he doesn't want to tie up too much money until he is 65 because he wants to focus on property investment, which he considers to be a vastly superior investment.

I'm too old for KiwiSaver

If you are already 65 years of age, then you are currently too old to enrol for KiwiSaver. However if you are under 65, I promise you are not too old, nor too young, for KiwiSaver. In January, I helped a client review her portfolio. I mentioned KiwiSaver to her and she asked, 'What is the point of KiwiSaver? I'm 60 years old and have a pittance of a superannuation fund coming to top up my investment earnings soon.' So I showed her the maths:

Owner contribution	Government contribution	Total annual contribution	Investment returns	Closing balance	Date
$0	$1,000.00	$1,000.00	0	$1,000.00	30 Sept 2010
$1,050	$521.43	$1,571.43	$22.50	$2,593.93	30 June 2011
$1,050	$521.43	$1,571.43	$77.82	$4,243.18	30 June 2012
$1,050	$521.43	$1,571.43	$127.30	$5,941.90	30 June 2013
$1,050	$521.43	$1,571.43	$178.26	$7,691.59	30 June 2014
$1,050	$521.43	$1,571.43	$230.75	$9,493.77	30 June 2015
$5,250	$3,607.15	$8,857.00	$264.40	$9,493.77	30 June 2015

By putting $5,250 of money down over five years in a conservative KiwiSaver fund, drip-fed by depositing in $1,050 by 30 June of every year, plus her conservative fund earning a net 3% return, she would have $9,494 as a nice sixty-fifth birthday present. My client is now looking forward to a simple $3,607 in government contributions and a little extra ($264) in interest, and getting a return of more than 70% in just over four years' time.

If you have a child under 16 years old, then there is no matching government contribution. However, the $1,000 kick-start applies at any age. My son Liam got into KiwiSaver when he was just five weeks old, and daughter Emily at two weeks old. So why not get your child started on the right financial footing and do the best you can for them too? There are KiwiSaver providers that have fee exemptions if you deposit regular amounts into your children's KiwiSaver funds. Maybe it can be a fun way to teach them the importance of saving and investing when they grow a bit older. It could be the start of their lifelong savings habit.

My recommendation on KiwiSaver

Get a KiwiSaver account; pass go and collect $1,000. Put at least $1,042.86 in it every year (and $1,045.71 in leap years). For many New Zealanders it is not easy to save this amount — so if you genuinely can't put this much in after applying as many debt reduction techniques as possible, then put in as high an amount as you can. The government will at least be giving you 50c for every dollar you put in.

If you can make a payment as high as the government's matching contribution level, that's great. To do this I recommend you, as an employee, select the correct percentage for you, whether that is 2%, 4% or 8% of your salary. This would be $13,075 at the 8% KiwiSaver payroll deduction rate, $26,150 at the 4% rate, and $52,300 at the 2% rate. You will get 2% of your salary contributed from your employer, too, which rises to 3% on 1 April 2013.

However, I am not a fan of contributing more than the amount of the matching tax credit from the government. This is because I would rather put my money into property, which has proven itself to be the best investment performer for a long time now.

2 | Why should I invest in property?

Now that you're convinced you need to invest and prosper, you need to decide what to invest in. There are many asset classes to invest your money in including:

- term deposits/cash
- forestry
- derivatives
- shares
- managed/pension funds
- art and antiques
- annuities
- bonds
- intellectual property
- futures
- Bonus Bonds
- currency trading
- commodities (such as gold, milk solids and oil).

Many people find the range of options extremely daunting; they can all be excellent choices, depending on your circumstances. Each option has its own set of risks and returns.

Low risk, low reward

Term deposits are extremely low risk. Even in the depths of the Global Financial Crisis in 2008, the government moved to guarantee New Zealand banks and accepted finance companies' deposit holders. But . . . in my work as a legal advisor and wealth mentor, I have met a huge number of wealthy people and none of them has made it by investing their money in the bank. Bank deposits are a great way to store some of your wealth but they are not a great way to grow your wealth. Property is far better for growth, though it is riskier than having cash in the bank. Well-managed forestry is low in risk, too, though not as low risk as term deposits. It's also low in reward; in recent times returns have gone southward due to reduced demand.

Medium to high risk, medium to high reward

Derivatives, shares, managed funds, bonds, futures, annuities — and property — all fall into this category. The more you understand each market, the better choices you can make. It's a lot simpler to learn the variables and drivers of the property market than it is to gain a thorough understanding of derivatives, for instance. Also, with property, you have much more control over your asset than you do with any of these other investments, which makes it my favourite investment choice.

High risk, high reward

Currency trading, art investing, antiques and commodities are all more likely to result in the loss of money and produce no income over time. If you make it big, the returns are huge. But if you get it wrong, it could cost you everything.

Property investment is my pick

Why do I love property investing so much? Unlike other investments, this is what property offers:

○ an inflation-protected investment with rents generally rising at least with wage inflation, providing you with a stable long-term income

○ capital growth for your investment — which is currently tax-free if you sell your property (unless you are a property trader)

○ leverage (using other people's money) — to magnify your investment returns

○ debt reduction — by repaying principal off your investment property loans over time, you have a forced savings plan, which rewards you with even greater cash flow and more equity

○ the greatest potential for huge returns as an active investor.

Many of the other investment choices mentioned in this chapter don't even provide a mechanism to keep up with inflation. Several of them you cannot borrow against. Investments like Bonus Bonds and term investments offer no capital growth.

The great thing about property is that everyone needs a place to live. Along with food and water, shelter is a basic human need. Slightly over one-third of the New Zealand housing market is owned by property investors (including the biggest investor of them all, the government's Housing New Zealand Corporation). Even after huge natural disasters like the 1931 Napier earthquake, which killed 256 people and decimated buildings in the Hawke's Bay region, and the September 2010, February 2011 and June 2011 Christchurch earthquakes, the housing markets in these areas did not collapse. Compare this to New Zealand's great financial disaster, the 1987 stockmarket crash, where the NZ Stock Exchange fell nearly 60% in less than two weeks. Even the till at the bar of the exclusive Auckland Club was robbed on Black Tuesday! Volatile markets such as commodity trading, where silver prices fell nearly 50% in four days in 1980, gold prices which lost half their value within a year (from US$850 per ounce in 1980), and subsequently fell to US$251.70 per ounce many years later in August 1999, show the risks of other types of investment. Property is a proven safe haven in New Zealand.

In my view, the New Zealand housing market is built on emotion. This is because nearly two-thirds of the market are homeowners, who do not care about the return they will make on their property. While capital gains are nice, they are not the driving force for their decision to buy a home. The distance to their work, family and friends, schools, tertiary institutions, shopping centres, and community facilities like churches and sporting grounds, and the number of bedrooms and bathrooms, are far more relevant factors. As a frequent attendee of auctions, I regularly see people who simply pay too much for their home, because they are emotionally attached to the property. Homeowners stay in their homes for a number of years, whereas investors in shares and commodities typically have much shorter ownership timeframes. Many homes are passed down through generations, particularly through smart ownership structures like family trusts. A simple comparison of listed companies 25 years ago compared to listed companies today shows how few have actually survived. All of this helps to stabilise the property market.

Even the banks think it's 'safe as houses'

In the past, I've tried to get loans from banks to buy their parent company's shares. Both banks I tried this with told me no, even when I wanted to borrow just 30% of the shares' market value. But both banks were more than happy to help me finance 80% of the purchase price of properties in New Zealand. Feel free to test this yourself! New Zealand's banks are renowned for being good at managing their money. So if banks will not lend on shares, even their very own shares, but they will lend on property, isn't this telling you something about the safety of property investment?

Furthermore the arbitrage opportunities available from direct property investment are tremendous. By 'arbitrage', I mean taking advantage of a difference in price — buying below cost and selling above cost. There are so many ways you can add value to your property or increase the cash flow you receive. Can you paint gold to make it more valuable? Nope. Can you buy shares below the current traded price on the sharemarket? Almost never. Can you give 60 days' notice to your bank that you are putting your term-deposit interest rate up, as you do when you are raising your rents? You wish!

The arbitrage opportunities in property are fantastic. You can add value and create value in so many different ways. Of course, while property investment can be an active investment or a passive investment, it will never be as passive an investment as owning a bar of gold, or having your money in term deposits. You will have to account for rental income received and file an income tax return. Gold does not provide you with an income stream (unless you are an active gold trader, buying and selling frequently).

And wait there's more — adding value through regenerating properties

You can also buy properties that are a bit tired or even extremely run down, and add value to them. This could be as simple as putting a couple of coats of paint on the walls. Or, you could build a permitted self-contained two-bedroom flat with its own kitchen and bathroom under the house, or reclad a house, or even change every surface area inside including new electrical and plumbing fittings, new kitchen and bathroom, or any of the numerous other refurbishments that I talk about in Chapter 22. I haven't been able to add value to shares I own in listed companies around the world.

Isn't property investing going to be a lot of work?

The short answer is yes. Property investment is an active investment in that you have to be actively involved in managing it. You need to go out and find the right property to buy, and do your research on it. In addition you have to ensure the cash keeps flowing, so even if you have a property manager (as opposed to finding, screening and dealing with tenants yourself), you still have to manage your property manager. You have to supervise and be responsible for any renovations, repairs and maintenance work, and pay for all outgoings. This all takes time. Direct property investment is an active investment. It is hands-on and is not without its risks.

If you choose a passive investment, you don't have to do all this work. For instance, you could buy a gold bar and put it in your fire- and theft-proof safe for a number of years. Or you could buy into a managed fund that tracks a sharemarket index, or invest in a term deposit, or buy shares in a listed property trust (like the AMP NZ Office Trust or Goodman Property Trust). These investments are much less work than property. The downside of a passive investment is the same as the upside: you have very little input. While that's great from a time-management perspective, it means you have little control over your investment and can do nothing to help improve your returns.

Because you can influence the outcome of a property investment to reduce the risks and increase the returns, I think the rewards on offer greatly outweigh the hard work. Plus, by avoiding the mistakes that most property investors make and by buying well in the right locations, you can set yourself up to thrive. Hours of polishing a gold bar won't make it more attractive to a buyer, but hours of polishing the presentation of your property could earn you thousands of additional dollars in annual rent or sale price.

3 | What do I need to know to get started?

Property investment is all about building an asset. Returns are mainly made from rental cash flow and long-term capital gain (the result of property values rising over time).

There are four ways to make money from property investment:

○ rental returns — net income from your property generated by the rent your tenants pay to you

○ capital gains — the value of your property rising over time

○ reduction in loan principal — leaving you with more equity in your property (the difference between what you owe and what it's worth)

○ tax rebates — the taxes you would otherwise have paid that are offset by some of the costs of being a landlord.

Let the rent flow in

A property which pays its own way is a great method for making money. This is the reason I love property — it can replace your income from work so you can have the freedom to choose how you spend your time.

This is what the numbers look like on a property I bought in 2004, a four-bedroom, no-frills weatherboard house and a three-bedroom minor dwelling in West Harbour, a north-western suburb of Auckland:

Total rental income	$38,740 per year ($745 per week)
Mortgage payments on loans of $280,000 at 6.5%	$18,200
Expenses on the property (rates $2,920, insurance $480, maintenance $2,500, property management fees $2,675, extras $300)	$8,815
Total pre-tax cash flow	$11,725 per year (just over $10,000 per year after tax)

Positive cash flow — it's not just a myth

I am sick of hearing there are no positive cash flow property investments left in Auckland. I am often told this by other investors, and sure, it can be hard to find positive cash flow properties in the major cities, but it is simply not true to say that they no longer exist. On a stand-alone three- or four-bedroom home this is unlikely to happen, but you have to think outside the square:

○ consider multi-income properties

○ what about building additional structures (with the council's permission)?

In early 2011, some clients bought a property in Auckland's Sunnynook, which is in a highly sought-after school zone. It was a home-and-income property with a self-contained flat downstairs.

The combined rent was $705 per week. The property had rates, insurance, repairs and maintenance and other expenses of around $5,300 annually. My clients were able to fix their mortgage at 6.49% for two years, giving them approximately $4,400 per year in positive cash flow — fully financed — in an area very well poised for significant rental and capital growth.

Values just keep rising

What were properties in your area selling for 10, 20 and 30 years ago? In almost every case, the prices were a lot lower than they are right now. In 1955, my grandparents purchased a section from a farm subdivision in Kohimarama, with fabulous sea views, for £600. Well, a lot has changed since then; that section is now worth $2,000,000. Even better, zoning changes have occurred over that time, so 55 years later it is sub-divisible into three lots, helping to lift the value even further. I had the title to this Kohimarama property mounted and framed, and it hangs in my office at home — it reminds me every day why I love the property game so much.

Here is why long-term capital growth is so powerful:

Growth in market value of my grandparents' section

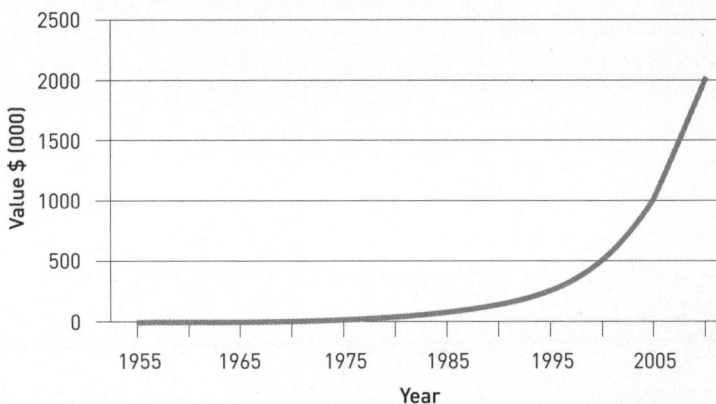

The hard work was done in 1955, by buying the land at a good price and choosing a great location. Since the early 1990s the growth has been virtually exponential — this is a fine example of money being allowed to do its thing and multiply. Money is very good at making more money.

With growth like this, and no reason to suspect that over time property prices will not rise handsomely as they have done for most of the past 100 years in New Zealand, why wouldn't you invest and prosper with property?

The rule of 72

I am a huge data geek. I love statistics and subscribe to virtually all of the statistical reports I can. It might not be most people's idea of fun, but I get the latest releases from Statistics New Zealand, all the leading New Zealand banks, the Reserve Bank of New Zealand, and numerous other providers in New Zealand and around the world. I read anything and everything related to property statistics. By looking at all the data, I can draw a picture of the state of the housing market at every level. I'm not saying you need to do this to be a successful investor, but it has certainly helped me.

My love of numbers started early, and one of the first property-related tricks I learned was from my grandfather. He taught me the rule of 72, which calculates the time it takes for an investment to double in value — the time taken (in years) for an item to double in value, multiplied by its growth rate, is equal to 72. Check it out for yourself. All you do is divide the growth rate by 72 to get the number of years that your property will take to double in value:

The rule of 72

Growth rate %	Apply the rule of 72	Years to double
36	72 ÷ 36	2
24	72 ÷ 24	3
10	72 ÷ 10	7.2
9	72 ÷ 9	8
8	72 ÷ 8	9
7	72 ÷ 7	10.29
6	72 ÷ 6	12
5	72 ÷ 5	14.4
4	72 ÷ 4	18
3	72 ÷ 3	24
2	72 ÷ 2	36
1	72 ÷ 1	72

Why do I like looking at this so much? Over the past 50 years of data, New Zealand has an average annual capital growth rate of 8.1%. This means that properties will double around every nine years. In Auckland, the nation's economic hub and by far our most populous city, the demand for housing means the annual capital growth rate is even higher at 9%, which indicates that properties will double every eight years.

The power of leverage

How to magnify your investments with leverage

Smart use of leverage can magnify your capital gain, and it can be the tool that gets you started in property investing. Here's a simple example of leverage at play:

A friend, Victoria, recently purchased a three-bedroom, 90m² house in Newlands, Wellington, as an investment property for $280,000. If the area's annual capital growth is a conservative 7%, the property's projected value in 10 years will be around $550,000.

If Victoria leverages her investment by having a bank loan, that loan will not grow. If she has an interest-only loan, it will stay the same. If she has a principal and interest loan, where she starts to pay off some principal, the loan will begin to reduce.

Let's assume she takes a 10-year interest-only loan. Victoria had saved up $56,000 of her own cash, (which included $6,000 borrowed from her parents) and the bank was prepared to lend her 80% of the purchase price. (I'm ignoring income and expenses for now, just to illustrate the concept of leverage.) Take a look at this graph, which shows the projected capital growth of the property Victoria purchased at $280,000 with an 80% loan of $224,000:

Capital growth over 10 years

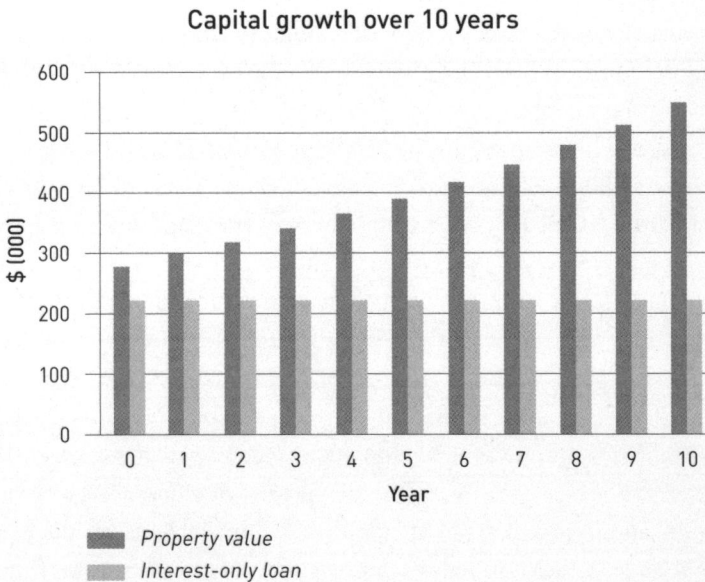

Victoria's property is worth $551,000 in 10 years' time, yet her loan balance has stayed the same. This means that Victoria will still owe the bank $224,000, but her equity in the property will have skyrocketed to over $320,000 once she has reimbursed her parents for their $6,000 interest-free loan.

Using leverage to get you started

My first direct experience of leverage was when I tried to open a margin loan account with a stockbroker (an account where the broker lends the buyer some of the funds to purchase the shares). I knew that margin loan accounts on shares were common in overseas markets; even though I'd set up an online margin loan account in the United States in the late 1990s, I wasn't able to set one up in New Zealand. Fortunately, senior stockbrokers told me that because of the erratic and general underperformance of the New Zealand stockmarket, margin loan accounts were seen as far too risky by the lenders and investors alike. (Apparently such loan accounts now exist, but they are still not widely used at all.)

There was absolutely no point getting a margin account to invest in term deposits or cash — I would be losing money. The length of time and the risks associated with forestry didn't appeal to me. There were no other investments which I understood well enough to consider. So the first time I used debt to help fund the purchase of an asset was also the first time I purchased a property.

I bought a house in South Auckland for $140,000 in 2002, with a 95% loan plus $7,000 I had saved. After some quality time with agents visiting a number of properties over a couple of weekends, and my own personal research into the area, I made an offer on this property. The bank charged a low equity fee or lender's mortgage insurance premium (as is typical for loans greater than 80% of the lesser of purchase price or valuation) of $2,200, which was added to the loan principal of $133,000, so my initial loan was for $135,200. With a bit of assistance from my work colleagues at Russell McVeagh, I was able to do my own conveyancing work and slash my legal fees on the job. By asking lots of annoying questions to property solicitors and legal executives at staff drinks, I was able to get the hang of the legal side of the deal. I also scrounged hordes of information from the property team to study in my own time — hey, I know it's probably not your idea of fun, but I love learning!

Well, not much happened to values in the first year. I didn't care about that; I was getting a positive cash flow from owning the property, and some attractive tax rebates. I also managed to pay the loan down to under $125,000, resulting in lower interest expenses and greater equity. From 2003 to 2004, the property's value went up by around 10%, to $154,000. This meant my equity in the property had climbed from $7,000 to $29,000 — not bad. The year after that, it appreciated about 10% again. A registered valuation valued the property at $169,000. So, even without reducing my loan balance between 2004 and 2005, I now had $44,000 of equity.

In three years my equity in this property had risen from $7,000 to $44,000 — more than 600%. That is leverage in action. Back then I simply couldn't have afforded to purchase the property without leverage — so leverage has been very helpful to me. How many other investments can make you over six times your money in three years?

For newbie property investors, you'll often need a high level of leverage — perhaps even 100% if you are borrowing against the equity that you have in your own home. As you grow your portfolio, your lenders will check your debt levels and try to reduce you down to a 65% or lower loan-to-value ratio (LVR). The LVR is the percentage of loans that you have against the value of the property or properties you own. For example, if you had a $300,000 loan secured against a $400,000 property, you'd have 75% LVR on that particular property. If you had a $5 million property portfolio (by value) and $2 million of loans against it, you would have a 40% LVR.

Leverage in action

Julia is buying an investment property for $290,000. Assume that the properties all have interest-only loans (a loan with no deduction to the loan principal), the capital growth rate is an even 7.5%, and we ignore income and expenses for the purposes of this demonstration. There are three debt scenarios for us to examine:

○ no gearing (no loans) at all — the top dark-grey line in the graph overleaf

○ 50% gearing — the middle grey line

○ 90% gearing — the bottom black line.

Now which line do you think shows the best return on the funds Julia committed? It may appear at first glance to be the top line (the property with no leverage on it) as it is higher than the other lines. However the bottom line is by far and away the best return on investment.

Why is the bottom line the best result? Because Julia is only contributing $29,000 (10% of the purchase price), which balloons up to a value of $597,000 (the property's total value of $858,000 minus the borrowings of $261,000). This is a truly massive internal rate of return (IRR) of 131%.

Julia's net equity under different gearing scenarios

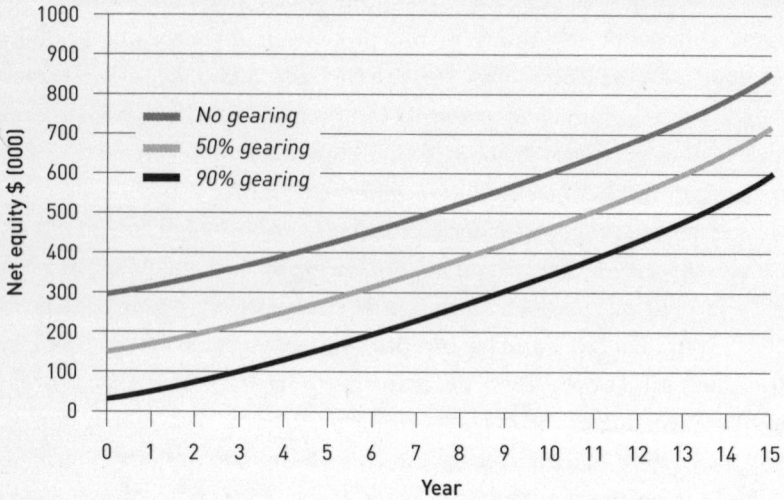

The 50% leveraged property also performed well with a very good 26% IRR, but the unleveraged property was far more mundane in its returns, achieving a 13% IRR.

Leverage lets you grow

Now (cue dramatic music) fathom the massive power of leverage on five properties! If you had $290,000 to invest, instead of just buying one property, why not put down a 20% deposit ($58,000) on five properties, each worth $290,000. Look what happens to your equity over time:

Leverage in action

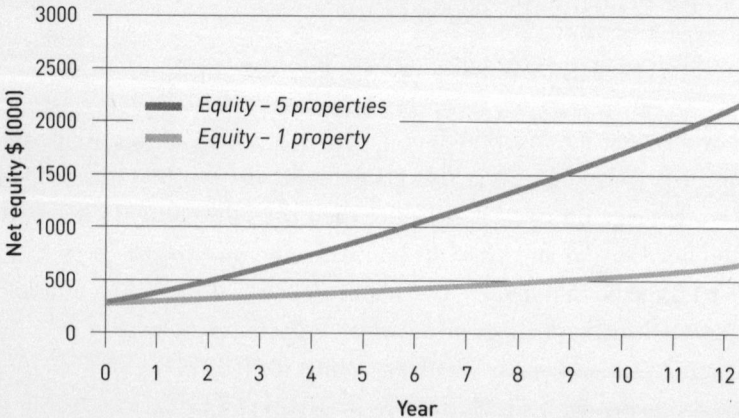

So if you had $290,000, your wealth would grow far more quickly if you could purchase five properties, putting $58,000 down on each purchase. Instead of having $800,000 in 15 years' time, you would have amassed an amazing $2.84 million. A sensible amount of leverage on appreciating assets is the key to wealth.

The leverage available in property investment is the reason why I believe that property investment is the best investment you can make. Sure you can get leverage on share accounts to 50% of the value of your portfolio in New Zealand now (and in overseas jurisdictions to 70%), but the interest rate that you pay for the margin loan is much higher, the loan terms are shorter (how many share investors get 30-year loans?), and the shares themselves are more volatile. As a result you may have 'margin calls' on your loans, which require you to suddenly put in equity when the value of the shares drops, to keep your loan-to-value ratio in check. This is extremely common with margin investment, and is risky for undercapitalised investors.

Many share investors became insolvent during this last recession when the sharemarkets dived over 20% in September and October 2008, which older traders compared with Black Tuesday in 1987 — a date powerful enough to still conjure nightmares for many New Zealanders. Our stock exchange index took nearly a full decade to recover from Black Tuesday, but property was hit far less severely and took just a fraction of the time to recover.

A word of warning on leverage

The property market doesn't actually move in a straight line, but in cycles. Towards the end of a property boom, access to credit frees up and products like low-doc and no-doc loans come into being again, as the eyes of the finance company owners light up. It's at this point when people think that prices have been rising for so long that they can never come down. Sadly, leverage works just as effectively, and often more brutally, when values fall. I know investors who were heavily leveraged in 1997 and 2007, then when the market turned and values dropped by 10%, they were forced by their lenders to put in more equity. They couldn't put in any extra cash, because they didn't have any, so they had to 'fire-sell' their properties at a bad time in the market to reduce their debt to keep their lenders off their back.

We have distinct property cycles in New Zealand and this was merely another one. 2008 was a negative year for property investment, with values dropping 11% across New Zealand. There was a mini-recovery in 2009, only for values to drop a little in 2010. The market is by no means uniform

Do you want to be an investor or a trader?

Property investing is not the same as property trading. Property trading is where you own properties for a short period of time and then sell them, aiming to turn a profit. Property trading is a business activity by itself, and is likely to be a 'taxable activity' under the Goods and Services Tax Act 1985, so it's subject to GST as well as income tax on profits made.

Property trading includes:

▷ buying a property below its true value and on-selling immediately

▷ renovating a property and selling it for a profit

▷ developing a property and adding a room or dwelling, then selling it. Additions could include an extra bedroom, doing a garage conversion, constructing a sleepout, minor dwelling or additional house on your land

▷ subdividing a property and selling all or part of it.

If this may apply to you, make sure you read Chapter 20 for more information, as becoming a property trader has big implications for all of your property investments.

either, so some areas may be going backwards, some doing nothing and others going forward nicely.

If you have under $500,000 of borrowings, your banks will probably not mind if the property market goes down by 10% in value, even if you bought at the peak of the cycle just a year prior. They have bigger fish to fry, and catch up with, so will generally just ignore you as long as you remember to meet all of your loan repayment obligations.

Debt reduction

It is critical to keep your own level of borrowings in control. Just because you have qualified with a lender for a loan, it doesn't mean you are safe — you need to do your own risk analysis.

Property investment can be like a forced savings plan. Often banks ensure you have principal and interest loans, so every payment you make includes some repayment on the principal (reducing the loan balance). If you have your own home, this is the number-one priority for payments — because it's not tax deductible. When you own investment properties and a home, you should negotiate with your lenders so that you have your investment properties on interest-only loans as much as possible. This allows you to be as aggressive as possible when it comes to paying off your own mortgage. You want to have a freehold home because interest on it is not tax deductible (unless you are using the loan for a business), and for the additional security it gives.

Tax rebates

There are a number of tax benefits in having an investment property. Almost every expense relevant to running your property business is tax deductible. However, in the May 2010 budget, New Zealand finance minister Bill English announced that a tax deduction for depreciation on building structure would be scrapped. This change took effect on 1 April 2011. Investors have never been able to depreciate land — the government is smart enough to realise that land goes up in value over time.

4 | Could I really become seriously rich?

If you are serious about becoming wealthy, even an exceptionally high salary won't cut the mustard. Income is merely one part of the equation. You need to invest and prosper.

My clients include Ian and Amanda, who work as a florist and a cleaner, two jobs which don't earn them high salaries. Another couple are Graham and Rebecca, a doctor and an accountant (in fact, Rebecca was a partner in a decent-sized firm) and these two earn a very impressive total income fully six times greater than Ian and Amanda.

Would you be surprised to hear that Ian and Amanda, the florist and the cleaner, were millionaires? Yet Graham and Rebecca were nowhere near achieving the same kind of net worth. Ian and Amanda had been investing a lot longer — so they had their money out working for them, while Graham and Rebecca were busy being busy, and not making saving a priority.

If you spend all you earn, it doesn't matter whether you earn a paltry $20,000 per year or a massive $2 million per year. The point is that you need to save money. Your savings become your assets. So put aside only what you need, and convert the rest into an asset like a property, which then becomes your savings. This asset will be working for you to increase your wealth.

Make money while you sleep

Passive income is what every investor wants: making money while you sleep (or read, or sunbathe, or manage other investments). Your tenants work for you by paying their rent. The market works for you to increase wage inflation and rents, as well as give you capital growth. So your income from property keeps flowing irrespective of where you are or what you're up to. When it comes time for you to stop getting an income from your job or business, passive cash flow will provide for you.

How you get your passive income is your decision to make. I employ a diversified strategy where I have a strong foundation in shares, managed funds, cash and property, but as property has overwhelmingly performed the best for me, I have my investment portfolio heavily focused on property investment. I'm not the only investor to discover this; many of New Zealand's most prolific landlords began investing in shares and managed funds only to find that property outperformed their other investments.

I believe that when it is the right time for you to draw income from your investments alone, that you should not be overly exposed to one asset class. A mix of cash (term deposits), shares/managed funds and conservatively geared property is likely to be most desirable investment mix. However, if you have millions in equity and fantastic cash flow from your property portfolio, diversification will not be as important for you.

Your most precious resource: time

The greatest asset you have is time. We all have the same amount of time, and none of us can make more of it. Time is the only constant factor in property investment. In life we need to be able to master our use of time. If you were designing the life of your dreams, how much time would you allocate to working? The idea of working from the age of 22 to 70 (a grand total of over 12,000 days) sounds a bit like voluntary slavery to me. So I am living life my way and getting a buzz out of helping others to do the same.

I want to empower you to open your eyes to a better way of life. If you are an employee, your income is dictated by the hours you work at your job. If you are self-employed, your income is still dictated by how many hours you work, though it's nice to have more flexibility and some tax breaks. The ideal scenario is when you have streams of passive income. By becoming the owner of a business with assets (like property), you can put people and/or technology in place to work for you.

This is how it works for me: I own a number of investment properties, which provide me with solid streams of rental income, plus I receive dividends from shares, distributions from managed funds, income from my property mentoring business, and royalty and licence fee income for intellectual property I own or control.

If we let assets do the work for us to set us up for life, we don't have to work thousands upon thousands of days to achieve this. I know I keep saying it, but this is what I really believe: invest and prosper.

Owning assets is absolutely vital. These assets provide you with a passive income, and equity growth, to fund your retirement, and allow you to provide for your family's needs. And, if you are successful enough at making money, they can provide you with some or all of your wants as well. Passive income gives you options in life.

The truth about money

Here's the thing: money has no personality. It really is very boring. Money is really only reliably good at one thing — it's excellent at making money. It doesn't know or care who owns it — it just wants to go out to work and make more of itself. The world's money supplies are not dwindling. Quite the opposite. In Britain and the USA, whose economies were severely hit by the global financial crisis, there has been a large amount of quantitative easing going on. Or, more bluntly put, printing money — many billions of dollars. As much as you might like to print money for yourself, that's not an option, but you can make a serious amount of money legally if you can follow these three rules:

▷ master the art of being disciplined

▷ put aside at least 10% of your pay into savings

▷ employ sensible money-making strategies.

Money is not the root of evil and it's not the path to happiness. Sure, there's no doubt some of the world's money is put to evil purposes. But there's nothing inherently amoral about a dollar. You can help to change the old saying by being a good person and putting your money to good use. With enough money for yourself, you can give a lot of time or money to your chosen not-for-profit organisations. From being on the committee of your local tennis club to funding cancer research to helping at your child's school or volunteering at the City Mission, the choice is yours. Rather than being a force for evil, the more money and time you have, the more you will be able to devote and give to your charity or community.

5 | Should I buy commercial or residential property?

I love property, whether it's commercial or residential. I love the outstanding returns that can be achieved in both fields. For me, there are five types of commercial property: office, retail, industrial, hospitality and farming.

The differences between commercial and residential property are significant. For starters, in commercial property you have a lease and the Residential Tenancies Act 1986 doesn't apply. Also, comparable sales take a massive backward step in commercial property. The yield is far more important, and valuations are done by the capitalisation rate method (see Chapter 23 on valuations for more on this). Vacancy rates are often higher and you have far less control over them.

The five types of commercial property

Offices

As an investor in an office, you purchase a property that is set up for a business to operate from, usually in the CBD, but sometimes in service suburbs of cities or small towns. Typical clients are lawyers, architects, engineers, accountants, bankers, insurance underwriters and brokers, and other similar businesses. Office buildings are often extremely expensive to purchase, particularly in Auckland and Wellington. As a result, prime (first-grade) office property is very hard for individual investors to finance and acquire. One of the most well-known commercial property owners is the AMP NZ Office Trust. The trust owns an impressive portfolio which includes the Auckland properties 21 Queen Street, 151 Queen Street, and the PricewaterhouseCoopers Building; and in Wellington, the State Insurance Tower, Vodafone on the Quay, HP Tower, and 125 The Terrace.

Retail

Retail tenancies range from small shops and dairies all the way up to giant department stores like Farmers and The Warehouse. Location is critical for retail; tenants rely on foot traffic for sales and much of this is dependent on location. Giant malls like Sylvia Park in Mt Wellington, Auckland, make it much harder for smaller retailers in the surrounding areas. However these malls also command high rents, so the market soon settles down.

Industrial

These properties house our nation's manufacturing industry as well as other industries like shipping, storage, petro-chemical plants, timber yards, brewing, mechanics, panelbeaters and numerous suppliers and distributors. The properties are often constructed in tilt-slab concrete or solid block, and have a concrete-slab foundation. They are usually hard-wearing and difficult to damage.

Hospitality

This category's tenants include motels, hotels, restaurants, nightclubs, hospitals and entertainment centres such as cinema complexes.

Rural

Farms are the key tenants for rural property. Different areas will be suitable for different uses. Farms are leased for things like dairy farming, viticulture, aquaculture and horticulture. The terrain, cost of acquisition of the land for the owner and climate are important considerations.

Many commercial property investors say you'd have to be nuts to manage residential rentals. They believe that commercial property is brilliant because all you have to do is check your rent each month and get a competent property lawyer. However, the catch with commercial property is that many investors cannot tolerate high vacancy rates, and this last recession has been particularly tough on commercial property owners. An investor I know had a property in Glenfield (on Auckland's North Shore) vacant for nine months in 2009 and 2010. Other commercial investors have had properties vacant for over two years in smaller provincial towns, and I heard from one investor that his just-built office and industrial warehouse (in Auckland's Albany) couldn't find a tenant for 18 months at the start of the last downturn.

Sadly, statistics indicate that over 80% of companies do not survive their first five years. Therefore tenant selection is very important. If you can master the art of finding good tenants relatively quickly, then commercial property can be a fantastic investment.

With commercial property it's all about dealing with contracts, whereas with residential property you are dealing with people.

Comparison between commercial and residential property investment

	Commercial	Residential
Vacancy rates	Low–medium usually	Low usually
Capital growth	Good	Very good
Valuation method	Cap rate	Comparable sales
Management	Easy	Hard
Rates	Tenant usually pays	You pay
Repairs and maintenance	Tenant pays for operational things like painting exterior; you pay for structural things like reroofing	You pay all repairs and maintenance costs (although you might get away with the odd light bulb that the tenants pay for)
Entrance	Harder to get into	Relatively easy access to this market
Financing	Based on the valuation	Based on valuation or purchase price, whichever is lower
Your contribution required	30% to 40% of valuation	Usually 20% to 30% of the lesser of purchase price and valuation

Financing commercial property is usually more difficult than residential property, too. You need to present an attractive proposal to a bank and have a deposit of 30–40% of the valuation of the property. At the time of writing, most lenders are not lending on vacant commercial property.

Commercial property investment works as follows: the tenant leases the property from you, and typically will pay you a monthly rent. The tenant will generally be responsible for all outgoings (including land rates to the relevant council(s), repairs and maintenance, water charges). The terms are covered off in a deed of lease (or lease agreement) between the landlord and tenant.

This deed of lease will generally provide for rent reviews, so the tenant has at least one right to renew the property for a certain fixed period. For example, you may have heard of a '5 + 5 + 5' tenancy. This is a five-year lease on a property, which gives the tenant two further rights to renew their tenancy, so after five years they can renew their tenancy again, and after 10 years they can renew again. A deed of variation to the deed of lease or new deed of lease could be signed up if the tenant wanted to stay in the same property for a longer period of time.

Rent reviews are an important mechanism in commercial property. Often rents are adjusted upwards by the Consumer Price Index (CPI) amount every year, or by a fixed rate as agreed by both parties each year. Sometimes a valuation is done on the property at a regular interval (say, every three years) to provide and reset the new rent level.

In times of high vacancy, such as during the 2008 and 2009 recession, rents can go down, as landlords with vacant property will reduce their rents just to get some income coming in. A number of commercial leasing agents have told me that commercial rents for second-grade office properties in 2010 were much the same as they were in 1987. Location is clearly vital in office property.

Can I buy commercial property without much money?

While I am usually sceptical of buying properties with no money down, with commercial property I feel a bit more positive. Occasionally, financing commercial property can be easier than financing residential property — and with no money input required. This pleasant situation typically happens when you find a tenant to go into a vacant commercial property, and sign up the tenant to occupy the property conditional on your purchase settlement of it. In your agreement with the vendor you have the purchase conditional upon finding a tenant.

Since valuation of commercial property is based on capitalisation rates (cap rates), an area may have a cap rate of 7%. With no tenant the property still does have a value, often the land value only. You would purchase the property for a song, say around $500,000, and then when you get a tenant signed up to pay $56,000 rent per year + GST + expenses, you would declare your agreement unconditional. You would then instruct the valuer to appraise the property and give them the tenancy agreement for the new tenant you have signed up. They would apply the area cap rate of 7% and thus a value of $800,000 would be achieved. Note that in commercial property the purchase price isn't very relevant — the valuation is key. If your bank's lending policy was to lend 65% of the valuation, then they would offer to lend you up to $520,000 (65% of the valuation figure of $800,000). Remember that your purchase price was just $500,000, so after spending around $2,000 in valuation fees, $3,000 in legal fees, $1,500 loan establishment fees and $500 in other costs, you would actually receive $13,000 from purchasing this property.

This is not easy to do, as it is a real skill to find a tenant that wants your vacant property and to negotiate a purchase with terms flexible enough to ensure a no-money-down deal like this can occur. It's particularly hard when tenants have a lot of choice with hordes of 'for lease' signs in windows and websites flooded with properties to lease. However, it is possible, and the wise investor who can pull it off can make a lot of money.

Commercial versus residential property

Let's be honest, I like almost every kind of property. Both commercial and residential investments can be fantastic ways to get the lifestyle and retirement of your dreams. Equally, either can turn into an absolute shocker that stresses you out and actually harms your finances! But that only happens if you are reckless, have poor property knowledge or make a poor decision.

The difficulty with commercial property is that it is a lot harder to finance, and the market is hard to read. The mainstream media all regularly report on the residential property market. However, the commercial property market doesn't get anywhere near as much coverage. The commercial property market is perceived as a bit of a male-dominated 'old boys' club', with commercial valuers, agents and investors being predominantly male. Compared to residential property, commercial property is far more closely held, with massive holdings owned by big players like New Zealand's rich-listers, big offshore companies, massive national institutions and super-annuation funds.

The average commercial property deal is more expensive than a residential one, and you will need to put in around 35% of its value from your equity. Therefore commercial property is generally harder to finance. Usually only small apartments (less than 40m²) and leasehold properties are as difficult to finance in residential property. You have a much smaller pool of potential tenants in commercial than residential property. That said, when you find a tenant they will in all likelihood be with you for much longer periods of time. As a commercial landlord, you are intrinsically linked to the success of your tenant's business.

With the average residential property being far cheaper than commercial property, and the fact that you will generally need to only put 20% of your equity into the purchase, it is relatively easy to finance residential property. Plus, there are vastly more residential properties for sale than commercial properties. It is pretty easy to tenant properties, and low vacancy rates are the norm. If a tenant moves out of a residential property in a city, *c'est la vie* — just advertise and replace them with another.

When I add up all these factors, I think commercial property is a great investment when you have built up a significant amount of equity. This amount will vary depending on where you like investing, and your own risk tolerance and investment profile.

6 | What do I need to know to be a great investor?

To be a successful investor, you need to minimise the number of mistakes you make. To do this, you need to have your finger on the pulse when it comes to what's happening in your industry, go to seminars where the presenters have this knowledge and the ability to communicate this information or get a skilled mentor. By understanding and tracking the factors which drive the New Zealand property market, you know where to buy, how much to pay and when to raise rents. These are the factors which influence your market:

- ○ population growth/migration
- ○ interest rates
- ○ affordability
- ○ serviceability/indebtedness
- ○ new housing consents
- ○ liquidity
- ○ global factors
- ○ housing sales volumes
- ○ rental growth.

Population growth/migration

Long-term and permanent migration 1925–2010

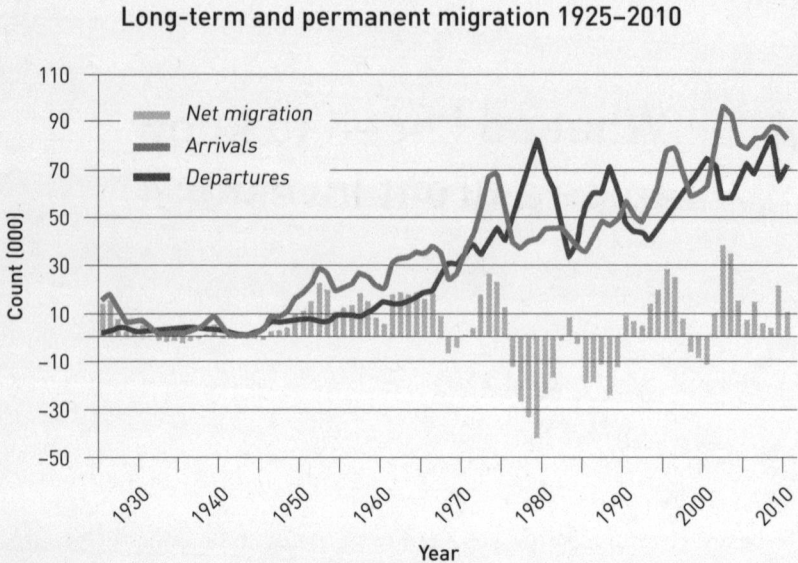

Source: Statistics NZ

Net migration is the difference between long-term arrivals and long-term departures. This typically runs at around positive 10,000 people per year. This means every 48 minutes we have one more New Zealand resident as a result of net migration. Around two-thirds of immigrants settle in the greater Auckland region, at least initially. As a result migration-influenced housing demand is most pronounced in Auckland.

In addition, at the time of writing, New Zealand has a birth approximately every 8 minutes and 10 seconds, and a death only every 20 minutes and 7 seconds. Other demographic trends include the move into cities, and the northward drift trend.

Interest rates

Interest rates are an important indicator for the property cycle. When interest rates are low, people are less scared of borrowing and are more able to service debt. Interest rates do not necessarily correlate with house prices; rising interest rates from 2003 to 2007 were paired with a rising house market, while when the market crashed in 2008 the interest rates were lowered.

Floating and 5 years fixed interest rates

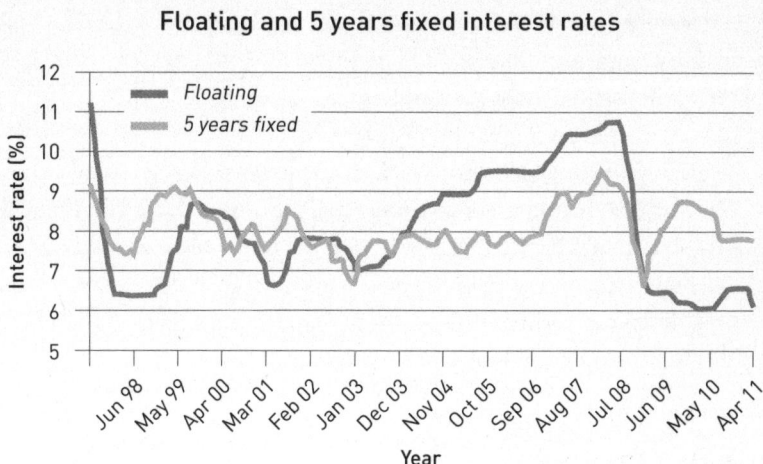

Source: RBNZ, BNZ

Affordability

An important measure of the property cycle is affordability. The main statistic used is the proportion of the average weekly household earnings required to service a 25-year table mortgage based on the two-year fixed rate, with a 20% deposit put down on the median-priced house (using the Quotable Value statistics for this median price).

Housing was hard to afford in the mid-1990s until the downturn from 1998 to 2002, then the boom from 2003 to 2007 saw unprecedented levels of unaffordability caused by high house prices and interest rates. The proportion of an average wage needed to service an average mortgage reached nearly 60% in the November 2007 peak of the market. Then the market crashed in 2008, with interest rates falling sharply at the end of that year too, and momentarily we needed about 40% of the average weekly household earnings to service the mortgage. A mini price recovery and interest-rate increase then occurred in 2009, which somewhat reversed in 2010 and is now in the process of stabilising.

Serviceability/indebtedness

New Zealand has a large amount of household debt as a percentage of nominal disposable income. The percentage is slowly reducing as we save more and pay down debt. Interest rates have come down and the servicing of household debt as a percentage of disposable income has come down too.

Serviceability is about relating interest payments to income, while indebtedness measures the level of debt relative to income. The large amount of household debt as a percentage of disposable income proves that New Zealand is not a nation of savers.

Since 2008, in the downturn phase of the property cycle, indebtedness has been slowly reducing as we save more and pay down debt. This is largely because interest rates have come down, with floating rates at around 40-year lows. The servicing of household debt as a percentage of disposable income has come down too. When interest rates go up we can expect serviceability to again become more difficult.

New housing consents

New housing consents increase supply, so when consents are running high this is not a positive factor for property investors. Currently, they are running quite low. A lot of criticism has been levelled against the Resource Management Act 1991 and Building Act 2004 and councils for their high fees, and contributions and interpretations of these acts. Before you join in the criticism, remember that by making life difficult and painful for developers and builders, these Acts are the investor's best friend. If consents are very low, we are under-building, which results in a reduced supply of rental accommodation, which drives rents up, vacancies down and makes landlords very happy. In recent times building consent numbers have been falling significantly to around 40-year lows, despite a population greatly higher than 40 years ago.

New Zealand building consents for dwellings

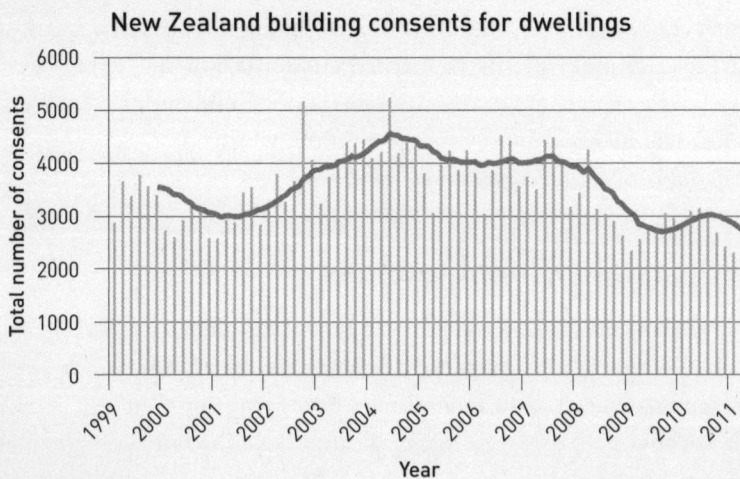

Source: Statistics NZ

Let's look at the correlation between median sale prices and New Zealand building consents (for dwellings).

Median sales prices and New Zealand building consents

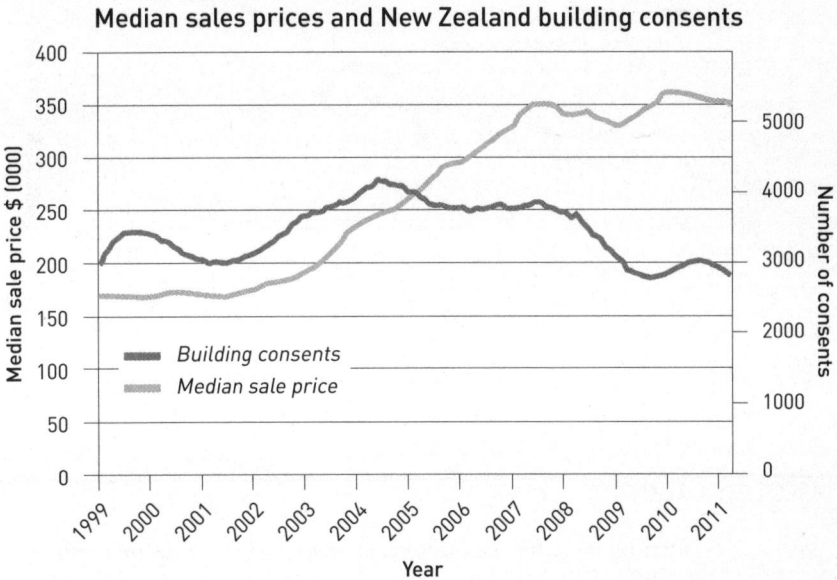

Source: Statistics NZ, BNZ

The New Zealand property market needs around 26,500 building consents each year to meet the annual growth in household numbers of 21,190 (since some consents aren't acted on or are for secondary houses such as beach houses). With annual net migration averaging 10,000 extra New Zealanders per year, this means we should be building around 2,100 houses per month. This is not happening right now and consequently we have a housing shortage. This undersupply is a positive factor for landlords — a limited supply of places to live causes more competition for existing rentals, driving prices up and allowing you to be more choosy when it comes to tenants.

Liquidity

The graph overleaf overlays median house prices with the growth in private sector credit (PSC) to gross domestic product (GDP) ratio. At the time of writing the issue is not so much the availability of PSC, but actually finding enough suitably qualified borrowers that want it.

You can see that credit growth/liquidity and the house prices are fairly well correlated.

Credit growth and median house prices

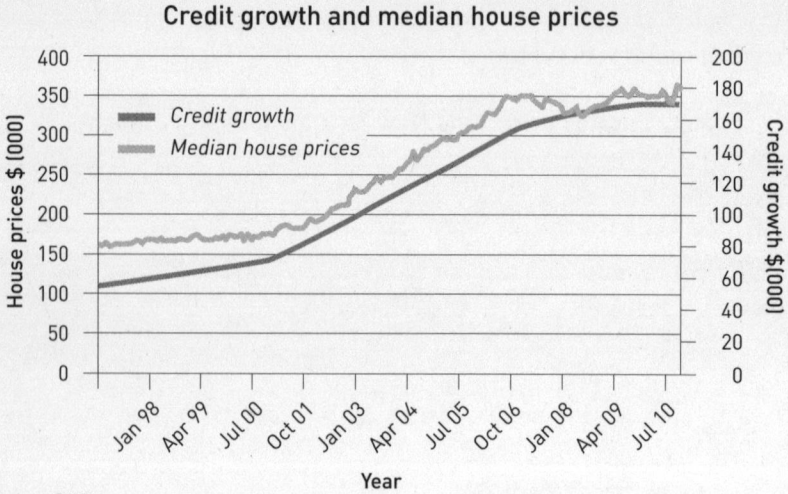

Source: BNZ

Global factors

What is happening to other economies around the world is increasingly important to New Zealand. Particular attention needs to be paid to our closest neighbour and overwhelmingly our largest trading partner, Australia.

House price movements in the largest cities in Australia, the United Kingdom and United States are only partially correlated to house-price movements in New Zealand. Property investors realise, however, that New Zealand is increasingly part of the global economy, and that trends in overseas markets may also have an impact here.

Housing sales volumes

There is no question that housing sales volumes seem to lead values. When few houses sell, we are in a downturn. A downturn is characterised by a tough pricing market, more days to sell a property, and a large inventory (many properties for sale). When lots of houses are selling we're in a boom, characterised by fewer days to sell a property and a smaller inventory.

The decade average from 2000 to 2010 is about 89,000 house sales per year, according to the REINZ. In the calendar year 2010, just 56,303 houses were sold. Interestingly, 1998, 2000 and 2008 were negative growth years for the housing market, and they were also years with comparatively fewer sales to normal.

Median house prices and volumes

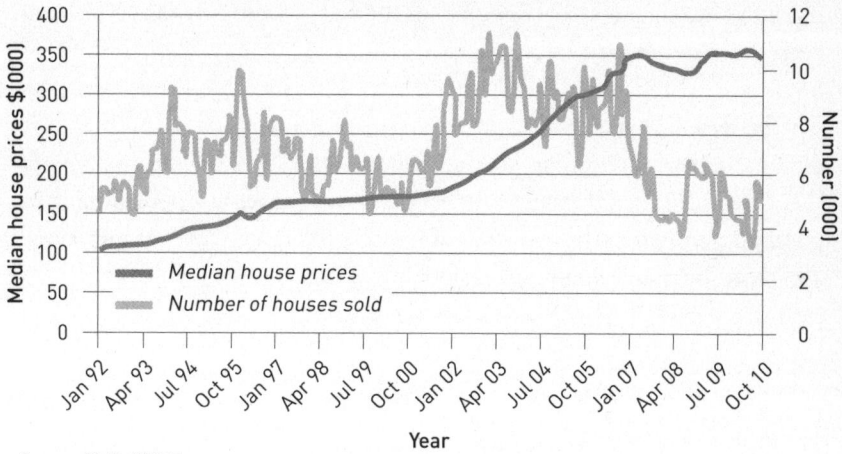

Source: BNZ, REINZ

Rental growth

Growth in rental income is important to investors as it is the cash flow which services our debt repayments and pays for other expenses. Therefore strong rental growth is useful — it's indicative of a recovery or the early stages of a property boom. Declining rents are indicative of a slump. Take a look at this graph for the median rental annual growth rate, on a three-month rolling average:

New Zealand median sale prices and annual rental costs

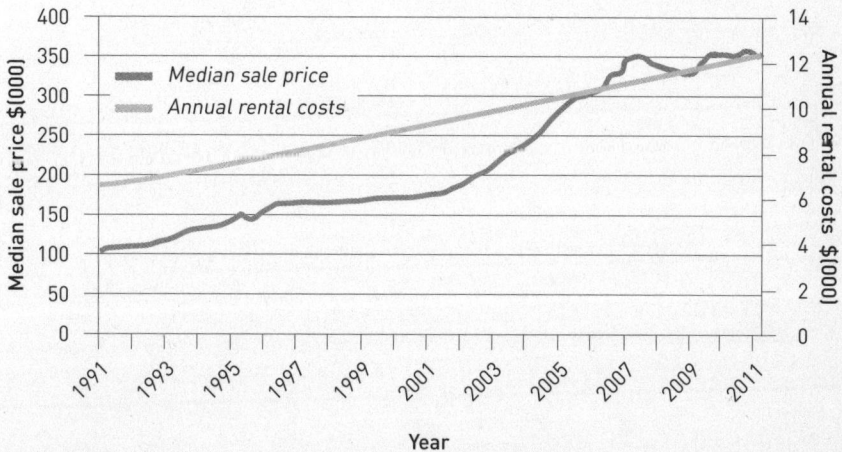

Source: BNZ, DBH

If you put all of these factors together you get a clearer picture of where the market is heading. It's very rare that all the factors point the same way. You need to look at the statistics available to you and learn to interpret them or find some trusted commentators.

The data I have provided in this chapter is intentionally brief as it is only current at the time of writing, when we are in a downturn. I think that downturns are the best time to purchase property: opportunities to purchase good property are more common as interest rates are at low levels, and there are not as many people looking to buy.

7 | What kind of goals should I set for my success?

by David Leon, BSc, life coach and Director of NZ Wealth Mentor Ltd

Goal setting

In my years of experience working with individuals and groups of people to achieve excellence I can certainly say that goal setting is the definitive difference between success and failure. We have all heard the clichés about goal setting that seem to only resonate for a few seconds before they disappear off into distant memories (SMART goals anyone?).

You see, the first problem with 'goal setting' is the name itself. The connotation we so often subconsciously associate with this phrase is 'Unattainable Dreams'. If this is the real meaning of goal setting for you, then you must change the phrase to another one that will assist you in your endeavours. I personally replaced it around a decade ago with 'outcome design'. Outcomes are just consequences that naturally occur as a result of one's actions. This means that they *will* occur if you follow a plan of action. Design refers to the creative process that must also be present at the beginning and during the process.

Outcome design is just the beginning of the process. Once the master design is finished you need to add several ingredients to make sure your outcome is as tasty as desired. The four extra ingredients you must add are:

- measurement
- accountability
- rewards
- mentoring.

I will cover these topics in detail after we talk in depth about outcome design.

Outcome design

When it comes to property investing-specific outcome design there are steps that must be followed in this order:

1. Why?
2. Money
3. Strategy
4. Area
5. Property.

Know your WHY

Without knowing the reason why you are undertaking this journey you are very likely to fail. Having a clear 'why' is the first step to efficient and successful outcome design. You need to know 'why' you are willing to work harder and take risks.

Your 'whys' need to be clear and you need to not just think about them but feel them, see them and hear them. The clearer they are, the more likely you will be to achieve them. For this reason, quite a few educators like Anthony Robbins encourage the use of vision boards. Vision boards are just a collection of photos (ideally with you in all of them) already showing what you want your outcome to be. For example, if you want to live in a beautiful home in an upmarket suburb with coastal views, go to your target neighbourhood, visit some open homes and ask someone to take a picture of you outside your dream home. Vision boards also need to be time con-strained. This means that you could have several vision boards going at one time. For example you could have a 12-month vision board as well as a five-year one. Vision boards are great to get a picture of your outcomes clearly cemented in your brain.

Affirmations are another tool that some professionals use to help with the auditory channel uptake of your outcomes. Affirmations are positive self-talk statements about what you will achieve or who you want to be. Using the example of the dream home, this means that you say to yourself on a daily basis that you *are* the proud owner of such a home. A walk-through video of such a home from a real estate agent's website would also create a very similar picture. This creates a clear image for all your senses so that you can focus on your path to making it happen.

So do it *now*. Design your 'whys', create your vision boards, go out there and have fun doing it. Don't attempt step two before you finish step one.

Money — how much money is it going to cost you to achieve your 'whys'?

I know what you're thinking right now. What if my 'why' was to spend more time with my family? Well, my answer to that is to ask another question: 'How much more time do you really want to spend with your family?' Usually an extra 10 hours of quality time is the average answer. My second question is: 'How much is that going to cost you?' What I mean by this question is that if you are currently working 40 hours per week and you want to spend an extra 10 hours with your family you may have to downsize your working week to 30 hours. How much income would you lose if you were to downsize your working week?

You see, there are two types of money: regular and recurring income, and lump sums of cash. To get the dream home you need a big lump sum of cash to come your way, while to spend more time with your family you need to create income that will occur on a weekly basis without your direct involvement (passive income).

Work out exactly how much money it is going to cost you to reach your 'whys'. This is the reason that your 'whys' must be very specific. You can't just say 'I want a new home': you need to know the type of house, number of bedrooms, preferred suburb and everything else you need to put a dollar value on it.

Most of the people I've helped through this process are very pleasantly surprised about how little they will need to achieve their initial whys. For the average person their goals feel so far away that they never even start the process of working them out.

Strategy — what property-investing strategy is best suited to achieve your target income?

If I want lump sums of cash to get my dream home, I would be more likely to look at a trading strategy rather than a buy-and-hold one for my property investing. If I want to spend more time with my family, I will be more likely to use a passive income-producing strategy like lease options or multiple income stream property rather than an active strategy like renovations.

At NZ Wealth Mentor we aim to help our students become strategy experts. We help them to define their own individual strategy and work to achieve it so they can beat anyone at it. Playing to your strengths is the only way to profit in today's market.

Time to work out your strategy and to follow it! Do not lose your focus. If your strategy is trading and you see a great buy-and-hold deal, have the courage to say *no*. Saying no will keep you focused and profitable. If you want to be an expert at studio apartments, then don't start looking at three-bedroom stand-alone houses in the outlying suburbs. It's too easy to lose focus and then justify it by saying it is 'too hard'. Stay focused!

Area

You can choose an area only when you have decided on your property-investment strategy. There are two questions that you must consider when selecting an area:

Is it realistic?

Can you really find deals that fit your strategy and financial capacities in that area? You have to be realistic about property. Yes, we all find amazing deals every so often but you're not looking for just one amazing deal; you want a string of them. You're actually looking for quite a few of deals that are 'just very good' rather than amazing. Those very good deals must be realistic and you must be able to find them in your area.

Is it close to home?

You are more likely to stick to your strategy if you don't have to waste several hours of your day driving on a regular basis. In most occasions you will also have to take very quick action when a deal comes to the market and being close to it gives you an edge over the rest.

Don't be sidetracked by the next silver bullet: by going outside your strategy and area and investing in products like, for example, US tax deeds or liens, which we sometimes see. If they are such outstanding investments why aren't more of the 310 million Americans buying them?

Property

Only when you know your area and your strategy should you start looking at property types, property inspections and placing offers. If you are looking at a buy-and-hold strategy in your predetermined area, you will firstly talk to property management agents so that they can tell you which property is in the highest demand from a tenant's perspective. You can then stick to the properties in higher demand so you can minimise vacancies and tenant issues and maximise your profits.

I can't emphasise enough how important it is to follow these steps in this order. You can truly create a lot of wealth through property investing if you follow the plan.

At this stage you have now fully designed your outcomes. You will now enter the hardest part of the process: successful implementation.

Successful implementation

As stated before, there are four ingredients that you must add to the formula to get your desired results:

- measurement
- accountability
- rewards
- mentoring.

All are equally important and all of them work together to produce outstanding results. Let's start describing them:

Measurement

Since you now have time-limited outcomes you can start measuring whether they are coming to fruition or not. I like to set at least one hour per week to evaluate progress and measure success. Allocating this time in my calendar makes me do it. It is non-negotiable. Measuring your success is essential because you will find two main results:

- You are on your track to achieve your desired outcome. That is fantastic news! This should keep you motivated to keep working hard. It may also alert you that your outcomes are a bit too easy to achieve and you can push yourself harder.

- You are failing to achieve milestones. This is a wake-up call so you can identify what issues are hindering your process. It takes introspective study to figure out what is wrong and how to fix it but this is the most powerful lesson you will ever learn. Make sure you spend the time analysing all the factors, from the feasibility of your outcomes to your personal skills.

Accountability

People will do more to please others than to please themselves. This truism seems present in every culture around the world. Other people can hold you accountable to reaching your outcomes. The easiest way for this to take place is for you to tell everyone around you about what you are doing and ask them to keep you true to your word. This action in itself will ignite your passion and results. Make sure you take this step seriously. When you set an outcome you must feel deep inside you that you are already there. That certainty will be transferred to the people you speak to. If your certainty is not high enough, people will not take you seriously; this is a tell-tale sign that you need to do more work on your design, personal focus and belief.

One of the ways I keep myself accountable is with the help of mentors/ coaches. These people have your best interests as their main concern and are paid to assist you to get more out of your life. This kind of accountability is essential. Run your life like a business owner runs their business. Many successful businesses employ coaches to help them achieve more. Why should your life be less important than a business?

Rewards

When you reach significant milestones you should reward yourself. The road to your outcomes might be a long and windy one and you must keep focused on results. Rewards help to keep you focused and reignite your passion. Make sure that the results fit the milestone. Do not over- or under-reward yourself.

Mentoring

I believe it is extremely important to have a mentor to guide you through this process, especially if it involves property investment. Mentoring is an ingredient that will add profits and will decrease the time to get to your outcomes. Talking with someone who has already taken your path will be invaluable, and help you to avoid the same pitfalls and costly mistakes.

One of my favourite quotes says it all:

'Smart people learn from their own mistakes, but the real
sharp ones learn from the mistakes of others.'

Brandon Mull, best-selling author

Some assistance to help you set your own desired outcomes

Many of our mentoring students are looking to attain financial freedom. This means different things to different people, as it is a subjective term. I think that financial freedom is where you have the ability to retire from earning income from your own personal exertion, and lean back to live off the cash flow and equity from your assets (investment portfolio).

This will take varying lengths of time for different people, depending on a range of factors including the mindset of the investor; their current financial position; their ability to raise finance with lenders; their own commitment to the desired outcomes they set; their skill as an investor; and the quality of their desired outcome monitoring regime. You wouldn't want to say 'I will be financially free five years from today' without giving much thought as to how you're going to do this, particularly if you are a fresh investor. You will need to set some very aggressive desired outcomes and then fully focus on achieving them through your unwavering total commitment to excellence and financial mastery.

I think if you have a desired outcome of financial freedom, as so many people do, why not consider what level of income this would require, and what level of assets this would entail. Then drill this further down to the strategies that you will use, and establish a set of buying criteria for properties.

Let's say you decide that you need a passive income of $150,000 per year. Remember that the tax breaks on income from your personal exertion (salary, wages, drawings etc) won't be there any more. I had a client earning over $700,000 per year, but when they stopped work they were foregoing over $70,000 in tax deductions alone, so they missed their desired outcome. They decided to work part time to hit their own $300,000 passive income a year goal, so they can spend time overseas in the Cook Islands, Mauritius, Florida and the Mediterranean, with a touch of skiing in the Swiss Alps for good measure.

Summary

Why not set your desired outcomes today? If you have set them already, then take time out now to review them. Otherwise you are just having a bit of a stab in the dark and have an unknown journey ahead to an unknown destination. Put your desired outcomes in a handy place like in your desk drawer, and back them up on your computer. Above all, review them very regularly.

Think goal-setting is unnecessary?

If you think you're doing perfectly well without writing down your goals . . . think again. A review of goal-setting studies by the University of Washington showed the following results:

▷ Specific and challenging goals lead to higher performance than easy goals, 'do your best' goals, or no goals.

▷ Goals affect performance by directing attention, mobilising effort, increasing persistence and motivating strategy development.

▷ Goal setting is most likely to improve task performance when the goals are specific and sufficiently challenging.

---

8 What investment strategy is best for me?

Your strategy as a property investor defines your choices, your plans and ultimately, your success. But there's no one-size-fits-all solution. You always want rental growth and capital gain; these are the crucial factors which make your portfolio work. You need to choose a strategy which suits your lifestyle and your personality. Your strategy may develop over time or you may have firm ideas about what you want to do from the outset.

Remember that strategies will differ for different people. As you get closer to the point where you wish to (or have to) retire, cash flow will be more important for you, as the cash flow will be what you use for day-to-day spending. If you have a job or business that gives you good cash flow, then you can afford to have a strategy that is more equity-dominant. The strategy that will be best for you depends on your own individual needs and situation. If you can't work out what strategy is best for you, consider seeking the help of an experienced property mentor.

Classic long-term strategies

My favourite strategy is also the most common, and is known as buy and hold; this is a long-term strategy. You purchase a property for its long-term cash flow, and also derive benefits from capital appreciation over time, plus tax rebates. You can also pay down principal over time to increase your equity in the property.

There are a few variants on the buy-and-hold strategy, such as:

○ buying a property and renovating it to add value

○ buying a section and building on it

○ subdividing land you own and building on it, then keeping the redeveloped property, which will generally have increased rental income and greater equity as a result of the redevelopment

○ buying a property and constructing another rent-generating building on-site, such as an extra dwelling or retail outlet.

This last multi-income strategy is a real favourite of mine. It gives you enhanced cash flow by creating multiple income streams from the same title — which can quickly add up to rents which cover the costs on the property. I have mastered the art of construction for investment, and I have a number of excellent home-and-income properties dominating my portfolio. It runs in the family; my grandparents favoured blocks of flats, where they would have a number of units on a property and rent them all out. Multi-income properties are also easier to manage and maintain — instead of managing tenants at two properties, you can get the same income from one site. Of course, it does take more money to buy them.

All these strategies are for the long term — when you buy the property you have no intention to resell. So if you do sell your property, a long-term strategy means that there is no tax payable — you are said to be holding this kind of property on 'capital account'.

Trading strategies

If you don't fancy the long-term commitment of those classic investor strategies, there are always the property-trading strategies. In the past the simplest property-trading method involved you getting a property under a conditional agreement for sale and purchase, and then assigning this to an investor buyer to settle themselves, in exchange for a finder's or assignment fee. Nowadays this method of finding appears to breach the Real Estate Agents Act 2008. As a result, property finders settle properties themselves and therefore take an ownership position before they sell to a third party.

Here are the common trading strategies:

○ buying a property and settling it contemporaneously (back-to-back)

○ buying a property, doing nothing to it and selling it at a profit when the market moves up

○ buying a property, renovating it and selling it

○ adding additional buildings to a property (such as a sleepout, minor dwelling or house)

○ buying a section, building a house or houses on it, then selling it

○ buying a section, building a commercial building on it, then selling it (individual units or as a whole).

These types of property trading aim to build the capital value of your assets and then to sell them in the short term. The timeframe varies from quick renovation and sales, which might take just weeks or a few months, to large multi-lot complex subdivisions requiring full-blown resource and building consents, which may take up to three years. Because your intention when you purchase is always to sell within a short time period, usually under three years, you are said to be holding these properties on 'revenue account'. Consequently, when you sell these types of properties you are liable to pay income tax.

When you're trying to decide on a strategy, remember that ultimately it is about the numbers. As the great Sean Fitzpatrick used to say, 'It was a game of two halves'. Well, property investment is sometimes like a game, and there are two very important parts to it, each of which is critical: equity and cash flow. You need to build both of these to make property investment work for you. Neglect one at the expense of the other and you will have to change your game plan — or worse, give up the game. Neglect both and you are on the fast track to failure. It is up to you to choose the strategy that is most likely to work for you. To determine what type of strategy will suit you, ask yourself some questions, such as:

○ How much money do I have to invest? Obviously this will have a big impact on your strategy — buying 10 multimillion-dollar commercial properties in the CBD could be a great idea, but few people have enough money available to fund that kind of strategy. If you're a little low on equity and cash, you may well prefer to begin with a single rented unit or apartment, for example.

○ How much risk am I comfortable with? If you love to take a risk with your money, you might like to put it into riskier strategies — you may tackle a development with a complicated consent or approval process, for instance. If you're more conservative, you might prefer to take your time, keep your debts relatively low and hunt around for low-cost cash flow-positive projects.

○ How much time do I have to spend on property investment? If you are going to work on property investing as your full-time job, you'll have the time to manage even a very complex project (like developing a subdivision). But if you're going to try to make your property investing fit around your other job, your family and your hobbies, you'll need to choose a simple, low-stress strategy (like a few buy-and-hold properties managed by a property manager).

○ What aspect of property investing really appeals to me? If you love the idea of renovating a property, you may want to concentrate on property trading by buying a 'do-up' and selling it for a profit. If you want to be a landlord, you'll choose a buy-and-hold strategy. If you are passionate about building, you might concentrate on creating new homes on sections.

I have employed virtually all of these strategies myself and have helped literally hundreds of people to utilise them with a high level of success over the past eight years.

Residential property investment strategies

Buy and hold

This is a plain vanilla strategy, but, just as vanilla is a very popular flavour, buy and hold is a very popular strategy that works for most investors. The strategy is to buy property and rent it out. It is a great strategy, particularly if you are time-challenged, or not sufficiently skilled (or sufficiently interested) to do a renovation. An example would be buying a new brick-and-tile house, which is low maintenance and has Master Builder warranties. Or it might be buying an older house and doing nothing to it, other than renting it out. While you are not changing the nature of the property, you will do well as time makes the property rise hugely in value.

Over time this basic property strategy works — because rents rise with wage inflation and the property gets capital growth as it cycles gradually upward in value. I believe that this strategy has a lot of merit; however, I think that you can get better returns from employing some of the more advanced strategies to create further equity and cash flow for yourself.

Stand-alone houses versus multi-income properties

In residential property most properties are stand-alone — that is, one house per property. But there are several types of properties with more than one house or dwelling — such as a sleepout, minor dwelling, two houses on one title, a block of flats, units and so forth. Often a stand-alone property will have a house, garage, garaport or carport and possibly a front yard. Alternatively, it might just be a single unit, terraced house or apartment. Essentially by 'stand-alone' house I mean one dwelling unit per property. There are considerably more stand-alone houses than multi-income properties; think of how many people you know who live in stand-alone houses or apartment blocks on their own title.

A multi-income strategy depends on having more than one dwelling on a property's title. With just one plot of land, by receiving extra streams of income you get more rent — and therefore a higher proportion of income to the property's value. The multi-income strategy is known as a high-yield strategy, and is more common with experienced and skilled investors. I use this strategy myself — it performs really well for me in terms of both cash flow and equity.

Blocks of flats are a typical example of this type of strategy. Here's a great example, courtesy of one of my mentoring clients. He is lucky enough to have a significant amount of money on term deposit and no property debt on a valuable portfolio (OK, it's not just luck, he also gets great advice!). We recently found a multi-income earner that was a fantastic buy:

Property: A block of eight one-bedroom flats in Mount Wellington, Auckland, quite close to developing suburb Sylvia Park

Purchase price: $1.3 million

Rental income: $98,000 per year

Expenses: $10,000 per year (excluding interest costs)

Gross yield: 8% (calculated as the gross annual rent divided by the purchase price)

The highest interest rate they could get at the bank was 5.5% to tie their money up for a ridiculous five years. It was an absolute no-brainer for me to recommend they move into this high-yielding investment. Because, instead of getting only $73,000 per year interest on a term deposit, they would earn a net rental of $88,000, and be able to increase their rents and add value to the property. At a cap rate for the area of 7.2%, the property's value is $1.361 million, so he's buying at $61,000 below value — term deposits just don't provide that kind of return.

Property trading — the classic method

Property trading, in its simplest form, is the process of buying and selling real estate. It can be a fantastic way to replace your employment income, and it can be a scalable business to suit your needs. Successful trading is a great strategy where the profits can be used to complement your long-term buy-and-hold properties, and fast-track your goals.

However, it is fraught with risk. Many traders do not make money. Many traders actually lose money. So it's imperative that you have the information and confidence to correctly trade property. You must also have a system set up to best enable you to achieve success. Importantly, you need a buyer in place to whom you are able to sell your property. In cities the size of Auckland, Wellington or Christchurch this is normally no problem, but in small towns or rural areas this is often extremely difficult.

The key issues are always price and the presentation of the property.

Typically, you would buy a property under conditional contract and do thorough due diligence and research on the property including the following:

○ the likely weekly rental income in its current state and, if applicable, in its renovated (done-up) state

○ the likely sale price of your property

○ renovation costs (if you plan to do a renovation)

○ holding costs (interest on loan, rates, power, water etc if you plan on settling the property)

○ legal due diligence (a title search)

○ full budget for the project (particularly if you are settling and holding it yourself for a period of time)

○ other useful information such as land size, house size, school zones, proximity to the city or town centre, shopping centres, major employment — any factor which has an impact on the value of the property.

There are two ways to trade property:

○ No funds? If you don't have funds and/or financial approval, you will be unable to settle on a property. So you are best to consider doing a contemporaneous or back-to-back settlement to place the property you found with a new buyer. This means that you settle the property and on-sell it on the same day you bought it.

○ Some cash to spend? If you do have funds available and can add value to the property (for example, doing a renovation or building improvements), then settling the property may be a better option. You would then aim to on-sell the property to your buyer at a higher profit than you would by just assigning the contract.

A word of caution: In recent times the Real Estate Institute of New Zealand has been clamping down on property traders operating by way of deed of assignment or nomination. REINZ believes that if you are buying properties, whether privately or through agents, and then on-selling them to a third party, you are acting like a real estate agent. The argument is that you are performing a service, in trade, on behalf of another person for the purpose of bringing about a real estate transaction.

I agree with their analysis and think that traders in property should be acting as a principal and back-to-back settling a trade instead (or owning it for a longer period of time to allow for your add-value steps). This may change again over time, so I have also included the deed of assignment method in the property trading strategies diagram on the next page.

Buy, build and hold

Time to take the complexity up another level. For this strategy, you purchase a property with a big enough section to build at least one additional dwelling for you to rent out. This can be a fantastic strategy for investors and is one of my personal favourites. I have employed this strategy many times over and find it an excellent way to create wealth. Often an investor-buyer will purchase a section, or a house on a big section, and then construct another dwelling. The benefits of getting a brand-new dwelling built include:

○ New buildings are much easier to rent out.

○ You get a higher weekly rental amount from a new building.

○ If you are diligent you can sometimes get good amounts of equity from a brand-new house.

○ Your new building has a high depreciation amount as you already own the land.

○ New houses look better, smell better, are nicer to touch, and give a great feel-good vibe.

Property trading strategies

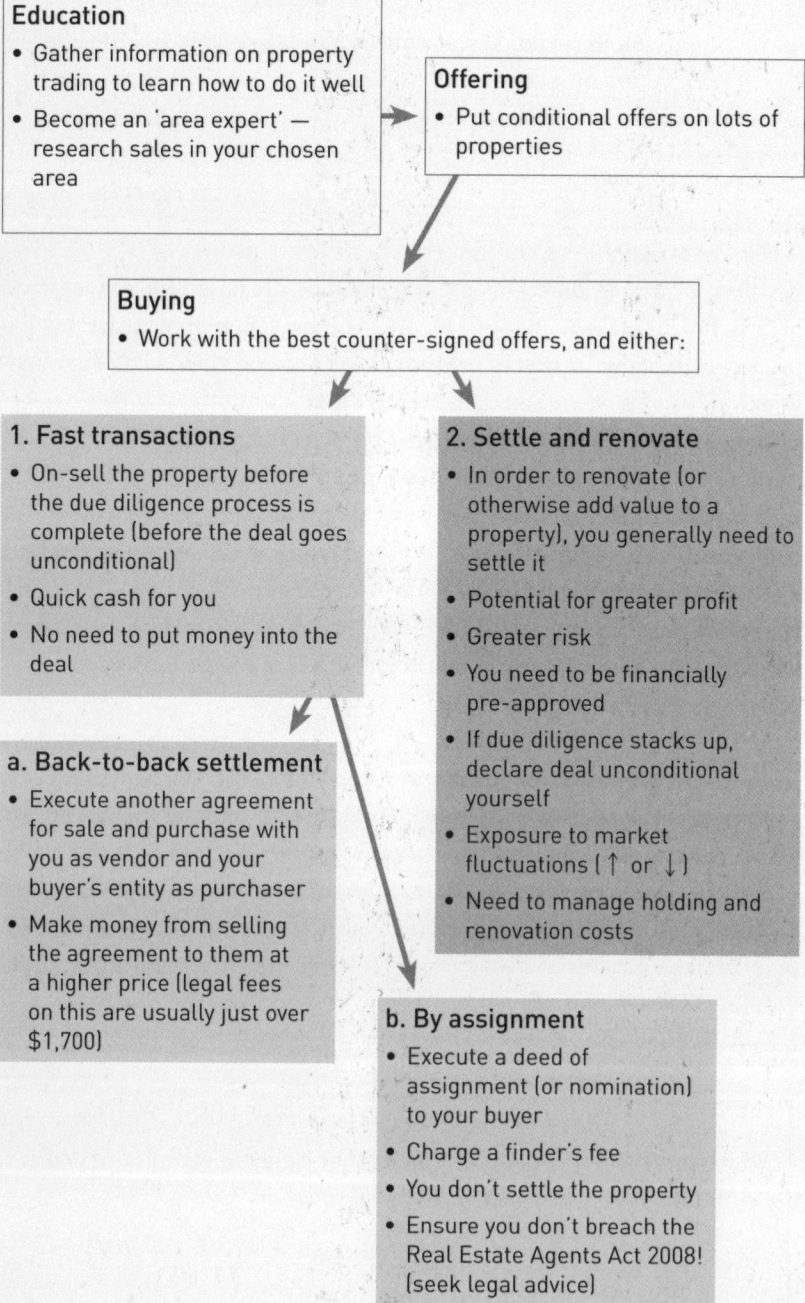

Education
- Gather information on property trading to learn how to do it well
- Become an 'area expert' — research sales in your chosen area

Offering
- Put conditional offers on lots of properties

Buying
- Work with the best counter-signed offers, and either:

1. Fast transactions
- On-sell the property before the due diligence process is complete (before the deal goes unconditional)
- Quick cash for you
- No need to put money into the deal

2. Settle and renovate
- In order to renovate (or otherwise add value to a property), you generally need to settle it
- Potential for greater profit
- Greater risk
- You need to be financially pre-approved
- If due diligence stacks up, declare deal unconditional yourself
- Exposure to market fluctuations (↑ or ↓)
- Need to manage holding and renovation costs

a. Back-to-back settlement
- Execute another agreement for sale and purchase with you as vendor and your buyer's entity as purchaser
- Make money from selling the agreement to them at a higher price (legal fees on this are usually just over $1,700)

b. By assignment
- Execute a deed of assignment (or nomination) to your buyer
- Charge a finder's fee
- You don't settle the property
- Ensure you don't breach the Real Estate Agents Act 2008! (seek legal advice)

The downsides of building a new dwelling include:

O The fact that construction is much more difficult than it used to be with a more stringent and comprehensive Building Code.

O Council inspectors are becoming far stricter under the requirements of the Building Act 2004.

O Construction finance is slightly harder to get than when buying a stand-alone property.

Think outside the box

Don't feel limited to just building a house. When it comes to build, buy and hold, there are so many options:

O Building a two-bedroom sleepout with a bathroom and lounge (though no kitchen), which increased my rent by $220 per week.

O Numerous three-bedroom minor dwellings (with kitchens), which have been rented out for between $315 and $385 per week, depending on location.

O I know investors who have built apartment buildings and blocks of flats, with great results.

O Home and income buildings have been incredible earners for many investors I know — one friend built a four-bedroom, 110m² house and a three-bedroom, 65m² smaller house under the same roofline.

O Don't forget terraced houses, duplexes and triplexes.

O You can add to not only the house, but the garage, by building bedrooms and a bathroom on top of a garage.

An example of the buy, build and hold strategy in action

A friend purchased a section in Rototuna, which is on the expanding northern fringe of Hamilton. They bought the section for $182,000 and paid a construction company to build a four-bedroom, two-bathroom brick-and-tile house with an internal garage.

The total cost to build was $194,000, including council contributions, fees, levies, all professional fees (surveyor, architect, engineer), as well as all construction fees including the retaining wall, driveway and landscaping as well. The building was to be a 'turn-key project', which means the code of compliance certificate was handed over at the end of the project.

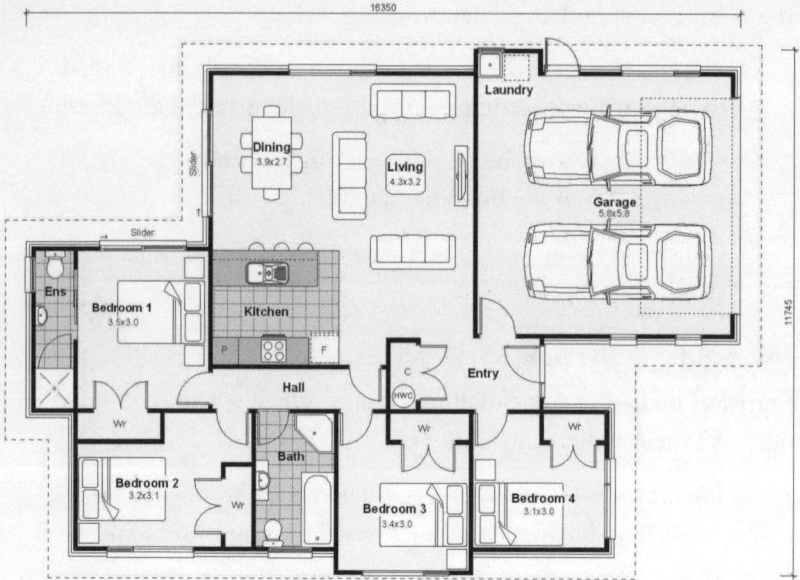

Source: Investor Homes Limited

The project cost was $376,000 and the project was valued at $437,000, meaning $61,000 of equity was created. The property also was tenanted at $450 per week, and will have lower repairs and maintenance costs, being a brand new brick-and-tile home with a 10-year Registered Master Builders' guarantee.

Renovations

You can add a lot of value to a property by renovating it. Smart property traders always look for properties that only need a cosmetic renovation. Structural renovations take time, and generally require an architect, a licensed builder and council building consent. These can take a long time — and therefore cost money as you pay interest holding costs while you service your loan.

What should you look for to identify a good prospect?

○ a dirty house which you can easily water-blast

○ dated interior colours

○ tired-looking kitchens and bathrooms that you can modernise

○ old interior fittings: new door handles, door stops and light fittings are inexpensive but very effective

○ worn carpets: this helps you get a good price as new carpets really lift the appearance of a property.

The run-down house my wife and I bought in 2008 is a great example — it looked terrible but the work required was actually only minor. The property really was an eyesore. The rot under the vanity unit, toilet and kitchen sink was so bad that the floorboards needed to be replaced. The living-room walls had been graffitied, the curtains were dilapidated, the light fittings were 1960s shockers complete with layers of fly dirt and discoloured by years (if not decades) of smoking inside. The ceilings were an interesting yellow-brown colour with pockets of mould, the weatherboards had lead paint flaking off to expose the timber, the fibre-cement baseboards had holes in them. With two leaky taps, the originally vanity unit had cupboard doors and drawers that were totally swollen, and the scene in the 1960s worn kitchen wasn't much prettier.

I knew that with its big garage, large section size and great bones that this property would be a good deal. It was not really that hard a do-up. Best of all, I did none of the work but just project-managed the renovation.

Purchase price: $265,500 including finder's fees

Valuation at purchase: $312,000

Cost of renovations: $25,600

New valuation after renovations: $365,000

Profit from renovations: $27,400

Total equity gained: $73,900

Fantastic.

I have so many examples from clients' investments around the country. Another client purchased a house in Saint Kilda, Dunedin for $165,000. It needed a cosmetic renovation; he had the kitchen cabinetry powdercoated, added new handles to the cupboards and doors, did some painting, added new carpets and Lino, a new letterbox and tidied up the garden. After spending $8,000, taking a week of annual leave and quite a few hours doing the renovation, the property valued up at $208,000.

Purchase price: $165,000

Valuation at purchase: $180,000

Cost of renovations: $8,000

New valuation after renovations: $208,000

Profit from renovations: $20,000

Total equity gained: $35,000

This was an excellent result; they achieved a $35,000 increase in their equity within six weeks of going unconditional on their purchase of this property.

Building

Building can be a fantastic way to make extra cash flow and equity for your portfolio. There are horror stories, though, and my clients, family members and I have all experienced the problems that can come with this strategy. To avoid encountering these problems yourself, you need to ensure you get it exactly right.

Leaky building perception

You would be hard-pressed to build a seriously leaky building now, following the enactment of the Building Act 2004 and its ancillary Building Code. The laws have toughened enormously and in addition the council's inspection regime is much tougher. However, in the property game perception is reality, therefore I would advise caution if you are planning to construct residential buildings with the following characteristics:

○ no eaves (soffits)

○ buildings with internal guttering

○ plaster houses, also known as 'monolithic clad'

○ Mediterranean-style homes (which just aren't suited to New Zealand's comparatively wet climate).

Even though the new regulations mean that you will have a good cavity system on your plaster townhouse and use treated timber throughout, this isn't enough to overcome the current 'leaky home stigma'. Potential buyers will often not take more than a glance before thinking 'Not for me, thanks'. There are some investors who excel in purchasing leaky buildings and then fixing them up and getting a new code of compliance on the corrected property. They make great returns from buying leaky houses well below value. I would advise extreme caution in this area, and a heavy reliance on suitably qualified architects and engineers.

Development

Whether you are doing a large-scale subdivision or just converting an over-sized garage into an extra bedroom, you are 'developing' your property by changing the nature of a part or all of it. Do it well and your cash flow and equity can soar.

With property there are just so many options. This is yet another reason why I prefer to have it as my dominant class of investment. There are so many possibilities and things to do when you set your mind to it. Yes, you need some resources (money, know-how and/or the time to do it) behind you to make these happen, but you don't have to think too big. If you do a larger development, why don't you consider keeping some of the houses? The cash flow that this can create, along with the equity, can be outstanding.

Some of the developments investors do to add further cash flow and/or equity to their portfolio include:

○ adding extra bedrooms to a house

○ garage modifications to provide more habitable living area

○ building a sleepout

○ bringing on a cabin for extra returns

○ building a minor dwelling

○ relocating a house

○ building a new house

○ building a home and income

○ building green investment housing (One day in the not-too-distant future this will also provide economic returns as energy costs increase, green materials like rammed earth, solar panels and self-composting systems come down in price and gain wider market acceptance.)

○ building multiple houses like duplexes and triplexes

○ building a block of flats, terraced houses or other multi-rentals

○ medium- and large-scale subdivisions, including stand-alone houses, gated communities, lifestyle developments, coastal developments with luxury houses and marina berths on the estuary or harbour frontage.

Developing is a great way to accelerate your returns. My portfolio growth has been far faster than most investors', because I quickly gained the ability to develop properties to keep for my buy-and-hold portfolio. I consider myself a bit of an expert on property development, having built over 175 new houses or minor dwellings for my portfolio, my family's portfolio and for clients.

However, I am different to most developers. This is because I like to develop to keep, rather than develop to sell. In my view, it is generally far more expensive to buy back what you have just sold. Also, when you sell property, this triggers adverse financial consequences in terms of paying income tax (as you are selling your trading stock) and payment of GST (as you generally are well over the threshold that rules out small businesses and you do have a taxable activity).

Once you have built up your property-investment experience and the equity in your portfolio, I would recommend very strongly that you consider some of these development strategies for your investment properties. I mentor several investors who have made use of at least one of these techniques and increased their cash flow and equity. Now obviously if your portfolio consisted of six apartments in Christchurch, Queenstown and Wellington, then sure, you will really struggle to do this. However, if you have a good-sized piece of land, then why not think about your options? Perhaps even consider doing something at your own place for investment returns? Call the local council and ask to speak with the duty planner so you know what processes you will need to go through.

Minor dwellings

Building minor dwellings can be a fantastic way to make money from property, so even though it is a type of development it warrants its own section. You can typically build another three-bedroom dwelling for around half the price of the existing house and land. Not all councils permit minor dwellings, however most do. Minor dwellings are an option if you have 600m² or more in section size and in cities with a sizable population. In towns you generally can't get a high enough return on investment, as they will cost much the same to build (or often slightly more than) in a big city, but the weekly rental figures will be much lower, meaning a poorer return on investment.

I did this in West Harbour, a suburb in north-western Auckland. We bought a house with views over Auckland's stunning Waitemata Harbour. The house itself only rented at $350 per week, so as a stand-alone investment it certainly wasn't an equity play. We didn't even get this property much below registered valuation. However we were hunting for properties that had sections over 600m² in certain suburbs of West Auckland, with a view to building a minor dwelling on them. This house had a section well over 800m², so fitted the criteria well.

Purchase cost: $287,500

Rent prior to development: $350 per week

Cost of building minor dwelling: $131,000 including holding costs and ancillary site works

Rental income on new minor dwelling: $350 per week

After the extensive luxury landscaping, exposed aggregate paths and drive-way, carport and fencing works we did ancillary to the construction of the minor dwelling, we had the property revalued.

New valuation: $560,000

Equity: $141,500

The cash flow side was just as nice as we combined the $3,000 negative passive cash flow (from costs such as rates, interest, insurance and property-management fees) the property had as a stand-alone three-bedroom house with the positive $6,000 passive cash flow from rents, to make $3,000 for the combined property in a highly sought-after area in West Auckland. This was all thanks to the minor dwelling, which was a huge cash flow and equity performer.

Lease options

Lease options are basically rent-to-buy home ownership schemes, where a prospective purchaser ('tenant buyer') wants to buy a house from the investor owner. This requires having two agreements:

○ residential tenancy agreement

○ option to purchase agreement.

A tenant buyer will not have qualified for a loan for a 'normal property'. This means that they will have bad credit, insufficient funds to contribute towards a purchase, or both. The investor makes their profit on this by charging market price on the property, when they bought it under value themselves. The weekly rental figure will be similar to what a mortgage on the property would be, so with a higher sale price, there will be a cash flow 'spread' that the investor makes money from. The best way to see this is by giving an example, doing the lease option the way I like to see it done. The outcome for the investor is a deferred trade.

Let's say Kylie buys a property below value for $195,000 in Wainuiomata, Lower Hutt, renovates it for $10,000 and has the property revalued, which comes back at $245,000. Tony wants to buy a house, but his credit-card debt got out of hand and he had to do a No Asset Procedure (NAP) under the Insolvency Act in 2008, when his hours at the factory were trimmed back. Tony is very excited that someone is giving him a second chance at his dream of home ownership, so he can house himself, his wife and their three kids in one location without being given notice that the landlord is moving in, or selling the property, just as he felt he was settling in. No one in his family has owned a home for themselves for generations.

Tony is now out of the NAP and sees a 'rent-to-buy' as a way out of the poverty trap. So he responds to Kylie's advertisement on TradeMe, inspects Kylie's house with his family and since he likes the house so much he completes an application form. Kylie then does the credit checks and approves Tony as the buyer. Tony enters an option to purchase agreement with Kylie for $245,000 in two years' time, pays his deposit of $7,000, and agrees to pay $460 per week in rent under a standard residential tenancy agreement.

Kylie has fixed a loan for two years with her bank at 7.2%, meaning her interest cost on a $205,000 loan is $284 per week. Kylie pays for the insurance and rates on the property, which amount to a further $24 per week. Kylie's weekly net income (the 'spread') is therefore $152 per week. However, Kylie is also giving Tony a 'rent credit' of $60 per week.

Rent-to-buy schemes are 'consumer credit contracts' and are governed by the Credit Contract and Consumer Finance Act 2003. Tony sought legal advice about this and his lawyer mentioned that the CCCFA provides that a lease option is indeed a caveat-able interest. As a result Tony puts a caveat on the title of the property to protect his interest.

In two years' time if all goes to plan, Tony will have saved just over $6,000 in rent credits to add to his initial deposit of $7,000, and the property's value will have risen by 5% a year for two years to now be worth $270,000. The rent credit schedule as evidence of savings, plus the initial deposit, and a good banker or mortgage broker will get finance for Tony for $232,000 (ie. the $245,000 option to purchase at the price agreed two years prior, less the $6,000 in rent credits and $7,000 initial deposit). Tony then exercises his option to purchase, so he can cash Kylie out. At this time an agreement for sale and purchase would be entered into, recording the terms of the option to purchase agreement signed two years earlier.

If during the rent-to-buy period Tony can't keep up with his rent payment, Kylie could renegotiate with him a lower rent amount and extend the term and, failing that, Tony would forfeit any rent credits he had received and walk away with nothing if he got into serious arrears — just as if a bank were in Kylie's shoes. Rent-to-buy is a form of vendor financing and is a deferred property trade for Kylie. It works best in a rising market.

In a declining market, however, it is a bit of a recipe for disaster. Imagine if you were an investor doing lease options in 2007, when the recession started to fully bite. Even if your rent-to-buy tenant was able to keep up with all the rental payments and rent credits, the chances were extremely high that with tough bank credit criteria in 2009 they would not be able to get finance to cash the investor out. Additionally, the property was often worth slightly less than what was paid for it with the market going down in value in 2008. Some investors were left high and dry as they could not sell the property for what they paid for it, and found 2009 a tough market in which to find interested rent-to-buy tenants, so they were forced to sell their property for a small profit or in some cases a loss, or rent it out in a negative cash flow situation.

On balance I would only advise this to certain interested investors as a good cash flow strategy if they are well heeled and fully educated in the concept. While rent-to-buys are an extremely common form of property transfer/financing in the United States, they are still not common or popular in New Zealand.

(Lease options have overtaken 'wraps', which were big in the 1990s. Wraps are when you sell a property to a tenant buyer, but keep the ownership of the property's title in your own name, and you as the 'wrapper' skim a margin from the tenant's payment of your loan. So there were two sets of payments: (i) the tenant paying money to you for your loan to them; and (ii) you paying money over to your lender. Interestingly, some lenders have a clause in their lengthy loan agreements to prohibit this type of financing arrangement without express written permission.)

It is critical that you have lease options contracts that are legal! This means that they must be compliant with the CCCFA, and you need to issue various legal disclosure statements to comply with this Act. I would argue that you need to at least be a Registered Financial Adviser when offering lease option deals. Unfortunately there are some rogue educators operating in the New Zealand market and some of them (and their students) have been taken to court successfully by the tenant buyers to whom they should have sold their houses. Lease options can be a fantastic strategy but you must make sure your contracts are win–win, comply with the law and are ethical. Ensure that you have sufficient deposit, rent credits and time to ensure that you can give your tenant buyer the very best opportunity to complete the purchase of their house. Don't get too greedy with lease options! Also seek taxation advice from a professional skilled in dealing with lease options to ensure you meet all your tax obligations in relation to lease options.

Various combinations

There are numerous combinations that can work for investors. For example, stand-alone houses may be able to be bought below value and renovated to be kept as a buy-and-hold; larger properties may be able to be subdivided, and then the 'new' section built on. The new house could then be kept as a buy-and-hold while building a sleepout on the 'old' section to trade or sell. It is absolutely a numbers game. By mastering a greater number of strategies, the better your success with property investment will be, and the faster you will attain financial freedom.

There are so many options in property and it is quite hard to be a master of all of them. However with time, application and education from skilled practitioners, you can achieve fantastic results.

I will give special emphasis in this section to applying multiple cash flow- and equity-making strategies on one particular property, which I call grand-slamming — something I always aspire to achieve on every property deal I do, as the results can be simply amazing. Next up is an example of multiple strategies at work:

Grand-slamming

My wife Bridget and I bought a four-bedroom, two-bathroom, 1960s-built property in early 2006 for $255,000. This was on a subdivisible section on the foothills of the Waitakere Ranges in the gentrifying region of West Auckland. We knew we had an absolute bargain here as we could add a minor dwelling on the front of the section to save on the cost of my services. This property also had sweeping views of the Auckland CBD skyline.

The story of how I bought this property is a lesson in getting your priorities right — I almost missed out because I was playing tennis. My game was scheduled for a Thursday morning when I got a call from a friendly agent with whom I do a fair bit of business. He said that he had a pretty special deal.

I told him I had a game of tennis in 45 minutes' time, because what's the point of being a property investor and setting your own hours if you can't enjoy some free time and flexibility? He said, 'I think you're in for a treat on this one, David'. So I knew he meant business. I interrogated him on its value, likely rental return, the lowest price the vendors would take, conditions they wanted and how far I could make the due diligence period stretch.

But unfortunately, part of setting your own hours is that you have to work when the call comes. So I postponed the tennis, which as it turned out saved me $177,000. (You can buy an entire tennis court for that amount!) I went to the property, arriving just 30 minutes later, and after 15 minutes on-site I had signed a conditional contract on the property. The friendly agent had arranged for the vendors (at their home) to counter-sign the agreement. I knew I had a winner.

My wife and I used multiple strategies to create cash flow and equity on this deal, to create a grand slam. I bought the property below value from vendors who didn't understand the full value of their property, combined with what I call 'a vendor circumstance': they needed money fast. I gave them what they wanted with a fast settlement (less than three weeks later), and got the rest of what I wanted in terms of a fantastic price and a very low deposit. I had the property with a short due-diligence period, just five working days to do my council checks on whether it could take a minor dwelling or not. I found out it could, which was a nice bonus, since I would have bought it anyway for the price and renovation potential.

Bridget spent $26,000 and project-managed the renovation: a new kitchen, new bathrooms, ripping up the old carpets and polishing the beautiful rimu floors in the living areas, putting carpet in the bedrooms for warmth and quietness, new curtains, new light fittings, satin chrome electrical faceplates, new satin chrome tapware, painting the interior and having the bathrooms' walls tiled. The house was completely modernised and transformed.

During that time I also obtained building consent from Waitakere City Council (which cost me around $7,000 in professional and council fees at that stage) to build a minor dwelling. I then had the property revalued. It came back at $362,000. We had the property rented out to a government department at $420 per week, which meant that after tax (depreciation) the property was cash flow positive. We built the minor dwelling next — unfortunately we needed to put in a macerating sewerage pump to transport the sewerage uphill into the public drain at the top of my north-sloping section. There was no public stormwater drain on the property so we had to also get a detention tank and discharge the roof run-off via this into the curb outlet in the road's gutter. These were unexpected costs, but the house was on the front of the section so we had a short service trench, and in particular a short mains electrical cabling run.

The total construction cost for the minor dwelling and site works was $135,000. Including $5,000 in holding costs, my total project cost for purchasing the four-bedroom, two-bathroom brick-and-tile house, the renovation, the minor dwelling and associated siteworks was $428,000. The valuation on completion of all of these works, which took just under eight months from first seeing the property until code of compliance on the house, was an amazing $605,000. We had created $177,000 of equity, which is outstanding. In addition we created a total combined passive cash flow of over $7,000 per year, which is also pretty good.

And I still got to play tennis the following week.

Now it would have been extremely hard for me, even if I were a partner in an Auckland CBD commercial law firm, to save $177,000 after tax in less than eight months. The money I put into this property came from other properties I owned. You just can't create equity, or indeed cash flow, like this with 99.9% of other investments. If you can raise your property investment game to become a champion player, then why not become a master at a number of strategies?

Grand-slamming is where the wheat gets separated from the chaff. There are plenty of very successful buy-and-hold investors who can usually manage a renovation project with some degree of difficulty. However, these investors are more passive and would struggle to become fine-tuned professional negotiators, excellent renovation project managers, and excellent development and construction project managers. This is why property is so great — the rewards are brilliant for those who make the effort to learn what schools and universities do not teach you.

This is an example of a reward only an active investor could achieve. If I had played that tennis match (or been tied to a desk job), I would have been second in line on the contract as an agent from the same agency had a buyer there just one minute after the contract was signed up. They went in as a back-up offer on my contract, with shorter due diligence, a higher deposit and a slightly higher price. Timing can be important in real estate, so part of your success comes from knowing when to go to work on growing your investments portfolio. Here are the figures from this grand slam:

Purchase price: $255,000

Renovation on original house: $26,000

Rental on original house: $420 per week

Cost of getting building consent for minor dwelling: $7,000

Cost of construction of minor dwelling: $135,000

Holding costs (interest payments etc): $5,000

Total spend: $428,000

New valuation: $605,000

Equity in the property: $177,000

plus positive cash flow of over $6,000 annually

Bridget and I have made several grand slams. They have become a very positive habit for us. One of our very best property deals involved my wife buying well below value, then project-managing a cosmetic renovation, before I got my team to develop plans for both a minor dwelling and a sleepout, which we had built. This gave us over a 10% net yield and around $200,000 in additional equity.

Summary of property strategies

There are numerous valid strategies that can be employed in property investment to invest and prosper. Property trading is a cash-flow strategy, where you buy and sell properties as your business activity, adding value to them in some particular way. You pay income tax and GST when you are property trading. The buy-and-hold strategy is the most common property investment strategy. Over time you will reap significant rewards for this strategy, even if you paid slightly over the value of the property at the time you purchased it.

There are also numerous variations on the trading and buy-and-hold strategies. By mastering some of the strategies outlined in this chapter, you can add real value to your investments, and reach your goals faster.

9 | How to get a great deal

Buy below value. This is a fantastic strategy to create equity for you — but it's more than just a strategy that you might choose to utilise. It's the best and fastest way to make money on property. By buying a property below value you are instantly building the equity that you have in a property, which also keeps your loan to value ratio (LVR) in check.

In other words, never buy properties above their value. I teach this to all my mentoring students. Why not? Because you just don't have to! There are always great deals out there.

Take another property that we purchased for $265,000. It needed work done to it, like repairing the kitchen and bathroom floorboards, fixing a leaky bath tap and removing the worn 1960s kitchen. We knew it was a good deal, and after doing our regular due diligence checks my wife had a registered valuation done. On an 'as-is' condition the property was valued at $324,000. We made $59,000 equity, just by buying the property below value. How long would it take you to save $59,000 from your job or business? I can assure you that it is much easier to save by buying property below value.

Why would anyone sell their house below value?

The property market isn't a 'perfect' market. Houses don't always sell for the prices they should. Some sellers want an early settlement as they have bought elsewhere and need the money, or are going overseas. When dealing with agents or private sellers I always ask 'Why is this property for sale?' The answers can be most revealing and give you an insight to what the vendors want out of the transaction. (More on this topic in the chapter on property negotiation.) Here are some reasons why a vendor would sell a house below its true value:

- O not knowing its true value — this happens far more regularly with private sales

- O poor presentation — for instance, unmowed lawns, an untidy house and section

- O a property in a state of disrepair — for instance, holes in the floorboards, foundation subsidence, a hole in the ceiling with water dripping through, big water stains on the carpets and so on

- O divorce sales — where a property is sold in forced circumstances due to a divorce

- O estate sales — for example a person has died and his or her will provides to distribute funds equally among all the children, and the loss in value from underselling the property is spread between them

- O mortgagee sales can sometimes create opportunities

- O vendor circumstances forcing a quick sale — where a vendor needs to move on quickly, and will be amenable to a quick sale or a long-term settlement, in exchange for a good price

- O vendor overly emotional — so sells it to a 'nice family', who say they cannot afford to pay top dollar, but will take great care of it and the old owner is welcome to revisit the home in the years ahead

- O poor property marketing

- O buyer-friendly real estate agents

- O long-term settlements

- O options to purchase.

Not knowing a house's true value

Too often there is a twist in a property that cannot be seen or taken advantage of by the vendor. This most often happens when there is a combination of strategies which could work with a property — such as having enough land to develop a minor dwelling or sleepout — which the vendor would not have considered. Another common example is being able to fix a problem with a property that the vendor either cannot figure out how to solve or simply can't be bothered. The most common reason, though, is just not knowing the state of the market and what direction it's taking.

A friend of mine, Trevor, who is an extremely successful property investor, bought a property in 2004 for $280,000 when the market had actually moved in West Auckland, and the property was conservatively valued at $375,000. The vendors were simply not aware that the market had moved, yet as a prudent investor Trevor already knew that and obtained this deal. Of course, this also happens in the other direction when the market is in a downturn and the vendors don't realise this (or refuse to), and don't move their price down to meet the market.

Private sales

Unfortunately when homeowners sell their own home, they generally have an inflated view of its value. They will proudly put up a sign on their fence or front lawn: 'Private sale!' Sometimes the house is in a quiet cul-de-sac so really only the neighbours benefit from this. (Don't laugh — I have seen an investor do this in a nine-house cul-de-sac. The tenants were not impressed.) Owners will usually list the property on TradeMe, and possibly use the Homesell publication and private selling kits. After a month to six weeks many homes have not sold, because the high asking price burns off many of the serious would-be buyers. Also, unlike a real estate agent, homeowners lack a database of interested buyers in their area. Owners also lack the negotiation prowess of most agents. All these factors conspire to mean that no deal has been struck with the most desirable type of buyer.

So use this to your advantage. Once a property has been on the market for some time without selling, the owners will be getting desperate. They will be growing increasingly panicky and strongly thinking about engaging a real estate agent, who will of course charge a commission. Now you can generally negotiate at least the commission off the list price, but often significantly more.

My advice is to look for private sales. Call them, visit the property if it could fit your buying criteria, and be assertive in your negotiations with the vendor. Be aware that the house will often be mispriced on the high side, and that you will have to wait for reality to kick in. However, insist on presenting them a written offer. Then even if they don't make a counter-offer to you, just wait. Follow them up with a phone call in a couple of weeks' time. I have both achieved and seen great success this way.

What fascinates me is why agents tell homeowners their home is worth $400,000 to $450,000, yet they decide to list it themselves at $495,000 'to test the market'. Too often the house sells in the very bottom of the range that the agents tell them, if not below that level, several months after they began the sales process!

So to summarise, the opportunities arising from some private sales are:

○ mis-pricing the property (sometimes you get presented an absolute bargain)

○ lack of negotiation prowess

○ no access to a pool of interested buyers like the ones an agent may currently be working with

○ no access to network of agents that may have interested buyers, or a multiple listing service.

Poorly presented properties

My sister-in-law and her husband bought a property in 2001 — it looked like an absolute disgrace, but in fact all it needed was a cleaning crew working full time for two days (at a cost of less than $1,000). The cleaners removed all the grime from the tiled floors so they went from brown to the sparkling off-white colour they should have been. They painted walls from cigarette-smoke-beige to a soft grey colour. The oven was cleaned and looked immaculate. The exterior was waterblasted to remove moss, lichen and grime. The lawns needed a mow and the driveway, the paths and the fence needed waterblasting too. The house was in Remuera, an upmarket suburb of Auckland. It was purchased for $305,000, and after the tidy-up it had a true value of $370,000.

Another example is a house I went to in 2002 — it had over 50 cardboard boxes stacked from floor to ceiling. A grand piano took up one whole room. Sullen teenage boys were eating their Weet-bix, ogling prospective buyers. The lads told the real estate agent where to go when he politely asked them if they could turn the loud heavy-metal music down a bit for five minutes. Little wonder that one had been on the market for over 12 months. The owner probably blamed the agents for not selling the property as I noticed at least three agencies had tried to market that property at some point in time.

In 2009, some of my mentoring students in Wellington told me their story of a property-hunting sortie which takes the cake. The property in

Lower Hutt they visited had the homeowner's family all sitting around the table except the husband. My clients were thinking that the house looked pretty nice, apart from the slight stench of decomposing food. They looked at the exterior of the house, walked around the deck, and thought these were in good condition.

Then they heard a big 'thud'. It seemed to come from the direction of the garage. The agent wanted to find out what on earth this noise was, so she followed the sound. My mentoring students were a little bit shy and certainly weren't going to go into the garage first, so followed behind at a sensible distance. Upon opening the garage they saw not only eight chickens but also an axe, a tree stump, a chicken's head and neck, and a headless chicken running wildly around into the walls of the garage before it finally gave up the ghost. The scene was complete with CSI-style blood splattered on the ceilings, walls and windows of the garage (or should I say private chicken farm). The agent then vomited over the garage door and her shoes, and unfortunately got a little bit on my clients' shoes too — they were trying to hold their own stomachs in check as well. My students were pre-approved buyers but they just weren't interested in trying to remove the smells or owning an investment property like this!

As a postscript, the owners of this house got a 'special visit' and there are no longer chickens living at the address. I understand that the owners escaped a fine in this instance for religious or cultural reasons. The moral of the story is 'don't count your chickens until your property is sold'.

Properties needing repair

You can buy a lot of properties below value because of the state they are in. I refer to these properties as buying them below their 'true value'. I think of the true value as being the value they would sell for if brought up to the market requirements. Too many vendors don't have the money, the taste, the know-how or desire to bring their properties up to speed, or they do shabby things and take short-cuts, like painting the exterior of a house over mosses and lichens with a garden broom, to save time, only to find paint coming off at an alarming rate a few months later, or DIY disasters like building their own deck, with differing lengths and spacing.

One simple example is a Riccarton property bought by a friend of mine named Lee. It was owned by an elderly couple with failing eyesight, and they didn't really care what the exterior of the house looked like. So when it came time to repaint the exterior, they decided to save money and let their next-door neighbour paint it with some discount paint he'd picked up in a hardware store sale. There was a good reason the paint was on sale — it was mustard yellow. The red roof, the mustard-yellow weatherboards and the khaki aluminium joinery added up to very few viewings because the house looked so unappealing in the listing photo. Lee picked it up at well below value and her agent estimated that by merely repainting the exterior to an inoffensive cream (at a cost of $3,500), Lee had added at least $15,000 to the value of the house.

Divorce sales

Another sister-in-law and her husband bought a fantastic property in central Auckland in 1997. Originally listed at over $300,000, they eventually purchased it for just $240,000. The bathroom mirror had rude words written on it in lipstick, as well as lots of childish writing like 'How dare you talk to me like that?' and 'Grow up $^&#er' scribbled in pencil on the walls, and 'You bast@^d' written by a finger in the dust on the windowsill. One door had a hole punched in it. There were no other breakages, the pencil rubbed out extremely easily, and the lipstick wiped off in no time. It was in a good condition and clean enough too. The vendors were in a state of mind which meant that they just wanted out, so they accepted an offer around 20% below its true value.

Some real estate agent colleagues have told me even worse stories. Destructive events happen during messy divorces, like houses having windows smashed in. One particularly nasty break-up resulted in a home with spray-paint on the living room walls, the vanity unit ripped off the wall, couches shredded, holes kicked in the GIB plasterboard walls, the pantry emptied out vigorously onto the kitchen floors, and the fridge and freezer turned off for good measure so the decomposing food would provide the soon-to-be ex-spouse with that 'special aroma' upon her return home.

From an investor's perspective, divorce can represent an opportunity for you to get a house below its true value. Vendors getting out of a bad relationship are often keen to escape a house filled with bad memories, negative emotions and where one or both partners felt trapped. The focus is often on exiting the relationship, so you can be of service to them by offering them a price even if it isn't necessarily top dollar. The vendors may weigh up the alternatives: getting top dollar but having to spend possibly months in negotiation, versus a straightforward and rapid exit to a fresh start and freedom.

Estate sales

Estate sales are often a great way to profit from property at the time of purchase. You can regularly get a property well below its true value as usually the remaining survivor in a couple has died and his or her will (which technically creates a testamentary trust), provides for distribution of funds among its beneficiaries. The beneficiaries will generally decide not to keep the property as a rental property in some form of co-ownership together, and want to sell it. This is great for you as a buyer, as you can put in your offer for the property to get it at a good price. The loss in value between your offer price and true value is minimised between each beneficiary as it is spread among a number of them.

Amy and Chris, for instance, bought their home at the height of the real estate boom in 2007. The property had been owned by the same couple since it was built in the early 1980s and not much had been done to it since then. The wife died and the husband continued to live there until he was 93, at which age he — no, he didn't die, he moved into a very nice rest home. The children were charged with selling the property — they were in their late sixties and didn't want too much hassle. Amy and Chris put in an unconditional offer of $530,000, which was accepted. The agent admitted to Amy that another couple had put in an offer of $550,000 but the vendor's children weren't interested in waiting for finance approval and they preferred to sell the house to a 'nice couple'.

Mortgagee sales

Mortgagee sales are where the owner (mortgagor) has been unable to honour their agreement with their lender and has missed a few loan payments, and the lender has exercised their powers to sell the property over which they hold a mortgage in an attempt to reclaim the value of their security. This can present the opportunity to put into action a great strategy. In Dunedin in early 2011 some clients bought one property in this situation at more than 25% below value, and another property with an outstanding positive cash flow.

Typically properties that are presented poorly or need renovation work are the ones that you can buy below market value. I have also experienced success from buying properties off homeowners directly.

Vendor circumstances

You can buy properties below value by making the most of a vendor's particular circumstances. This is why it is very important to ask a person why they are selling the property. Sometimes a vendor simply finds the whole sales process rather stressful and traumatic and just wants it sold fast to alleviate the stress, without sufficient regard to the price. Other times a vendor needs money as they have bought a home elsewhere and need funds for their purchase settlement, so they don't have to arrange costly bridging finance — or worse they cannot actually obtain a bridging loan, so are staring down the barrel of a settlement default.

I once purchased a great property and saved the vendors' credit rating at the same time — so we both got a good deal. The vendors were in default on their home loan, and had been served the requisite Property Law Act notices. They were five months in arrears on their loan and the mortgagee sale was going to commence the next day. I dealt with an agent who dealt with the vendors, and I also dealt directly with their bank. Because I have a strong knowledge of insolvency and property law, I was able to convince the bank to accept my offer.

This was an example of a real win–win in negotiation as the property did not go to mortgagee auction, largely on the basis that the purchase price covered the bank's loan balance, penalty and interest fees as well as legal fees to date. There was even enough money in it for the vendors to pay off their credit card, book flights for a permanent trip to Australia in a couple of months' time, to pay for a bond on a place over the ditch, and for other relocation and start-up costs. I had saved their credit rating as there was no longer any bad debt outstanding. Also, there was the possibility that their house would have sold for much less at the mortgagee sale, which could have shattered their dream to join their family in Sydney.

Vendor overly emotional

This happens most often when the vendors are in love with their house, and have to move on. They often have to move into a rest home or move in with younger relatives, as ill health and old age kick in. Other common situations include relocating to another city for employment or family reasons. They don't think to keep their own home as a rental or they need the full amount of money for the next purchase. The owners don't like people that are going to chop and change the property around or demolish it and build three townhouses on the site, so they want to sell to another nice family. Their emotions get in the way of what they should really be focused on — price.

One couple who were selling their house in central Wellington had allowed tall trees to grow up all around the home during the 35 years they had lived there. The trees blocked out all the light entering the house and reduced its value dramatically by making the home unnecessarily cold, dark and damp. But the couple insisted that the property be sold only to a buyer who wouldn't cut down any of the (massive, overgrown) trees — so the property sold for at least $50,000 below value. It will be interesting to see how long those trees last!

Poorly marketed properties

Some properties are marketed extremely poorly. A great example of this is my home. It was advertised as a four-bedroom great family home. Nowhere in the advertising did it mention it had excellent views of Auckland's stunning CBD and Rangitoto Island, that it faced north so had excellent sun exposure, or that it had an ensuite bathroom. In addition, it had five bedrooms, not four. At the time it wasn't a great family home, with its 1960s-style light fittings, layers of wallpaper peeling off, shagpile carpet in some areas, nasty carpet squares in grey and pink in another bedroom, heavily worn curtains, and a red light bulb on the front door landing. It was hardly ideal for a crawling baby. The open homes had families coming in with their children in tow, but they left pretty quickly. It was just too much of a do-up project for them.

The agent had mucked up the marketing by advertising the property as a great family home and leaving out any mention of the sheer scale of the do-up. This property would have no doubt been a family home in the 1950s and 1960s but very little had been done since then. We got a great price by being the only bidders at the auction. Neighbours and around 10 real estate agents from the same agency were the only other people there.

Buyer-friendly real estate agents

While I don't particularly admire this practice, it does happen. There can be opportunities to work with agents that are quite friendly towards buyers, as opposed to property vendors, who they are meant to principally work for. Real estate is a funny game at times, and it can be rather cut-throat. The structure of real estate deals is all or nothing with regard to agents getting paid for their work. If the property sells they get paid. If the property doesn't sell they don't get paid. So they can at least be partially excused for trying to make a deal happen. But by forging a working relationship with a real estate agent, they will sometimes reveal all sorts of things they probably shouldn't. I am regularly able to find out the lowest price a vendor will accept — which is immeasurably important.

At the other extreme, I have heard of some outrageous deals where an agent has obtained a property for their best friend at a savagely low price. While the Real Estate Agents Act 2008 has tidied up some of the parasitic behaviour of certain real estate agents, you can bet your bottom dollar that just like every industry and profession, there will be a couple of agents that bend and break the rules to try to get themselves further ahead in life.

At the more honest end of the spectrum, Amy and Chris (mentioned above) dealt with a very helpful agent when buying their home, though the agent wasn't working on their behalf at the expense of the vendor. In fact, the agent had a great relationship with the vendor's whole family, and when she assured the vendors that Amy and Chris honestly were 'a nice couple' with a baby on the way, who would look after the property, the vendors decided to weigh that up in their final decision, which went in Amy and Chris's favour.

Long-term settlements

In a rising market you can benefit greatly from having long-term settlements (typically six months to two years). You buy the property at today's price or today's price plus a certain percentage. When it settles, if you have bought well enough and/or the market has given you a higher property value, you get to settle on a property well below value in the future.

For example, Warren entered into an agreement for sale and purchase to buy a property from Kent in four years' time in 2014 for $500,000. The property was worth $460,000 now, so Kent is happy as he thinks the property market will stagnate and be worth much the same as it is today. However, Warren is up with the play and knows that the council is likely to pass a vote on a zoning change that would enable the property to be subdivisible, which would greatly add to its value. Also, in 2014 the downturn should be over, and the property's value should therefore rise by far more than $40,000 over the next four years.

I find that most vendors don't want long-term settlements, finding them inflexible — they would prefer cash now.

Options to purchase

These are similar to long-term settlements, except you don't have to settle if the property goes down in value, or situations change and you can't obtain finance. You have an 'option agreement', which gives you a legal right to purchase a property from its owner at a certain predetermined price (strike price). You would pay the vendor a fee (the option fee) for the right to purchase their property at a certain price in the future. This is just like an option in a sharemarket.

Using the previous example, Warren would pay vendor Kent an option fee for $7,000 to have the right to purchase Kent's house for $500,000 on 31 March 2014. Kent couldn't sell his property to other people as there is an agreement on it with Warren — who should put a caveat on the property's title to best protect his interests as someone with an agreement on it entitling him to purchase it. If the property was worth more than $500,000 during the option period then Warren could exercise his option and purchase the house. Kent would pocket the option fee regardless and be free to do with it what he likes.

Like long-term settlements, most vendors are simply not interested in options, so this is a low-volume lottery strategy which is not widely employed.

10 How to find great properties

Once you have decided that property investment is right for you, and you have set some goals and come up with some ideas about what strategies will suit you, it is time to start looking for the right kinds of properties.

To do this you will need to set buying criteria that are right for you. Ask yourself questions like:

○ Do you only want to buy properties in your town or city?

○ Do you only want a brick-and-tile house?

○ Do you want an apartment?

○ Does the property need to have positive cash flow using an 8% interest rate? (This is approximately the 10-year average of all interest rates.)

○ Does the property need to have a house on it that you can renovate, and/or a subdivisible section?

○ Do you just want to buy a coastal section that you will build on and on-sell as a property trade for a profit?

It can seem rather overwhelming at the start with all sorts of properties available, varying in price depending on age, condition, type of dwelling, section size, and even the street and suburb. Selection is a crucial process. My property selection process is relatively easy as I have worked out the strategies that I want to use and I have created strong buying rules for myself. I also have good financial spreadsheets and excellent systems in place. If you want to be a really successful property investor you need to have buying rules, and good tools available to be able to distinguish a good deal from just an average deal.

Location

You've heard the cliché: location, location, location. It's been used as the title for more than one top-rating real estate TV show, and the reason that it's such a familiar phrase is that it's true.

The location of the property you are hunting for is crucial. It is so important that it can determine whether you are able to be financially free in 12 years or if it will take 60 years. For example, I had a mentoring student who lived in a remote and beautiful central North Island lakeside area about 25 minutes' drive from Ohakune. She didn't want to buy a property in Ohakune, or even in Taupo. She had observed that capital growth is typically lower in small towns, vacancy rates are higher as supply and demand fluctuates wildly between seasons and the towns are dependent on one or two industries (such as skiing in Ohakune). Instead she chose to purchase properties in Wellington (including Upper and Lower Hutt) and Auckland where there is plenty of tenant demand as well as the population growth to create constant demand for houses.

It is vital to pick a property in a good location. Would you really want your investment property to be in a town experiencing population decline, with a dependence on one core industry? Would you like to purchase in a suburb with over 20% unemployment among the working population, riddled with serious crime, and graffiti not just on fences, but on houses too? Or would you prefer to purchase in a good suburb in a city that is growing fast, with all indicators pointing to this continuing?

Do you have to buy close to where you live? I know that many people, including me, like to invest within half an hour's drive from their home. However, it's not possible for everybody to acquire a good investment property within such a short distance of their home. And even if it were you might be missing out on the best locations.

What is the perfect property?

There are three elements to property investment: cash flow, equity and growth. The closest thing to a perfect property would be in a location that has fantastic capital and rental growth, but is cheap to purchase. Sadly this is a bit of a fantasy; the most desirable suburbs typically have the best long-term capital growth as well as the best rental growth and are well located near the CBD — but they are expensive to buy into, and don't give a good cash flow. Conversely the cheapest properties in less desirable suburbs may provide good cash flow but have poorer long-term capital growth and rental growth prospects.

Therefore I believe that a combination is important. I don't like to invest in the bottom 20% of areas, nor the top 30% of areas, as the areas at the bottom end tend to have too many property-management issues. Also I am keen to get some good cash flow going so I typically do not look in the 'nicer' areas (and being in Auckland I simply need to cull the number of houses I am looking at).

Helpful software

The Real Estate Investar software has an amazing search tool where you can search for properties that have positive cash flow, discount property, development deals, vendor finance deals and so on, to focus your search. You can sort and rank the search results to narrow down the best deals for your criteria.

This software includes Property IQ's online iAdvise service, which is useful in seeing what houses in the area sold for, the features of properties you are looking at and of course what the current owner paid for the property. Other tools like PropertyGuru and RPNZ are useful in giving you comparable sales data, but I personally rate Real Estate Investar is the best as it is cheaper and contains:

○ iAdvise

○ the Investar Search tool

○ Property Analyser, which is a strong property analysis tool, and

○ Portfolio Tracker, which keeps track of your property values, loans, income and expenses.

Location factors

Now remember! You are buying a rental property, not your next home. The numbers are the most important thing, and if they add up then the nasty curtains and trashy letterbox are irrelevant. You don't have to live there yourself, you just have to make it liveable for a good tenant. The reason is that tenants rent on emotion. They are often happy to pay more for things like a better suburb, being closer to work, closer to public transport and other factors which make life more comfortable.

Location factors that I think are important are:

O sound school zones

O homes in the street and neighbourhood that are well cared for (for instance, no paint flaking off, rusted roofs, broken-down cars on the front lawn

O attractive gardens in the street and neighbourhood, with well-maintained lawns and landscaping (as opposed to knee-high lawns, overgrown gardens or no gardens)

O low crime rate

O low amount of graffiti and trash littering the place

O good proximity to schools, employment, large shopping centres

O good proximity to public transport routes (though probably not a house backing onto a motorway!)

O not in a declining part of town.

O no high-tension power pylon in the backyard, or high-tension power lines over the house (they can interfere with cellphones and other electronic devices, crackle from time to time, and simply scare the living daylights out of too many tenants and future buyers).

Selection process

When selecting property, we are blessed to have the internet. If you don't have a computer with broadband internet you are going to make life more difficult for yourself (in most respects, not just finding a property). There are so many tools that we literally have at our fingertips right now that you will be missing out on or taking a much longer time to find out about. Packages like Telecom's TotalHome Package have brought the cost of long-distance calls and using the internet right down.

Tools

TradeMe Property

This is an amazing resource featuring virtually all listed property in New Zealand. Just about every real estate agency in the country puts their listings on it, as well as most private sellers. Bookmark www.trademeproperty.co.nz on your internet browser if you haven't already done so.

Department of Building and Housing Tenancy statistics

This is a great resource featuring all of the information collected by the DBH from bond lodgement forms. DBH divides cities into suburbs and states the type of property and number of rooms (for example, two-bedroom flat, five-bedroom house) and it gives out the median rent, lower and upper quartiles and the average rent, as well as the number of bonds received, so you can disregard information collected for too small a sample size. The market rent tool is a fantastic resource. It's currently located online at, www.dbh.govt.nz/market-rent

Rating information

I have collated all of the New Zealand council's and territorial authorities websites and put them onto my own website for your ease of use. Go to www.davidwhitburn.com/nz-council-databases and select your council. Most councils in New Zealand have their rating information, including the capital value and its split between land and buildings, online. Some councils also include their public drainage data, scale maps, aerial photos, development contributions, and full zoning information on their website. Other councils have portions of this information.

Sadly a handful of councils are still in the Dark Ages of the last millennium and haven't embraced the full power of the internet and information revolution, including some with no websites at all. If this is the case you will just have to ring your local council to verify the rates for yourself. Remember that there will usually be a local council rate and a regional council rate. For example, if you live in Whitianga in the Coromandel Peninsula, you will have a rate charged by the local Thames–Coromandel District Council, and a rate charged by Environment Waikato as your regional council.

Interest rates

Information about current interest rates is available using websites like Good Returns' www.mortgagerates.co.nz, www.interest.co.nz and www.bnz.co.nz. It is always important to know what is happening in the interest rate market, so you can budget for the interest charges on your investment.

General property investment information

Go to information-rich sites like www.nzwealthmentor.com and www.davidwhitburn.com to get great general property investment information, which is searchable in my blogs. I like writing and update my readers regularly so I have a popular newsletter that I email out. I would highly recommend that you also join my database. I also blog frequently to share my thoughts on various aspects of the market. You should also consider joining your local property investors' association.

Property investment calculation spreadsheet

You want to calculate whether the deal is good or not, and if you, like me, have equity and passive cash flow as your criteria, you will need to measure how much.

How can I find good deals?

You owe it to yourself to seek out and take advantage of good property deals. Purchasing a hugely negative cash flow property that you need to tip money into from other sources (like your job, business or other investments), at above its true value, in a declining or remote area is not going to be a smart investment. Instead I believe that you need to focus on three foundations to property investment: cash flow, equity and growth.

To get good growth in both rentals and capital values, you are best to invest in cities as opposed to smaller towns. Within cities, the more centrally located and sea- or river-side suburbs tend to have the highest growth. Equity comes from knowing an area well, which gives you the ability to differentiate a good deal from a standard or bad deal. Cash flow comes from renting a property and it sure does help if you get the purchase price down to achieve a higher return from your property. As a result once you have selected a city to buy in, you need to become an area specialist and focus on a maximum of three suburbs. It is preferable that these suburbs are within 30 minutes driving distance so you can easily look for good investment properties, particularly if — like most Kiwis — you will be managing it yourself.

While real estate agents are the major source of quality property investment deals, they are by no means the only source. In fact some of best property purchases don't actually come via real estate agents. To me the buying process is like a funnel.

The property-buying process (the funnel)

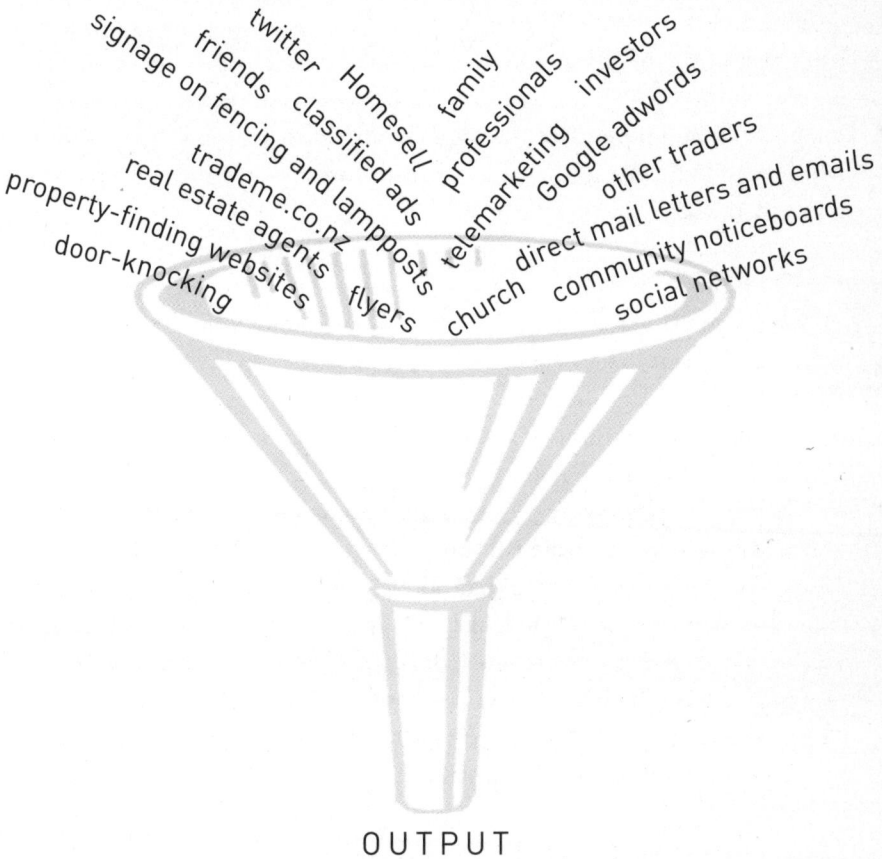

twitter
signage on fencing and lampposts
friends
classified ads
Homesell
family
professionals
investors
telemarketing
Google adwords
other traders
trademe.co.nz
direct mail letters and emails
real estate agents
community noticeboards
property-finding websites
church
social networks
door-knocking
flyers

OUTPUT

Great property deals

Great deals can come from surprising sources: a mentoring client of mine purchased an outstanding property via a supermarket noticeboard! He had read my mentoring manual about alternative ways of buying property, so he starting looking at community noticeboards including at churches, community halls and supermarkets in the area. He found an advert saying 'Need to Sell My House Now'. After a Christmas with no presents, no holidays, no food in the cupboard, the owners had realised they weren't able to comply with their bank's November default letter, which threatened imminent placement of a mortgagee sale. Stressed at the thought of having a fire sale and a shortfall leftover, and thinking they couldn't afford agents' fees, the owners did the advertising themselves using free methods including writing on the back of a leftover real estate agent's sign and putting small ads on community noticeboards. This is where my client found the property. He contacted the vendor and after a three-hour-long meeting, a price was decided and the house sold subject to the bank accepting the price. The bank did; as the offer was above 75% of the council valuation, and the decision-makers felt that a bird in the hand was worth more than two in the bush. In addition, there was a quick settlement in a fortnight's time, which was invaluable to the bank when the arrears situation was getting worse by the day.

Letter drop

Another example of a great deal was done by a friend of mine, Steve, a very successful investor in his own right. He purchased a property in Henderson Valley, West Auckland in 2003, before the boom took off, for $180,000. After he put a broom through it and ran a waterblaster around the outside, he got a valuation of $260,000.

He found this property by doing a letterbox drop, manually posting letters stating that he wanted to buy a house in the area. Most people didn't reply but by using a tool like RPNZ back then (iAdvise is another equivalent now) he was able to look at the properties he wanted (with a full section and at least three bedrooms), then target them with a private sale to save agents' fees. The strike rate was around two phone calls for every 100 letters, and only one of the phone calls would result in an appointment. However when appointments were made, sales were closed.

11 | How do I check out a property?

It is vital that you do some research to ensure that the property you are thinking of buying is suitable for your needs. This process is called due diligence. It can be as thorough or haphazard as you like. I want you to be thorough and to analyse all aspects of a potential property transaction so you can make the right decision.

Conditional contracts

A conditional contract is an agreement for sale and purchase that is live, but the property is not sold yet, because the buyer is in the process of doing their due diligence. A property is only sold when the agreement goes unconditional — otherwise it just has an agreement on it.

When you are looking at properties with real estate agents, a few will try to push you into making an unconditional agreement, where you get no opportunity to do a full due diligence as you have already bought the property. Don't fall into this trap — it is absolutely fine and indeed normal to make the agreement conditional. Most people use the Real Estate Institute of New Zealand and Auckland District Law Society standard form agreement for sale and purchase. You should familiarise yourself with the key workings of this document. I recommend that until you become highly experienced with property, and are able to do your calculations and due diligence in advance of making an offer, that you should only do conditional deals. That means you need to insert a condition into the further terms of sale (on page 2 of the agreement). The wording could be something along the lines of:

'This agreement is conditional on the Purchaser giving written notice to the Vendor, approving all matters that the Purchaser considers may affect the property or the commercial viability of the transaction within 12 working days from the date of this agreement. The Vendor warrants to provide the Purchaser and any of their invitees access to the property between the hours of 8am and 5.30pm Monday to Saturday on working days, as many times as necessary in order to carry out its due diligence investigation. This condition is inserted for the sole benefit of the Purchaser, and the Vendor may not enquire into the Purchaser's exercise of their discretion.'

Unless you are presented with an outrageously good deal (good enough to cover things that may be missed in the due diligence) and have the ability to recognise this and do your numbers quickly, do conditional contracts.

Your role in due diligence

Your main task in due diligence is to do the numbers to see if the property meets your buying criteria or not. There are a number of steps to go through in order to do this:

○ Liaise with your lender or mortgage broker to ensure that you have your finance in place, including satisfactory financial pre-approval.

○ Establish what the interest rates are. (If you are unsure what rate to use, consider using the 10-year average interest rate of 8% as weighted across the variable, one-, two-, three-, four- and five-year fixed-term categories.)

○ Record the rental level. (If the property is currently tenanted and the tenant is staying on, you know the rental level; otherwise get a property manager that is skilled in your area and is independent to the real estate agency, to appraise the weekly rental — this service is usually free if you use them as a manager or refer them business, or might cost you around $60 at worst case.)

○ Engage a suitably skilled property lawyer to investigate the title, LIM (Land Information Memorandum report) and draw up any special terms of sale. For instance, when a property I was buying had a rusty trailer, car, numerous beer bottles, tyres and other junk littered around the gardens on a property, I required a vendor warranty to remove the junk by settlement date or vary the agreement so the price for settlement would be reduced by $10,000.

○ Email, ring or get an online quote from your insurance company for the property.

○ Either obtain a property file (building bag) and discuss in person, ring the council to ask them about the property (sweet-talk them into releasing noise complaints in the street, and ask if is it in a hazard area), or obtain a Land Information Memorandum (LIM) report.

○ Consider talking to your prospective neighbours to find out if they are tenants or owners, and their thoughts on the neighbourhood.

○ Co-ordinate your lawyer, lender and other professionals that may be required (like a valuer, building appraiser etc).

Lawyers

You need to engage a specialist property lawyer or legal executive to help you settle your purchase of an investment property, unless you are one yourself. I did my own conveyancing when I worked at Russell McVeagh in 2002 with a bit of help from a friend who specialised in property. That was my first and last conveyance. Even though I am a lawyer holding a current practising certificate, I don't believe that I am best placed to do my own conveyancing as I am not a specialist and my time is better spent with my family, on property deals or on my businesses.

Property lawyers and legal executives are excellent at doing due diligence. They will usually do a number of things at a good price of just over $1,000 including GST when you purchase a property. If you are very active in the property market, you may be given discounts on your fees.

12 | How do I structure my property ownership?

While your rental income and capital growth don't change because of what name you put on a property's title, you need to be aware of potential taxation and cost consequences that may restrict or cost you financially in the future. There are many choices available and it is very important that you think carefully about this — it can be very expensive to change your mind, particularly with potential taxation issues, but also with conveyancing fees and refinancing fees to a lender. There are a number of ownership structures you can choose to own your assets in. These include:

- own name
- look-through company (LTC)
- 'ordinary' limited liability company
- partnership
- limited liability partnership
- trust
- offshore structures.

I will not include fringe structures like an unincorporated joint venture as very few investors use them. The main thing is to weigh up your goals from the ownership structure in terms of both tax optimisation and tax efficiency. Each structure has various advantages and disadvantages. While I am going to summarise each type of structure, you should seek independent professional advice from a suitably qualified accountant or lawyer who is skilled in property investment taxation issues and who can assist you to set up the best structure given your own particular circumstances.

Own name

This is the sole trader structure where you own the property under your own name.

Advantages:
It is very easy, and can have cheaper fees for conveyancing and accounting.

Disadvantages:
You have no asset protection.

Look-through company ('LTC')

This is an ordinary company incorporated under the Companies Act 1993, and has a tax structure created pursuant to the amending Acts of the Income Tax Act 2007. It has been created to replace the loss attributing qualifying company (LAQC), and took effect from the first day of the income year, which for the vast majority of investors was 1 April 2011. LTC shareholders are liable for tax upon the company's profit, as well as being able to offset the company's losses against their other income.

The key features of an LTC are:

○ For income tax purposes, the LTC is 'looked-through' and the owners of an LTC are regarded as holding the LTC's assets directly and carrying on the activities of the LTC personally.

○ An LTC's income, expenses, tax credits, gains and losses are passed onto its owners following their effective interest in the company.

○ Each owner of the LTC will then record any income or losses, as appropriate, in their own income tax return.

Advantages:
You can offset any rental losses against your personal income which can save you tax (some LTC owners save many tens of thousands of dollars in taxes). You have limited liability protection as it is still a company. Capital gains are considered as derived directly by the shareholders (therefore no liquidation of the company is needed to distribute capital gains to the shareholders).

Disadvantages:

You have no asset protection. If you make profits you may be paying a higher tax rate on them than you need to, and you cannot keep profits in the LTC. There may be higher compliance costs than by using other entities. There is a deemed sale of the underlying assets when you change shareholding, or exit from the LTC regime.

More details on LTCs are found in the next chapter.

'Ordinary' limited liability company

By 'ordinary' company, I mean a company incorporated under the Companies Act 1993. It is a separate legal entity comprising shareholders who are the legal owners of the company, and directors who have a duty to operate the company.

Advantages:

Limited liability protection. Lower tax rate currently at 28%.

Disadvantages:

Cannot offset losses against personal income. No asset protection.

Partnership

This is a structure that has two or more partners being jointly and severally liable for the debts of the other partners, and they share in assets, for example, property investments. Net income or losses go to the partners' own income tax return. For example: Walter, Eva and Richard are in a partnership. The partnership made $90,000 for the income year, so Walter, Eva and Richard each individually have $30,000 of partnership income to put into their individual accounts and income tax return.

Partnerships are relatively common structures for professional firms (such as law firms), but are less common for property investors. This is because more people use trusts for asset protection and succession planning on positive-cash flow portfolios, or LTCs for loss-making investors in salaried or waged employment. Partnerships are governed by the Partnerships Act 1908, which permits the drafting of a Partnership Deed or Agreement to enable partnerships to have their own rules (such as a compulsory date of retirement for a partner, rules for exiting the partnership and so on).

Advantages:

Can offset losses against personally earned income.

Disadvantages:
Jointly and severally liable for the debts of your fellow partners. No asset protection.

Limited liability partnership ('LLP')

This is a comparatively new structure established by the introduction of the Limited Partnerships Act 2008, which came into effect on 2 May 2008. These are special partnerships consisting of a general partner who is liable for all the debts and liabilities of the partnership, and a limited liability partner who is liable to the extent of their capital contribution to the partnership. The general partner needs to be resident in New Zealand, whereas the limited liability partner can and often is resident overseas.

This is a structure that is broadly similar to the US Limited Liability Corporation (LLC), the LLPs in the United Kingdom, Dutch BVs, Spanish SAs and German GmbHs, in that they allow for overseas investors to use them. LLPs in NZ are used mainly by overseas private equity investors to provide for a pool of venture capital money.

Advantages:
Can be a flexible way of bringing in capital to invest from overseas. Can offset losses against personally earned income. Limited liability partner is only liable up to the amount of capital they contributed.

Disadvantages:
General partner is liable for all debts and liabilities of the partnership. No asset protection. Higher compliance costs.

Trusts

Trusts are an excellent structure to house assets in. They comprise a (i) Settlor if only one person, or Settlors if more than one, who settle the property onto the Trust. Then they have (ii) Trustees who are the legal owners of the trust fund, who hold the Trust's assets on behalf of the (iii) Beneficiaries of the Trust.

Many believe the origin of trusts dates back to the fifth century AD where trusts were modelled on the Roman *fideicommissum* (where wealth could be transmitted to a beneficiary via a person who would be trusted to honour their moral obligation). This was used by priests to evade restrictions on inheritances to the clergy. The use of trusts became more widespread with the Crusades in the thirteenth century. The Crusaders would often leave for many years, not knowing whether they would survive, and they would leave their property in the hands of trusted fellow knights, relatives and friends for the benefit of their wives and dependants while they were at war.

Advantages:

Trusts are the only structure that can offer true asset protection. They are treated in many respects as separate legal entities (although legally speaking they are not technically separate identities but have the identity of their trustees, who are protected by the indemnity for the assets of the trust fund). They can last up to 80 years and have proven themselves to be a great succession-planning tool to transfer wealth between generations. The benefits include:

○ ability to split income among beneficiaries, which can result in tax savings. For example, Mike and Jan's trust has owned rental property for 12 years and earns $100,000 in investment income. Mike is on the high tax rate so doesn't get any money distributed to him. Jan does charity work so gets a distribution of $48,000 and pays a maximum 17.5% income tax on this amount, and their two adult children studying at university aged 19 and 21 respectively get the remaining $26,000 per year (note that while this is what a lot of people do, it is important that you can get this amount back off your kids!).

○ government subsidies — for example, aged-care benefits like rest home, medical, pharmaceutical and nursing subsidies

○ succession planning — trusts can provide a coherent inter-generational wealth protection structure

○ creditor protection — property owned by your trust will not be exposed to personal guarantees, so if you have to offer a personal guarantee to a supplier, and you or your business are not able to meet your payment obligations, you don't have to use your trust's assets to meet this debt obligation.

○ accident protection — imagine you are a bit disorganised and your car is a week late in getting its registration and it crashes into a beautiful brand new Mercedes Benz. This will cost a small fortune as insurance companies don't like paying out when they don't have to (it is a condition of the vast majority of car insurance policies that your car is registered). The Mercedes driver's insurance company will probably not sue you if you have no assets, since the trust has them. It is not worth their while trying to get blood out of a stone.

○ divorce — by having a trust before you enter into marriage or a serious relationship, you can have this property treated as individual property and not relationship property.

○ death — if or (unfortunately what is more likely) when estate and death duties get brought back in, trusts provide a great way to minimise them.

Trusts are a whole lot easier to transfer and gift assets nowadays with gift duty being abolished on 1 October 2011. This means an end to the accountant's or lawyer's fees for template gifting programmes, and a saving of $250 to $700 per year for most people gifting money each and every year to trusts.

Disadvantages:
The only disadvantages of trusts are the set-up costs and the current fact that you cannot offset tax losses against your own personal income. In terms of set-up costs, trusts are typically more costly than any of the previously named structures to set up. But these costs are minimal when you consider that trusts can last for up to 80 years. When you consider all of the other benefits trusts give, the set-up cost is generally a no-brainer.

Most people (particularly accountants and tax advisors) state that the problem with trusts is that they don't have the ability to offset tax losses against personally derived income (your salary and wages, for instance). This stems from the fact that trusts are taxed in two ways:

○ trustee income — at the rate of income tax payable on trusts, currently 33%; and

○ beneficiary income — at the marginal tax rates of the beneficiaries.

Many trusts distribute income to their beneficiaries during the income year, or when the tax return of the trust is filed (a significant number of trusts are on a tax agency listing enabling an extension of time to file their return until 31 March the year after). Any income which is not distributed to beneficiaries becomes trustee income, which is taxed at the trust tax rate.

Offshore structures

There are a huge variety of offshore structures with which to own New Zealand property, including Australian individuals, German GmbHs, Spanish SAs, US LLCs to Panamanian foundations and British Virgin Islands Trusts and many others. In any event, if there is income sourced from a New Zealand property (such as rents), a New Zealand tax return needs to be filed.

I encourage readers who are not New Zealand tax residents to seek professional advice from a suitably qualified professional in relation to any proposed New Zealand investment purchases. Too often people don't know their obligations, and I have heard of New Zealanders investing in cheap properties and property products in the United States who have been stung by costly accounting and tax return preparation fees. This is the same in reverse; people overseas have to prepare accounts and file tax returns for their New Zealand rental properties.

Loss attributing qualifying companies (not available any more)

LAQCs were the single most common tax structure for property investors until recently. In the May 2010 Budget, Minister of Finance Bill English stated that he would be looking at LAQCs with a view to rendering them impotent. This has since happened, with legislation abolishing LAQCs from 1 April 2011 onwards. As a result if you had an LAQC you needed to change your ownership structure, or just run a Qualifying Company with no ability to attribute losses against personal income.

LAQCs were very popular because investors could attribute tax losses against their own salaried or waged income. When LAQCs make tax losses (tax deductible expenses exceeding taxable income), the losses are attributed to the shareholders in the percentage in which they own the shares. Conversely if an LAQC makes a profit it has to attribute this profit to the shareholders in the proportion that they own the shares.

13 | What do I do about paying tax or getting tax rebates?

The Loss Attributing Qualifying Company (LAQC) was a common tax structure that became enormously and increasingly popular in the past property boom of 2003–2007.

Active LAQCs — value of losses claimed

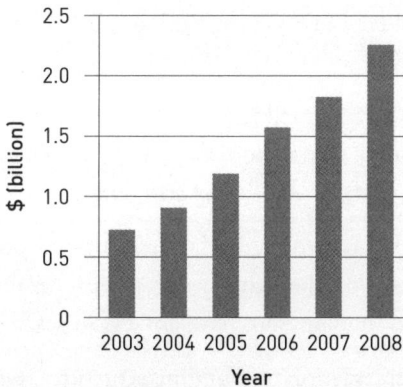

Source: Inland Revenue

With LAQCs rising in popularity, combined with interest rates reaching cyclical highs (floating rates were over 10% in 2007 and 2008), the government saw net losses (from all property investors aggregated together) for the first time in 26 years in the 2007 income year and this net loss was repeated in 2008. The government commissioned Victoria University to assemble a Tax Working Group to consider options for tax reform. Unfortunately in my view, the group included all sorts of representatives from the managed fund industry, academics, economists and the CEO of the NZ Stock Exchange. It had no representation from the NZ Property Investors' Federation (NZPIF), or any other property industry professionals. The fact NZPIF president Martin Evans and NZPIF vice president Andrew King had to pay to sit in the lecture theatre to attend some meetings, showed me, as president of the Auckland Property Investors' Association, just how welcome opinions from the property industry were in this Tax Working Group.

They proposed a number of scenarios that could be implemented ranging from:

O raising GST (which the government did to 15% with compensation to beneficiaries and superannuitants). This has hurt property investors as residential rentals are exempt from GST, but charges like rates, insurances, repairs and maintenance, management fees and professional fees have increased GST costs on them.

O imposing a capital gains tax (CGT). Both a comprehensive CGT including the family home and a targeted CGT where all real estate (not shares, businesses and commodities) except the family home would face a tax on the capital gain they make on selling the property.

O land tax. A 0.5% annual land tax on the value of land was proposed (much like an additional rate, but charged by central government instead of local government).

O risk-free rate of return method. Under this proposal, investors would be taxed on their equity at 6% with no ability to claim expenses and therefore not have any tax losses.

O removing depreciation on building structures. Depreciation rates for buildings were 3% diminishing value and 2% straight line, and the recommendation was to make this 0%.

O removing the 20% depreciation loading on new assets.

The Tax Working Group didn't mention structure changes in their recommendations. However in the May 2010 budget, the government announced changes to LAQCs, where they would be abolished and the groundwork for a new tax structure (the look through company) was announced.

Instead of the scenarios proposed by the Tax Working Group, the government chose to focus on property investors' depreciation. This was good news, as the worst option would have been the risk-free return method. Interestingly many investors felt relieved that it was only depreciation being impacted. However the impact of this is more than just a mere timing difference, as chattels appraisals had been used in the past at the time of sale to allocate as much of the sale price into land as possible.

Also just what constituted a building structure was redefined in April 2010. This was expanded in the eyes of many chartered accountants when the term 'building structure' was defined by the Inland Revenue Interpretation Statement IS10/01 (Residential Rental Properties — Depreciation of Items of Depreciable Property) as including items like partition walls, ducting, ventilation, electrical reticulation, plumbing fit-out, vinyl flooring and tiles. Then in the May 2010 Budget, Minister of Finance Bill English announced that building structure depreciation would be removed (rated at 0% just like land) with effect from 1 April 2011.

Depreciation impact

The cost of the depreciation changes is quite significant; the New Zealand Property Investors' Federation has surveyed its members and found an average cost of $43 per week per property. I surveyed a number of NZ Wealth Mentor clients in Auckland and found that the average cost of the depreciation changes to building structure is higher at $62 per week, which is over $3,200 per year. If you have a number of properties like me, this is a significant cost.

However I don't view this as a significant problem as my focus is on getting positive cash flow for my properties before tax, with the depreciation just being cream on top. I have heard from real estate agents that some undercapitalised investors with their own financial challenges have decided to sell, as these depreciation changes were the final straw. Conversely I know there were some investors who did not claim depreciation at all, viewing it as an added complexity.

I am still able to claim depreciation on building fit-out and chattels. This includes items like carpets, curtains, blinds, light fittings, fencing, driveways, stove, hob, rangehood and the letterbox. The loading for new assets is gone, but that wasn't a big deal to me anyway.

LAQC changes

The Budget highlighted some structure tampering with particular reference to LAQCs. In October 2010 draft legislation was issued which rendered LAQCs useless from 1 April 2011. This is because LAQCs lost their ability to attribute losses to their shareholders. Instead, if you did nothing with your LAQC it would become a qualifying company (QC). QCs only allow profits to be attributed to their shareholders in the proportion that they own the shares (and specifically not losses). This means that losses in LAQCs were able to be attributed against their shareholders' personally derived income only until the end of the 2011 income year (which is 31 March 2011 for the overwhelming majority of property investors who have the standard balance date), in the proportion that the shareholders own the shares in the LAQC.

Do I need to change my structure?

Since many LAQC owners are property investors who make losses, they will need to make a decision since LAQCs no longer provide the ability to offset rental losses against an investor's salary or wages. There are however some very friendly grandparenting rules to existing LAQCs (and qualifying companies) that allow tax concessions to change into a new structure.

The new tax structure: a look-through company

Legislation was passed in December 2010 to allow for the introduction of a new structure, a look-through company (LTC). The LTC rules came into effect from 1 April 2011. These structures are ordinary limited liability companies incorporated under the Companies Act 1993, but they have a special tax structure. Shareholders of an LTC are liable for income tax upon the company's profits and similarly they can offset the company's profits against their other income.

From an income tax perspective, an LTC looks through the company straight to its owners. The owners are regarded as holding the LTC's assets directly and carrying on the LTC's activities personally. All of the rental and any interest income, all expenses, tax credits, gains and losses are passed onto the shareholders of the LTC in the percentages they own of the LTC. This is done via a partnership (IR7) annual tax return for the LTC, and not via a company annual tax return. The individual shareholders then record their income or losses (subject to a loss limitation rule) in their own personal IR3 annual tax returns. The LTC is liable for all other tax types (eg. GST).

The look-through company's loss limitation rule

The LTC's loss limitation rule is very similar to that for limited liability partnership structures. The shareholders of an LTC can only offset tax losses to the extent that these losses reflect their true 'economic loss'. In practice, this means few investors will be denied losses. This is despite the fact that tax losses may exceed the amount of capital they have put at risk, as the rules have generously permitted that loans personally guaranteed by the shareholders (extremely common as lenders require these as a fundamental condition of loans) are included in the calculation. This means that losses claimed are very hard to use up, unless you are contributing a lot of equity into the initial purchase. If this was the case you would have far lower interest costs and be more likely to return a profit (and have a different tax structure, such as a trust). Any loss you cannot use gets carried forward and may be claimed in future income years, subject to qualifying under the loss limitation rule in those years.

Who can become a look-through company?

Only NZ tax resident companies can be LTCs. An LTC's shares must be owned by individuals, trustees or another LTC, and the LTC must have a maximum of five 'look-through counted owners' who ultimately receive any income or losses from the LTC.

Electing to become a look-through company

An IR862 look-through company election form needs to be filled out; this is available at www.ird.govt.nz (search under IR862), or you can get one from your accountant (at a small fee). All the LTC's shareholders must sign the election form, and the company's directors need to do this too.

You can find more information about existing QCs and LAQCs transitioning to an LTC in the Inland Revenue's IR879 guide, available at www.ird.govt.nz (or phone Inland Revenue on 0800 377 771), or by seeking expert advice from a tax professional.

What did investors do with their LAQCs?

Many investors decided to sell their property directly into a trust structure since they were receiving positive cash flow. The depreciation changes meant reduced expenses and some investors also achieved increases in rental income (in particular with the mini rental boom in Auckland in early 2011). Other investors did nothing and were converted into a qualifying company where there is no ability to offset losses against personal salaried or waged income. Instead losses need to be used at the company level.

The other main options with concessionary tax treatment were to:

○ revoke your LAQC election and be taxed as an ordinary company. Any new losses would have to be used by the company not the shareholders, and all dividends would be taxable to shareholders (but they could have imputation credits attached).

○ become an LTC

○ become a limited partnership

○ become an ordinary partnership

○ become a sole trader.

If you elected to become an LTC, limited partnership, ordinary partnership or sole trader, you were able to transition to these structures with no tax cost (no depreciation clawback!) if you did this prior to 30 September 2011. If you wanted to change shareholdings in your LAQC, you needed to have done this prior to 31 March 2011. Seek expert advice from a tax professional if you are unclear about any aspect of your structures.

Example of an LTC in action

Suresh and Shilpa own an LTC with two investment properties in it. If it makes a $30,000 tax loss in 2012, then they breeze in with the loss limitation rule as they have over $900,000 of bank loans they have guaranteed. So, with Shilpa owning 90% of the shares and Suresh owning 10% of the shares, $27,000 of losses pass through to Shilpa and $3,000 of losses pass through to Suresh. This means Shilpa doesn't pay tax on $90,000 any more, but on $63,000, and Suresh on a salary of $53,000 pays tax on $50,000. Have a look at this in the diagram opposite.

Associated persons rules

The definition of 'associated persons' in the Income Tax Act 2007 ('Act') was restricted in 2009, particularly with the introduction of a new 'tripartite'

Shilpa Sharma	Suresh Sharma
90% shareholder	10% shareholder

Sharma Properties Limited

LTC

Rental Income:	$50,000
Rental Expenses:	($80,000)
Net loss:	**$(30,000)**

Losses to flow through:

Shilpa	90% x ($30,000) = ($27,000)
Suresh	10% x ($30,000) = ($3,000)

Shilpa

Salary:	$90,000
Loss via LTC:	($27,000)
Taxable income:	$63,000

Suresh

Wages:	$53,000
Loss via LTC:	($3,000)
Taxable income:	$50,000

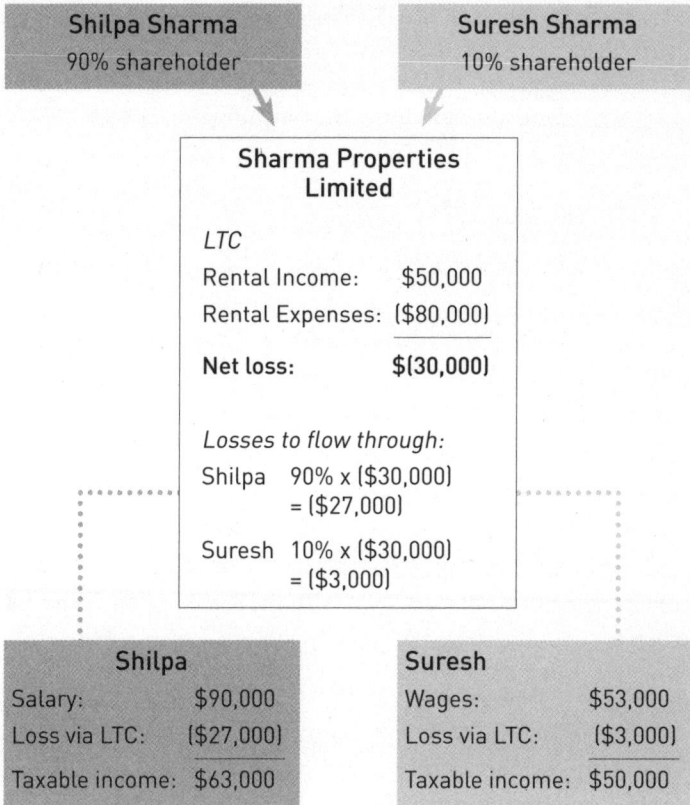

test for tainting. This targeted 'land transactions', which covers property investment specifically. In practical terms, investors used to be able to trade properties on revenue account (paying income tax on profits from trading, or deducting trading losses), and also have long-term buy-and-hold properties on capital account (no tax paid on gains on sale, and no losses deducted on selling at a loss). A trading trust would often be used for the property-trading activities and another structure would be used for the buy-and-holds. This was the case even if an investor traded several properties, and then if they sold one of their buy-and-holds after a couple of years, provided they had no purpose of resale at the time they acquired that property.

This is now not the case with a tripartite test being enacted (section YB 14 of the Act) which associates two persons if they are each associated with the same third person under different associated persons tests.

For the land taxing provisions, however, the reforms apply to land acquired on or after 6 October 2009.

The tests of association in the new associated persons definition are:

○ two companies

○ a company and a person other than a company

○ two relatives

○ a person and a trustee for a relative

○ a trustee and a beneficiary

○ trustees with a common settlor

○ a trustee and a settlor

○ a settlor and a beneficiary

○ a trustee and a person with the power of appointment or removal of the trustee

○ a partnership and a partner, and

○ two persons who are associated with the same person (tripartite part).

These tests mean that properties acquired by builders, traders and developers after 6 October 2009 will be 'tainted' by their activity and as such they need to hold these buy-and-hold properties in a separate entity from the tainted one, and also for at least 10 years. The rules mean that as a company (LAQCs and LTCs are still companies and not just tax structures) and its controlling shareholders (for instance, a husband and wife owning 50% of the shares each) are associated, and the husband as the settlor of the trading trust and the trading trust are associated, then this new tripartite (three-party tainting) test means the company and trading trust are associated. A buy-and-hold trust and a trading trust with a common settlor will now be associated too. Therefore properties owned by an LTC must be held for at least 10 years to prevent the properties being deemed to be on revenue account and income tax paid on the profits, or conversely an income tax deduction sought for losses. Since over time property values go up and you will make gains in more years than you make losses, I see this test as being more of a hindrance to property investors than a nightmare. Worse things in life will happen to you than owning a good investment property for at least 10 years!

The associated persons test is very difficult to circumvent. This is clearly a technical matter and you must seek independent tax, legal or accounting advice if you are in any way uncertain about how the associated person rules may affect you.

The writing was on the wall

Parliament's intent, when it enacted the current land tax rules in 1973, was that land dealers, developers and builders should generally be taxed on all gains on property sold within 10 years of acquisition, and they cannot claim to hold non-taxable investment portfolios. The Honourable Wallace Rowling, Minister of Finance, when introducing the relevant legislation, said:

> 'Profits and gains from real property will now be assessed when . . . the property was acquired by a land dealer and either was held as part of his land dealing business and later sold — in which case the profits will be assessable irrespective of the period between acquisition and sale — or, if it was not held as part of his land-dealing business but is sold within 10 years of acquisition, for example, claimed to be held as an investment but sold within this 10-year period.'

As a result investors who are also traders, builders or developers shouldn't feel too hard done by, as it was a deliberate decision nearly 40 years ago by the government that gains on land sold by property developers within 10 years of acquisition should generally be taxed.

Quite simply the previous definitions of associated persons were defective in that the associated persons definition for land sales contained legal loopholes which allowed land dealers, developers and builders to escape tax on buy-and-hold property held for less than 10 years by operating through closely connected entities. This loophole has now been slammed shut.

Good news

Many people investing in property who also build, trade or develop are still well advised to have a buy-and-hold portfolio. Why? Because of the impact time has on property investment. Where will rents be in 10 years' time? What will the value of your property investment be in 10 years' time? History shows that in New Zealand's cities, in every single 10-year period, property has gone up in value enormously. Unfortunately life sometimes gets in the way of successful long-term buy-and-hold property investing. But it's a good idea to keep property for a long time. If you learn how to time the property cycle, then you can use this rule to your advantage by holding property for at least 10 years — and then selling it in the boom phase.

14 | How can I find the money to invest in property?

The power of leverage is hard to overstate — but it also has associated risks.

You can accomplish far more with leverage, so borrowing (or gearing) your property investments is a smart thing to do for the overwhelming majority of property investors. This is even more so when you are starting out, as you are most likely to need to borrow to be able to afford the purchase price of a property. I consider my lenders to be my most important business partners in my own property portfolio.

Banks lend against residential property on the lesser of purchase price and registered valuation. For example, if you purchase a property at a retail price of $250,000, with its valuation also at $250,000, then it comes down to the credit criteria of the lender involved. Typically on your own home, if you have stable and significant income they will lend 95% of the lesser of purchase price and valuation, but only 90% of the lesser of purchase price and valuation for your first investment property. As your property portfolio grows, or if you don't have sufficient income, 80% will be the maximum loan amount. These percentages are also commonly termed loan to value ratio or LVR. This is the amount of the loan divided by the valuation, so it is a measure of the amount of debt relative to the value of the property.

When it comes to loan structure we have a number of choices to make as property owners. For the few investors who have paid off their mortgages, there is no need for a lender at all; they own their property 'freehold' or outright. Most investors, however, need the help of lenders to grow their portfolio. As a result you need to choose how to structure your loan. There are many choices available and these differ from lender to lender:

○ the length of your loan: 15 years, 20 years, 25 years, 30 years?

○ the type of loan: revolving credit, pooling/offsetting account, variable rate loan, fixed loan, mixed/split loan, capped interest rate loan?

○ whether to have an 'interest only' or 'principal and interest' loan?

○ whether to fix your borrowings or float, or a little of both (if this option is available)?

The next few chapters focus on financing your property investment. Most other property books only give this topic cursory coverage. However since I have been actively involved in mentoring hundreds of successful property investors in group mentoring and one-on-one mentoring, I have observed that to truly succeed in property investment, you need to have a good understanding of finance. The most successful property investors are acutely aware of what loan structures they are using and why. It is just as crucial to sort out your borrowing strategy as to sort out your property investment strategy.

It saddens me that many investors spend more time getting quotes for a new TV than they do when shopping around for a loan product that suits them. Over the years the wrong loan can and will cost you many tens of thousands in excess interest and fees. Your lenders are your most important business partner and you must work cleverly to pay them as little as possible over time. There are a number of other choices that we get, such as:

○ Which lender to go to?

○ What interest rates does your lender offer?

○ What are the early repayment and break fees?

○ What are the loan establishment fees and loan termination fees?

○ What are the ongoing fees?

The importance of finance

If a great deal comes up during your property searching, one that is well below valuation and producing positive cash flow in an area you think is well poised for growth, you need to be able to pounce on it. You will not be able to complete the purchase if you don't have your finance sorted out. You will need to have the money to put down as a deposit to secure it. Next you will need a loan to finance the rest of the purchase price.

We want to grow our property portfolios to secure a better financial future and to get to the desired outcomes in our lives. As time goes on we focus on building a property portfolio with a mix of cash flow, equity and growth. To do this it is imperative that we get support from a bank who will partner with us by lending us money. Your lender will make their money from interest and certain other fees, and we will make our money from the surplus cash flow in the property and equity gains (property value less loan amounts owing). It can and should be a beautiful partnership.

Have a good borrowing strategy

Everyone has a limited borrowing capacity, even Warren Buffet, Bill Gates, Carlos Slim and Her Majesty the Queen. It is just that their borrowing capacities are rather large. I see many investors set out excitedly to grow mega-million dollar property portfolios with a goal of $100,000–$200,000 passive cash flow per annum. Whilst this is very possible, it is also very uncommon. In fact most property investors own just one rental property. The next biggest group only own two properties, and fewer than 10% of property investors own three or more properties. While there are a number of reasons for this, one of the major reasons (I'd argue the major one) is the lack of ability and appetite to get finance. From my observations, there is a lack of understanding about how lending works. Finance is a real weakness for a great number of investors.

To succeed in property investment, we will need some degree of leverage, which means having an excellent borrowing strategy. We have to look at what banks want, and this of course is profits to ensure adequate compensation to their shareholders for the risks they have taken in investing their equity into the bank itself. Banks don't actually want to have mortgagee sales; they would much rather you honour your obligations by repaying your loan on time. It is far simpler for a bank to make a fair interest margin than have a long and slightly cumbersome legal process to go through to sell a property by way of mortgagee sale under the Property Law Act 2007. It is fortunate that mortgagee sales are nowhere near as frequent in New Zealand as they are in the United States. Over there in late 2010 over one in four houses were sold by mortgagee sale! Yet in New Zealand at the very highest point of mortgagee sales and at the worst point in the last property downturn, mortgagee sales were fewer than one in 50 sales.

Investors need to buy properties that will help them meet their goals. At the end of the day it is about balancing the scales of cash flow and equity. It is imperative that you can prove an ability to service the loan repayments, but you also need to have sufficient equity to keep lenders happy to continue to lend you more money. These are what I term your borrowing keys: cash flow and equity.

Often investors who are equity rich and cash flow weak buy their next investment property as another weak cash flow property with sound equity in it. Similarly investors who are cash flow strong and equity poor buy a good cash flow property that doesn't increase their equity. This doesn't help them get to their goals anytime soon and makes them hit the wall much faster. So let's get into the nitty gritty and look at how the finance process works.

Get pre-approved

To give you certainty that you will be able to buy the property you are looking at, you should get a financial pre-approval. This means that you know the bank will lend you up to a certain amount, providing certain conditions are met. A pre-approval certificate or letter on your bank's letterhead will state that you are pre-approved to borrow (say 80%) of the lesser of purchase price or valuation, which is up to a certain specified maximum loan amount.

We have previously looked at the concept of LVR or Loan to Value Ratio, which is the percentage that your loan is of the property's valuation. Your pre-approval will often have conditions stated in it, or refer to special conditions, such as not buying a leaky building, leasehold apartment, apartment less than 40m^2 in size, terraced house or leasehold property. If you do want to buy one of these properties, the LVR percentage will drop. Different lenders have different policies on these, which vary at different phases of the property cycle, as there remains a constant battle between risk and return (perceived bank profits), which shows in the credit criteria of various banks. To help fund your investment property purchases you will have money in savings, or more likely equity in other properties that you can draw against. The rest of the money will likely come from a lender, often with the property you buy being used as security alongside those properties being utilised for their equity.

Loan approvals look at two different areas:

○ the borrowers, and

○ the property being used for security.

Where your application is strong, banks can provide pre-approvals for customers looking at nearly any situation, including over 80% lending, apartments and so on. If the security is not known at the point of the pre-approval, then this will need to be satisfactory to the bank and a conditional pre-approval will be provided. When both elements are known, an unconditional pre-approval can be given.

A pre-approval allows you to bid with authority at auctions or put in strong cash unconditional offers after you do your due diligence and research. A cash unconditional offer is far more powerful and gives an ability to get a better price when it comes to negotiation as the certainty of the property selling is far more likely. Many real estate agents tell me it is more likely that homeowners (who comprise the majority of the market) rather than investors will not be pre-approved prior to looking seriously and offering on properties. How strong is an offer that has multiple conditions in it, like subject to finance and the sale of the purchaser's own home? These are weak offers, so as a vendor I would put in a short notice cash-out clause and expect a much higher price, as I know many offers that are subject to finance, and even more that rely on a third party (especially conditions requiring the sale of their own home) fall over.

The finance decision-making process in a nutshell

Get loan (pre-) approval

The bank may ask you to supply various documents to them such as:

○ proof of income such as two of your latest payslips if salaried or waged, the last three to six months of your transactional bank statements, or the last two years of your accounts if you are self-employed or a business owner, tenancy agreements and/or rental appraisals. For existing customers, many banks will accept regular direct credits to your account as a form of income.

○ proof of equity, such as a government or registered valuation of your own home and/or investment property, term deposit, savings or transactional accounts with your contribution towards the purchase price.

○ proof of your identity (copy of photographic identification as required under the 'know your customer' government regulations). This is not generally required for existing bank customers.

○ your current profit and loss statement and balance sheet (your
   assets less liabilities) on a signed loan application form.

Bank credit checks and financial analysis

The bank will look at your character, credit score and record. If this is
satisfactory the bank will then do their financial analysis to see if your
application meets their current credit policies.

The decision

The bank will either:

○ approve your request

○ conditionally approve your request, which means that everything
   looks to be in order but the bank will require you to provide
   further information, such as a registered valuation, a builder's
   report or evidence of your income. (By providing this information
   to support everything you have told the bank, your approval will
   be confirmed.)

○ give you a deferred approval. This is subject to certain things being
   done (which means you are close but no cigar — a typical example
   would be if you need to save at current levels for another six
   months to build your deposit, and if you can evidence this then the
   bank would in all likelihood approve you for the loan).

○ decline you.

If you do receive a pre-approval you will need to note any conditions and
comply with these to ensure there is no nasty surprise and that drawdown
actually occurs. Most of the conditions are fairly standard, such as:

○ producing a copy of the agreement for sale and purchase (and if
   applicable any relevant paperwork like a deed of nomination, deed
   of assignment or deed of novation to transfer the purchasing rights
   and obligations)

○ providing information about the entity you are buying it in (eg.
   deed of trust, certificate of incorporation, partnership agreement)
   — for example, banks will look at trust deeds to ensure they grant
   the trust the powers to borrow and to grant security (the mortgage)
   of the trust's asset (the real estate acquired)

○ providing a registered valuation if a private or contemporaneous (back-to-back) settlement

○ ensuring your property is not a higher risk classified property as previously mentioned (leaky building, leasehold apartment, terraced house, small apartment, tiny remote rural town and so on).

As a condition of your loan agreement, your property must be insured therefore your lender will ask for your solicitor or conveyancer to certify they have seen a copy of the insurance cover note (certificate of currency) or you may be asked to sign an insurance undertaking to evidence that the property being purchased has been insured prior to the drawdown of funds before settlement. As mortgagee on your property, your lender has a legal responsibility to ensure your rates are paid and an obligation to ensure your property remains insured. If you get behind in either of these payments your lender may force a payment through your account.

How do banks analyse loan applications?

The banks have their own calculators (generally developed on Microsoft Excel, but also on their own networked systems) and the financial information on the spreadsheet is keyed in by a banker. Understandably banks are conservative and are not looking for giant risk takers, so they will not be entertaining loans at 120% of the property's valuation, with interest capitalised into the loan (added to the loan principal) for three years for a property in a remote town. That is the kind of reckless lending that was far more popular in the mid-2000s in the USA, and precipitated the Global Financial Crisis.

Instead the bank will look at your rental income and scale this back by a percentage between 70% and 90% of the weekly rent annualised. The most common percentage is 75%. This allows for vacancy periods, rates, repairs and maintenance expenditure and property management costs. Lenders also typically add a margin to the two- or three-year rate to analyse the deal and your ability to repay it if interest rates go up. The bank will typically take 30% of your income into the mix; however, this is adjusted by all sorts of things like the number of dependants you have, your credit-card limits and whether you pay off your credit card(s) in full each month, and your living costs. (Note that if you report too low a living cost in your application your bank will often ask you for a budget to prove it as they think you don't know what you are talking about. In many cases they will look at your transactional bank statements and see you are spending several hundred every month more than the figure you put down on your loan application form as living costs.)

An example

Scott and Lois want to purchase a property for $260,000 which rents for $340 per week. They have a loan of $200,000 at 6.20% which costs them on an interest-only basis $238 per week. They think they are making $102 per week on top of their loan repayments. However their bank assesses this quite differently as they firstly scale Scott and Lois' rents down by 75%, and then add a sensitivity margin to the three-year rate on a 25-year period.

How Scott and Lois see the deal		How the bank sees the deal	
Weekly rental	$340	Weekly rental	$255
Weekly loan repayment (6.20% on an interest-only basis)	$238	Weekly loan repayment (7.99% on 25-year principal and interest basis)	$356
Cash flow excess/(deficit)	$102	Cash flow excess/(deficit)	($101)

This is a massive swing; Scott and Lois think they are making $102 per week, yet the bank thinks they are losing $101 per week. This shortfall in the bank's eyes must be made up from their personal income. And this isn't too bad a purchase, so you can start to see how investors can hit the wall. This is why it is important to analyse your own financial strengths and weaknesses and get yourself into the best financial shape, so you can submit a strong loan application that is difficult for your bank to decline. To grow a large portfolio you then need to buy good properties that balance cash flow, equity and growth. You should then strongly consider educating yourself on how to get great property deals, for example by going along to the Property Masterclass two-day weekend events run by NZ Wealth Mentor. These are great events packed full of useful content which I helped create to train good property investors.

Using equity in your own home for property investment

As time goes on we know that the overwhelming majority of properties rise enormously in value. Many homeowners use the increased equity in their home by refinancing it, borrowing up to 80%. Then this amount is put down as a 20% contribution on an investment property, and you would get an 80% loan for the remainder of the investment property. The steps to do this are:

O Obtain a valuation on your own home (often the government valuation or a simple e-valuer by Quotable Value is fine. In some cases a registered valuation may be required — check with your lender first).

O Go to your bank (or consider refinancing the lending to another bank) and let them know that you would like to buy an investment property using the equity in an existing property.

You may be able to borrow 100% of the purchase of your new investment property without the need to refinance your current borrowings or for you to contribute a cash deposit.

Take for example Patrick and Skyla. They purchased their home in Wellington in 1999 for $289,500 with a BNZ loan of $260,000 at the time, which they have now paid down to $200,000. Their latest rating valuation appraised their home as being worth $500,000. They went into their nearest BNZ branch and completed a loan application where BNZ offered them a loan of up to $425,000 against their own home, and they got pre-approval for an investment property loan at 85% of the lesser of purchase price and registered valuation. This meant they didn't need to put in any of their own money in to purchase their investment property. Also, they were told they could qualify for another investment property loan, so they would be able to own two investment properties, getting them closer to their financial goals.

What if you don't own your own home?

While the majority of property investors start with their own home as their first property purchase — don't worry if you don't have your own home. I didn't do it this way for a start. I was well read in property investment, studying it by reading New Zealand and a few Australian books from

2000–2002, so I took a different approach as it suited my needs at the time. It was also far cheaper to rent than to own, and I was buying properties that would go up in value, so it didn't feel like I was tipping my rent money down the drain.

I cobbled together $7,000 in 2002 and got a 95% loan to purchase my first property. I bought a development property off the plans in an outlying suburb of Auckland, where the house would be built soon after a staged development. I was able to save more by changing to a job with a higher salary, which gave me higher personal cash flow and more importantly increased borrowing capacity. The result was I bought even more property: my increase in equity, plus positive cash flow from the properties, meant I was making far more money from property investment than my day job despite only being able to put in a fraction of the amount of time.

Avoid the one-bank trap

Cross-collateralisation is not great

A word of warning, it may not be smart to have all your borrowings with one bank as you build a portfolio, unless you are doing so with conservative loan to value ratios (under 50%). This is because lenders may try to cross-collateralise your borrowings, which means that they secure their lending to you across all your properties that they hold as security.

In the downturn phase of a property cycle in particular, this can led to adverse consequences. For example, you might be selling investment property #3 and think you are clearing $100,000 but are instead are forced to use some of the sale proceeds to repay debt on investment property #2 with the same bank, to meet the current bank loan to value ratio rules for the downturn.

The only sure-fire way to avoid cross-collateralisation is to take away the bank's opportunity to do this, by spreading your borrowings. Each lender will want a (first) registered mortgage on the title of the property they are lending against. So if you have different lenders they will not be able to get security on the other titles as another lender will already have it! Note that if no banks will lend to you on fair terms except for the bank that you already have borrowings with, then you will no doubt still go ahead with that bank assuming the next property purchase also stacks up. Always discuss your concerns with your bank: just because using all available securities to support your lending is their preference, it doesn't mean they won't be open to other arrangements, particularly when you have reasonable levels of equity or are providing a cash deposit.

More banking relationships

In addition to spreading your borrowings, it is a good idea to forge strong relationships with a number of lenders so if one says no in the future you have another good contact to approach. Remember that banks' credit criteria are constantly changing and just because one bank has excellent credit criteria now and you have an excellent account manager doesn't mean that bank will be good for you in one year's time and your account manager could easily have moved along. I am a big fan of having a Plan B, Plan C, Plan D and Plan E just in case they are needed, as I have learned that in far more cases than not, those with one bank have problems in growing their portfolio. You should not be reliant on one bank for something as crucial as improving and securing your family's future when we are facing the tremendous likelihood of pension cuts and the age of pension eligibility increasing, as well as the real risk of higher inflation, when it comes to the important business of building your property portfolio.

Mortgage brokers can help you in this regard; however major lenders like BNZ currently do not use brokers, and nor do other industry players like Kiwibank, HSBC, TSB Bank, SBS Bank and others. As a result you have to directly approach these lenders. I have used brokers and found them capable of leveraging my time and providing a professional interface when dealing with other lenders. Some lenders exclusively deal with brokers so you cannot go direct to those lenders. Many asset-based lenders only deal with brokers, for example. Different people have different needs, and with far fewer lenders in New Zealand than in the UK and in particular the USA, brokers just haven't quite had the market penetration that they have in these significantly larger countries. This may well change in the future, as evolving technology means there will be new ways of distributing loans.

Interest-rate negotiability

I believe that the success I have in negotiating significant discounts off my floating and various fixed interest rates comes from lending with a number of banks. This is because I can point out the cheapest retail rates that other banks offer for that period of time to get the best available, and then when I get discounts I scan or screenshot loan statements from banks to evidence the rate that I am getting and ask them to beat it. My bankers usually have to take this to their pricing desk and they match it. This also requires negotiation skills, a proven track record of paying all your loans on time every time, and not pushing things to the maximum loan to value ratio. If you can save 0.25% on $200,000 of borrowings you save $500 every year. This rises to saving $2,500 per year if you can save 0.25% on $1,000,000 of borrowings. Now if you could save 0.4% on $5,000,000 of borrowings you would save $20,000 per year.

The first priority is to get the loan; then you can focus on getting the right terms. The interest rate is just one of these terms. I have seen too many property mentoring clients with a few properties all with one bank get no interest rate discounts. Yet when they refinance a couple of properties, suddenly they get better rates and when they leave one property with their original bank they then get discounts as they can tell that bank what the other lenders are doing for them.

Fee waivers

The same principle applies to fee waivers, like loan rollover fees, redocumentation fees and interest-rate fixing fees. When you are with other banks the threat of refinancing appears more real and you are in a stronger negotiating position to get your lender to waive these annoying fees if you spread your borrowings.

The following chapters look at other aspects of financing your property investments. Firstly I look at revolving-credit accounts in Chapter 15 including the market-leading pooling and offsetting BNZ TotalMoney account, then I look at the pros and cons of fixing and floating the interest rate on your loans in Chapter 16. In Chapter 17 I look at the various ways you can save money on your mortgage, before I analyse the various loan types in Chapter 18, and discuss ways you could structure your loan in Chapter 19.

15 | What is a revolving-credit or offset account?

Revolving-credit accounts

Revolving-credit accounts are loan accounts which have balances that fluctuate over the course of a period of time. They have a pre-determined credit or facility limit, which you cannot exceed (or if you can exceed it, you won't want to — you will be charged penalty interest rates which are often over 20% per annum). A revolving-credit account is secured against a property and therefore gets interest charged generally at the lender's floating rate. Note that some lenders also charge a monthly fee.

The reason you might want a revolving-credit account is for convenience. The convenience factor is huge because you don't have to keep going back to your bank and asking for a new loan. You can have the account set up for internet and phone banking, have a chequebook and use it just like a normal transactional account. The risks are that you perceive the difference between the loan balance and the revolving-credit limit to be spare money, and you spend this amount.

If you have poor financial discipline and think available credit is to there spend on non-essential items like cars, home entertainment, holidays and other gumble, then revolving-credit accounts are likely not to be the best accounts for you, as you will be servicing the interest on purchasing these items.

Credit cards are essentially revolving-credit accounts too. For example, Alpesh has a credit card with a $20,000 limit which he doesn't spend all of each month — in fact he can only come close if he is on an overseas holiday! So let's say Alpesh spends $4,000 in a month on, say, power and gas bills, home phone and broadband, groceries, clothing and entertainment.

This means there is $16,000 unused or available credit. He is presented with three choices at the end of the billing cycle:

○ paying the balance off in full (I do this always and encourage you to do the same if you can)

○ paying the minimum monthly balance of $200, and incurring high interest on the remaining $3,800 not cleared

○ paying an amount in between the minimum balance and paying the balance off in full.

For example if Alpesh chooses to pay $1,500, he is 'revolving' the remaining $2,500 into the next month. If he spends absolutely nothing in the next month then his statement would show the $2,500 as a balance brought forward from the previous month plus $42.47 in interest (at 20% interest and a 31-day billing cycle).

In this next month Alpesh has the same three choices, and he chooses to pay $1,000, and revolve the remaining $1,542.47 to the next month. This amount attracts a further $25.36 in interest. You can see how credit card companies make their money. If you don't like the service they provide, then always pay off your credit card in full, or don't use a credit card!

How to use revolving-credit accounts effectively

The most effective way of using a revolving-credit account for salaried and waged people is to have your salary or wages put into it. This is because you only pay interest on the balance that you borrow. Then put as many expenses on your credit card as possible. This will include power, phone, internet, Sky TV, groceries, fuel companies and many other suppliers. Then you pay off your credit card on or just before the due date so you don't pay ridiculously high amounts of interest. This gives you interest-free credit on purchases for 30 to 55 days. By retaining funds in your revolving-credit account for as long as you are able, you will be minimising the debit interest charged on this account, thereby creating a win–win situation. If you paid the expenses directly from your revolving credit account you would be paying interest right from the date of the purchase.

Remember that you only pay interest on the amount of the loan drawn down, so the less you spend the less interest you pay and vice versa.

As you grow your property portfolio, you will find revolving-credit accounts are excellent because of their many uses. Whether you have surplus cash from a bonus paid at work, an inheritance, selling or refinancing a property and so on, it is a great idea to pay money into your revolving-credit account as you only pay interest on money drawn down. Then if you want to use undrawn credit without seeking your bank's permission you can do so.

As a result I use revolving-credit accounts to pay deposits and settlement contributions on further property acquisitions, and also for funding renovations, as well as repairs, maintenance and improvement costs. Even if you just want a bank account to pay your rent into, revolving-credit accounts are fully functional transactional accounts so should be very strongly considered as a vital part of an active investors' financial arsenal. The extremely high degree of flexibility they give makes them a very popular choice amongst serious property investors.

Pros and cons of revolving-credit accounts

Pros	Cons
Convenience (internet banking, EFTPOS, telephone banking, chequebooks available)	Monthly account fees (in some cases)
You don't have to apply for a new loan when you want to draw money down (if you are below your facility limit)	Interest is charged at the floating rate (which may be higher than fixed rates at the time) and some lenders have slightly higher interest rates for revolving credit accounts
Flexibility — you can use the account as a buffer, for renovations, new property purchase deposits and so on	Risk of mixing your non tax-deductible personal expenditure with your tax-deductible property expenses and interest payments — a potential tax nightmare requiring careful apportionment to avoid increased accounting costs
Reduce interest costs by putting money into the account, as you only pay interest on what you borrow	Compound interest effect for ill-disciplined spenders (where you pay interest on interest)

Pooling and offsetting

Pooling and offsetting accounts are similar to revolving-credit accounts. Many homeowners and property investors are using the BNZ's TotalMoney loan facility to save on interest costs. In essence you take out a home loan, and you group together a number of other accounts that you have with BNZ. These may include transactional accounts (ie. rental account, bills and maintenance accounts) and savings accounts being grouped together, and the positive balances are offset against your TotalMoney loan. This drops your effective interest rate.

Your regular payments stay the same, but by lowering your effective interest rate you'll repay more of your original loan (the principal) each time. This is a very popular product as it takes many years off your home loan, saving thousands of dollars in interest. In addition the interest rates BNZ offers on this are very competitive and have often been the leading floating rate in the market. The total term of a TotalMoney home loan can be any length up to 30 years. The minimum starting loan size is $10,000.

The diagram below shows how TotalMoney lets your savings cut the interest you pay on your home loan:

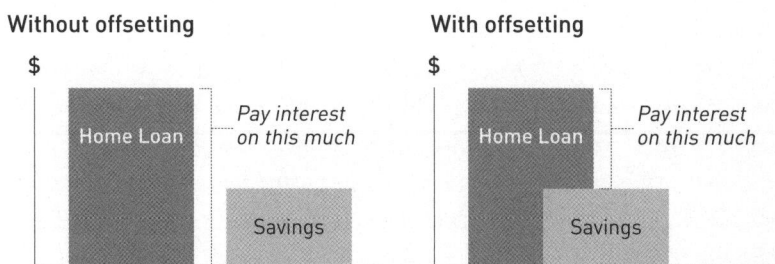

Without offsetting

$

Home Loan

Pay interest on this much

Savings

With offsetting

$

Home Loan

Pay interest on this much

Savings

Every dollar counts

TotalMoney gives you the flexibility to increase or decrease the amount you offset to suit your lifestyle. Even a small amount in your cheque and savings accounts can drop your effective interest rate. For example, if the TotalMoney floating interest rate was 5.59% p.a., $5,000 in your cheque and savings accounts offset against a $150,000 floating home loan can drop your effective interest rate by 0.19% per year.

I am a massive fan of BNZ's TotalMoney Account as this has saved me and a lot of my clients sizeable amounts of money. Not only do you get the benefits of pooling and offsetting, but you get the benefits of BNZ's proven track record of their TotalMoney home loan having one of the lowest floating rates across all major banks.

You could even pay zero interest

If the total amount in your offsetting accounts is the same as or larger than the balance owing on your TotalMoney home loan, you'll pay no interest at all on the loan and earn credit interest on the surplus.

16 | Fixed vs floating interest rates

Loan interest is my greatest expense, and it is my goal to minimise the amount of interest that I pay over time. To achieve this goal, we property investors have a number of choices in relation to choosing interest rates on our loans. We can float our loan, which means that we pay interest at our lender's variable rate. Or we can fix it for a certain period of time at a certain predetermined rate.

Floating-rate loans

You have no control over the movement of the floating rate. It can move downwards sharply — as it did in late 2008 and early 2009 when the recession and full force of the global financial crisis kicked in. The floating rate can also move upwards — and it does when the economy is perceived to be performing well. In New Zealand the Reserve Bank meets every six weeks and announces (on a Thursday at 9 am) whether the official cash rate (OCR) is staying the same, reducing or going up, and by how much. The OCR is influenced by a number of economic factors but the Reserve Bank is primarily charged with keeping inflation in the target band of 1–3%. Unlike many other countries, New Zealand's Reserve Bank is not charged with maintaining high levels of employment or a stable currency. The result is that the OCR can change dramatically in a rapid space of time. Just have a look at the history of the OCR on the Reserve Bank's website http://reservebank.govt.nz/monpol/statements/0090630.html, and the following graph showing the OCR and floating rates over 20 years:

OCR rate vs variable interest rate

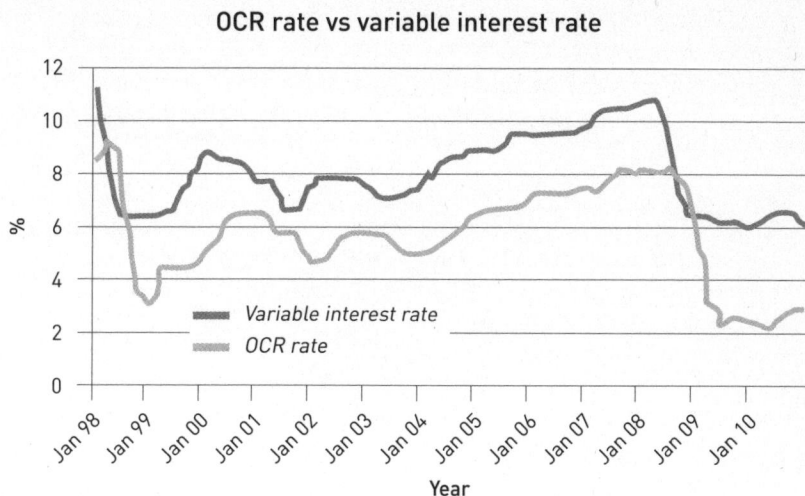

You can see that the floating rate is very closely — but not perfectly — correlated to the OCR. Lenders can move interest rates up and down of their own volition; it's a free market where they set the price. They are, however, under quite a high level of competition for market share, so any drastic moves could see many clients refinance to another lender to save on interest costs.

The choice is made for you if you have a revolving-credit account, or a pooling or offsetting account, as you cannot fix these types of loans. If you don't make a decision, your lender will automatically put it onto the floating rate. Similarly, if your fixed term expires without you choosing a new fixed term, your loan will automatically default to the floating rate.

Fixed-rate loans

If you don't want to let your mortgage rate float, you can choose to fix your loan for a period of time (typically in New Zealand these range from six months to five years, although BNZ does offer a seven-year fixed rate).

This is how fixed rates work: you have a loan of a certain length, for example 25 years. Then you might choose to fix this rate for two years, then float for 18 months, before fixing a rate for five years, then floating for 11 years before fixing again when a sharp three-year rate comes up, before floating again until the loan expires as it has been fully repaid.

You can see the flat lines on the graph overleaf where the interest remains unchanged for long periods of time are when the fixed rates are chosen. I know many investors have a preference for certainty and choose fixed rates

Typical interest-rate movements over the period of a loan

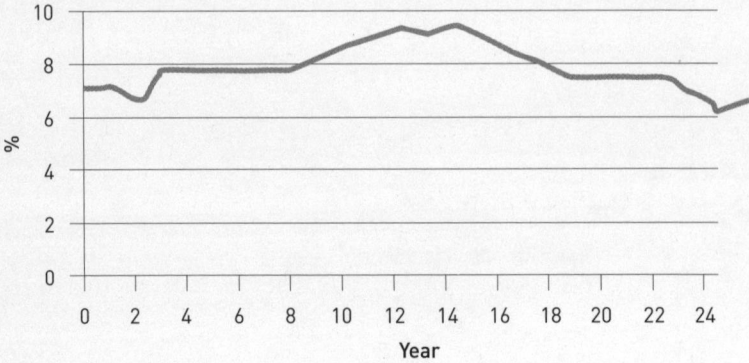

for as long a term as possible, while other investors prefer to ride the ebbs and flows of interest-rate cycles by choosing floating rates.

Currently New Zealanders have a preference for floating or short-term fixed rates (less than two years in loan term), as opposed to medium-term (two- and three-year fixed rates) and long-term fixed rates (four and five years). For example, below is a pie chart of the loan expiry statistics from the Reserve Bank of New Zealand at 31 May 2011.

Loan expiry statistics from RBNZ as at 31 May 2011

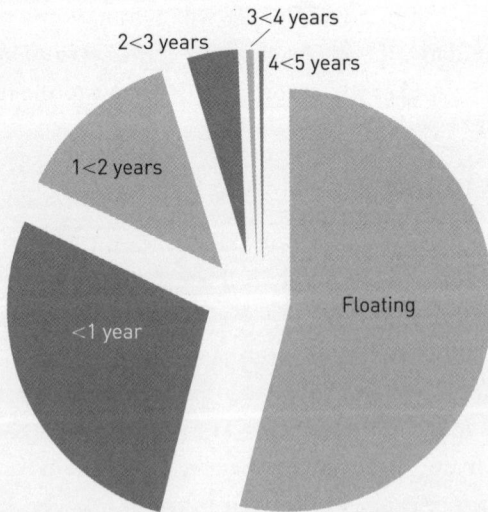

Pros and cons of fixed and floating interest rates

Fixed rates

Pros	Cons
Interest rate certainty — you know exactly what your repayments will be for the period of your fixed-rate term.	The interest rate may be higher than floating rates at that time.
The fixed interest rates available may be lower than floating rates at that time.	Fixed-interest rates may go lower during your fixed-rate term (and sometimes much lower).
You can incorporate a degree of flexibility by documenting a higher repayment than the minimum required, allowing the option to increase or decrease repayment levels — often without a fee being charged.	You may incur break fees if you sell or refinance your property (that is security for the loan). There are usually no break fees if fixed interest rates have gone up.
	You may not be able to repay any or only a small portion (5% of original loan balance) without incurring a fee.

Floating rates

Pros	Cons
Flexibility — you have the option to select a fixed rate at any time.	The floating interest rate may be higher than fixed rates at that time.
Floating interest rates available may be lower than fixed rates at that time.	No interest-rate certainty — the interest rate rides with the ebbs and flows of the market, which can rise steeply or fall swiftly meaning you have no certainty around your required repayments.
You can usually pay down the entire loan without penalty (100%).	

There is a lot to think about in terms of whether you fix or float — and there are a great number of choices and combinations. Assuming you have the goal of being financially independent and to stop working for your money, as opposed to making your money work for you (this is a crucial difference to note), you will be growing a portfolio using property investment as one of the key tools for your wealth generation system. Therefore you will be using leverage for your property investments, at least in the earlier and middle stages of your investment portfolio growth, and as a result it will be critical to try to minimise the amount of interest you pay.

To achieve this in the buy-and-hold property trusts I administer, I prefer a mixed approach where I have revolving-credit accounts on the floating rates, some standard variable-rate lending, and a wide variety of fixed-rate terms. I call this an interest-rate averaging strategy, which I feel is important enough to warrant its own chapter as it means that I am not unnecessarily exposed to interest rate spikes.

17 | How can I save money on my mortgage?

Interest-rate averaging is a loan management strategy that involves adopting a spread of interest rates that expire at different periods. It is basically a hedging strategy designed to ride out the interest rate 'storms' which hit the market from time to time. I would note that it is important to have good financial advice and this is particularly vital when interest rates are very low or very high.

For example, Jeff bought his first property, a three-bedroom, tired-looking house in a suburb not too far away from Auckland's CBD, for $380,000. He got a loan for $300,000 — which is 78.9% of the lesser of purchase price and valuation (valuation was $420,000). With this $300,000 in total borrowings, Jeff split it into six loans in this fashion:

○ $50,000 floating

○ $50,000 fixed for one year

○ $50,000 fixed for two years

○ $50,000 fixed for three years

○ $50,000 fixed for four years, and

○ $50,000 fixed for five years.

As a result, if interest rates were to suddenly increase by 3%, only one sixth of Jeff's borrowings would be subject to this rates increase. This means he would only be paying $1,500 extra for a year if the floating rate was raised dramatically by 3%.

Conversely, if floating rates were to fall by 3%, only one sixth of Jeff's borrowings would be subject to this rates fall, meaning he would save $1,500 in interest costs.

Now compare this to if Jeff had all his borrowings on floating and rates over the course of 18 months went up by 3%. This would mean that all of Jeff's borrowings of $300,000 would go up, so in 18 months' time he would be paying $9,000 in additional interest. That means that Jeff (who was already paying $50 per week to own the property) would have to find an additional $180 per week. He couldn't put his rents up on his property enough to cover that amount, so it would have to come out of his own pocket. If Jeff couldn't do this he would have to look at options such as interest-only finance, if available, or a loan-repayment holiday (which only delays the inevitable) or — like so many undercapitalised investors — he would have to sell the property. How would that make him feel? Dejected about property investment and possibly never considering it again, abandoning his goals? Struggling to make the repayments on your investment property is not uncommon in the New Zealand property market over the past few years. But property investment is a business and businesses need to adopt risk-minimisation strategies. No one has a crystal ball to predict all future interest rate movements across all rate terms.

So you can and should minimise any downside risks — and the potential of financial ruin for highly leveraged investors — by having an interest-rate management strategy. In particular, consider the interest-rate averaging strategy.

Watch out for loan rollover fees — interest rate averaging in action!

Now if you're like Jeff, most lenders are going to be unimpressed with your request to set up six separate loan accounts. Every loan requires a separate document and is an item to be managed. The main reason that I wouldn't advise doing what Jeff has done is that loans involving smaller amounts can, and often do, attract 'loan rollover' or 'fixing' fees. My experience in dealing with a number of lenders is that these fees are sometimes hard to negotiate away, particularly initially when you have a smaller portfolio and higher levels of leverage, as you have less bargaining power.

Therefore I wouldn't actually copy Jeff's strategy if I were setting out to build a portfolio. Splitting into three loans may work well. For instance:

○ $100,000 revolving credit (always on the floating rate)

- ○ $100,000 fixed for two years
- ○ $100,000 fixed for five years.

Let's say Jeff bought his property in March 2010. After a year had passed, Jeff would have the three loans: $100,000 still on the floating rate, $100,000 with one year to go and $100,000 with four years to go. Then Jeff, boosted by the confidence of rent increases and the now greatly diminished fears of a property crash, bought a second property, in March 2011. This one also cost $380,000 and he got a $300,000 loan for it. He split this loan over three fixed terms:

- ○ $100,000 fixed for two years
- ○ $100,000 fixed for three years, and
- ○ $100,000 fixed for five years.

Twelve months after the first purchase and having now acquired two properties Jeff's lending looks like this:

Loan expiry date	Jeff's property portfolio at 31 March 2011
Floating (current)	$100,000 (revolving-credit account facility limit — always on the floating rate, arranged in March 2010).
March 2012	$100,000 (fixed for two years in March 2010 on property A, and one year has now passed).
March 2013	$100,000 (fixed for two years in March 2011 with the purchase of property B).
March 2014	$100,000 (fixed for three years in March 2011 with the purchase of property B).
March 2015	$100,000 (fixed for five years in March 2010 on property A, and one year has now passed)
March 2016	$100,000 (fixed for five years in March 2011 with the purchase of property B)
Total loans	$600,000

In practice, it's not quite this simple. Seldom are you going to buy properties in the same month, and sometimes there will be amazing interest rates on offer. As a result, while I like the principle of an interest-rate averaging strategy as a hedging strategy, you should customise this to suit your own risk tolerance and the market interest rates.

For example, available for a very short period of time (around one week with some major banks) was a rate of five years at 5.95%. Also, for around six weeks there was a rate of 6.50% available for five years. So in February and March 2009, I advised in my blog at www.davidwhitburn.com that readers should fix long immediately! The rates were amazingly low, and the ability to get an extremely low interest rate for such a long time made it prudent to partially abandon the interest-rate averaging strategy I had. As a result my loan portfolio is heavily weighted with loans expiring in 2014.

That said, I didn't break loans to fix other amounts. I waited until they came off and fixed rates (with the usual interest rate discounts I ask for) like 5.4% for 12 months, then 5.8% for 12 months and 6.40% for two years. So unless the one-year rate in March 2013 goes above 8.50%, then perhaps the 6.5% rate isn't so good after all. But that said, there is value in certainty — and at the time it just felt the right thing to do.

Less than six months earlier (in late 2008) an author and property market commentator had said to people on his database and his mentoring students that they should fix for the long term (four and five years) despite these interest rates being between 8.6% and 9.4%. This was on the basis of what he perceived to be a significant risk of hyper-inflation (massive inflation typically over 10%) where interest rates would have to rise accordingly to attempt to control it. This 6.50% rate was the lowest since 2003. When interest rates are low, particularly longer term ones, it can be prudent to 'fix long' (fix your interest rates for a long period of time) as they are highly unlikely to go any lower and you get a lot of certainty by fixing for a long period of time. Conversely when the interest rates are high and have been for a while it may be prudent to have more loan amounts on floating and for shorter fixed-loan periods, so you can take advantage of the next downward cycle in interest rates.

I believe you should have the interest-rate averaging strategy as the basis of your loan management strategy and spread your borrowings so that they expire over a wide variety of loan terms. Then increase your financial intelligence by subscribing to relevant newsletters (like BNZ chief economist Tony Alexander's *Weekly Overview*) and network with a wide variety of people in the industry. This allows you to establish their opinions on the direction that interest rates are heading and why, then you can take advantage of your information to fix long when interest rates are at cyclically low periods, and fix short or float when interest rates are at cyclically high periods.

Save money by paying your lender less or getting a contribution from your bank

Banks charge quite a number of bank fees and you can save yourself a lot of money by paying fewer of them. In other cases and particularly when refinancing to take your lending to another bank or when applying for a new home loan, you can get a contribution towards legal and valuation fees.

Pay your lender less

There are a number of possible costs your lender may charge you, including account maintenance fees, electronic transaction fees, loan application fees, low equity premiums (lender's mortgage insurance premium), mortgage discharge fees, loan termination fees, break fees, early repayment fees, fixing fees (a fee to load up a fixed-rate loan). Most of these fees are actually negotiable, and depending on the bargaining tools and negotiation skill-set you have, as well as the strength of your banker or broker, and the relevant lender's policies at the time, you will be able to save money in some of these areas. I regularly save money by negotiating out of loan application fees; I say that it is my trust's policy not to pay these types of fees, and that XYZ lender isn't charging me this. Who wants to argue with policy, after all!

Loan-fixing fees are a particularly annoying charge to a number of property investors but I have found these are for most lenders pretty easy to negotiate away. However, it is harder to negotiate out of lender's mortgage insurance premiums. Even this is not impossible — back in 2002 I negotiated on a property purchase and was quoted $2,550 lender's mortgage insurance premium, which could be capitalised back into the loan. I said this wasn't for my benefit but for the bank's benefit and the banker explained that that's how it works since I was borrowing more than the bank's comfort level of 80%, so they needed to insure against the statistically increased risk of me defaulting and them losing money in the deal. I offered them an even $2,200 and they agreed to this some two days later. Sure it is not a very big saving, but it all adds up. The point with all of these fees and examples is that if you don't ask for a discount you won't normally get one! It is just like your tenants not telling you that their rent is too cheap.

Get a contribution towards legal and valuation fees

Many banks offer a financial contribution towards legal and valuation fees. A property mentoring client was being charged a $250 application fee, and just before they went ahead with this they asked their mentor about it. The mentor suggested he ask about a contribution. Upon politely complaining about the fee and stating other banks offer contributions, two hours later their personal banker rang them back with great news of a contribution of $1,000 towards legal and valuation fees. This was a net benefit of $1,250. They were about to take the easy path and simply accept the $250 standard charge, but two short phone calls later they received a $1,000 payment.

Get a contribution towards break fees

In some cases with strong borrowers and a good banker advocating your case, the bank will also pay your break fees (costs to break a fixed-term interest contract with a rival lender). The key thing to do is be professional and assertive but polite when you ask your bank or broker. If you are breaking a loan you need to keep in mind that as early repayment charges represent the economic cost to the bank, these fees are extremely hard to negotiate.

18 | What type of loan is right for me?

It is very important to know the type of loan that will suit you best. There are a number of loan products and structures available currently. I want to focus in on the main options which are:

- offsetting loans
- revolving-credit loans
- table loans
- interest-only loans
- accelerated-repayment loans
- reducing-balance loans.

Offsetting loans

Without offsetting

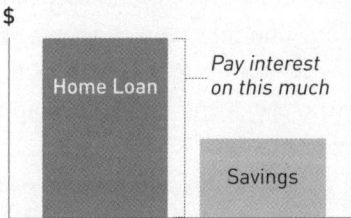

With offsetting

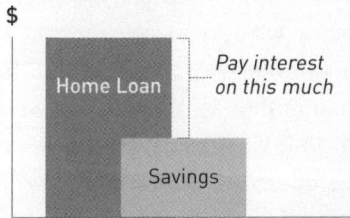

Offsetting loans allow you to put your separate cheque and savings accounts to work on your home loan. BNZ's TotalMoney loan is currently the market-leading offsetting account.

Here's how it works: the total amount in your cheque and savings accounts is subtracted from your home loan balance before the interest is calculated, which means you only pay interest on the difference. Offsetting home loans as a result can greatly reduce the amount of interest that you pay.

This type of home loan has a floating (or variable) interest rate. You can split your lending with a bank to tailor it to your needs by having some of your borrowings as an offsetting loan and the remainder on a fixed rate. You can even have an offsetting loan with interest-only payments.

As an example, Jane and Rahul have a variable-interest-rate home loan of $200,000 and $45,000 of credit balances in their cheque and saving accounts, so these credit balances are offset against their home loan and they only pay interest on $155,000 of their home loan. If you need a refresher have another read of Chapter 15.

Pros:
O If you regularly have money in transaction or savings account, you can save on interest and pay off your home loan faster.

O If you fully offset your loan balance with credit balances, you pay no interest.

Cons:
O As the rate is floating, it can go higher than fixed-term rates; if the interest rate goes up, so will your repayments, which could put a squeeze on your budget.

O If you offset you don't earn credit interest on your savings.

Revolving-credit loans

These are loans where you have a giant overdraft on one single transactional account, where you can transact including draining money against the loan without seeking permission from the lender up to a certain facility (maximum) limit. You can freely make extra repayments and redraw up to your limit whenever you like. A revolving-credit loan is sometimes called a line of credit. The idea is to help save on interest by keeping the daily balance of your loan as low as possible.

You can do this, for example, by direct crediting all your income into the account and then paying your bills and everyday expenses from the account as you need to. Revolving-credit loans have a floating (or variable) interest rate. Some people will mix and match by having some of their borrowing on a fixed-interest-rate term loan and some on a revolving-credit home loan. These differ from offsetting loans, as the interest is calculated on the basis of one single account, the revolving-credit account, and not the group balances pooled together as in an offsetting account. Note that many people simply put their savings and sometimes cheque account balances into their revolving-credit account.

The interest is calculated on the daily balance of your account, so by keeping the loan as low as you can, for as long as you can, you will pay less interest. You have the option of making lump-sum repayments and if you need the money again, you can redraw up to your limit at any time. Some revolving-credit home loans have a credit limit that steadily decreases (as they are useable on a principal and interest loan basis) to help you stay on track to the day you'll be debt-free, whereas others may have a set limit available for the life of the loan — effectively providing an interest-only revolving-credit account. Some banks set these up with a set fee per month for as many transactions as you make, whereas many others are set up like normal transaction accounts where the usual bank fees can apply for things like deposits, withdrawals and setting up an automatic payments. Have another read of Chapter 15 if you need more information on revolving-credit accounts.

Pros:
○ If you're good at controlling your finances you can repay your home loan sooner.

○ If your income is uneven, a revolving-credit loan may be best for you, because there are no fixed repayments but (depending on the product you select) your limit might reduce each month. You can help save on interest by putting spare money into this account instead of a savings account.

Cons:
○ You need self-control. If you keep borrowing up to your credit limit you'll end up paying interest on the full loan amount year after year.

Table loans

Table loans are also called principal and interest loans, where you have fixed regular repayments and a set date by which the loan will be paid off.

Loan balance on a interest and principal loan

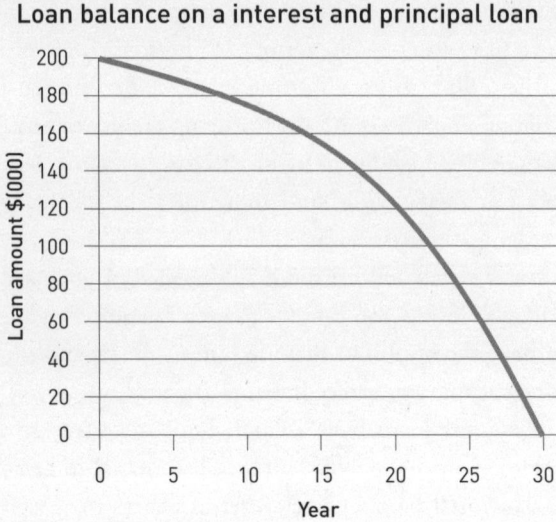

This is the most common type of home loan. Your regular repayments are the same each week, fortnight or month, unless your interest rate changes. Every single repayment includes a combination of interest and principal. Initially your repayments comprise mostly interest but as the amount you still owe begins to decrease, your regular repayment will include less interest and repay more of the principal (the amount you borrowed). Most of your later repayments go towards paying back the principal.

With a table loan you can choose a fixed rate of interest or a floating rate. With most lenders you can select a term (how long you'll take to repay the loan) of up to 30 years. Table loans can also be structured with an interest-only term or on an offsetting product.

Pros:
○ Table loans can help to keep you on track because they have regular repayments and a set date by which the loan will be paid off. They provide the certainty of knowing what your repayments will be (unless your interest rate changes, in which case repayment amounts can change).

Cons:
○ Fixed regular repayments might be difficult to make if you have an irregular income.

Interest-only loans

This graph shows a 10-year interest-only period on a 30-year loan.

Loan balance on an interest-only loan

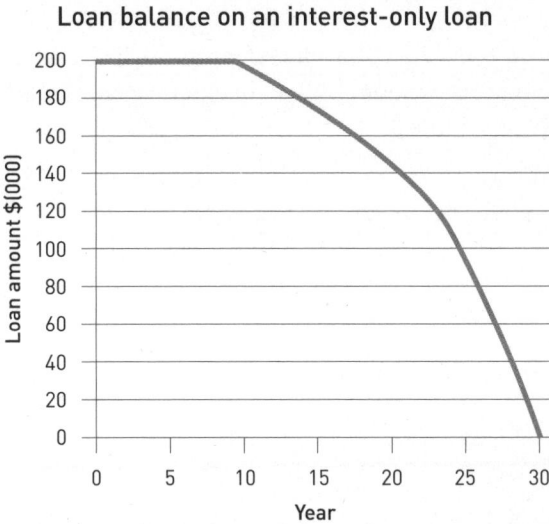

Your regular payments are interest only until an agreed time — then you repay the whole loan or you could request to switch to a table loan.

An interest-only loan can be ideal when you need a home loan, but don't want to pay off the principal (the original amount you borrowed) just yet. These loans are frequently used for property investment, and I would recommend all property investors with loans on their own home to have interest-only loans on their investment properties so they can focus on paying down the principal on their own home. Some people take an interest-only loan for a year or two and then switch to a table (P&I) loan. The BNZ currently offers a 10-year interest-only loan.

With interest-only loans you don't repay any of the money you've borrowed (principal) until an agreed time — then you can request to switch to a principal and interest repayment loan or repay the loan all in one sum (by selling or refinancing the property). In the meantime you make regular interest payments every week, fortnight or month.

Pros:
○ Because you're not repaying principal, you can free up cash for other purposes, such as owner-occupied property debt repayment, buying another investment property or renovations.

○ As the interest on investment property is a tax-deductible expense, utilising an interest-only term can be beneficial from a tax perspective.

Cons:

○ You pay interest on the full amount you borrowed until an agreed time because you are not paying off any principal, then you still have to repay the loan amount (or you might, for example, request to switch to a table loan).

Accelerated-repayment loans

Loan balance on an accelerated-repayment loan

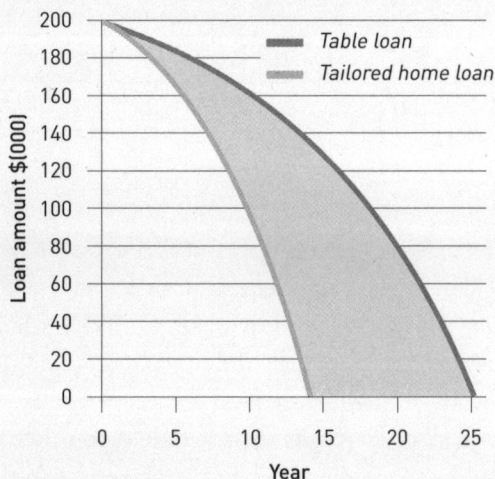

Accelerated-repayment loans, such as BNZ's tailored repayment options, assist you to pay off your balance faster, saving you thousands in interest. Typically as the years roll on your income will increase and sometimes your expenses may reduce. By choosing an accelerated-repayment option you'll be prompted each year to think about increasing your loan repayments. Keeping your repayments as high as you can afford can make a big difference to the total cost of your loan and the number of years it takes you to repay.

For example, by choosing fortnightly repayments of $250 rather than monthly repayments of $500, you'll make two extra repayments a year and repay an extra $500 off your loan. That's because there are 12 months in a year but 26 (not 24) fortnights. If you also accept small increases in your repayments each year, you can pay off your home loan even faster. This combination can give you surprisingly large savings in interest every year that could add up to tens of thousands of dollars over the life of your loan.

If your situation changes, the accelerated-repayment option allows you to change your repayments to better suit your budget and lifestyle.

Pros:
○ Can reduce the term of your loan by years saving thousands in interest costs.

○ More suited for borrowings on owner-occupied homes where debt reduction is a goal.

Cons:
○ Not as popular for borrowing on rental properties due to higher repayments, both initially and ongoing optional annual increases.

Reducing-balance loans

Reducing-balance loans are relatively uncommon. With this type of loan, you repay more of your loan in the early stages and pay less interest overall than you would under a standard table (principal and interest) loan.

Loan balance on a reducing-balance loan

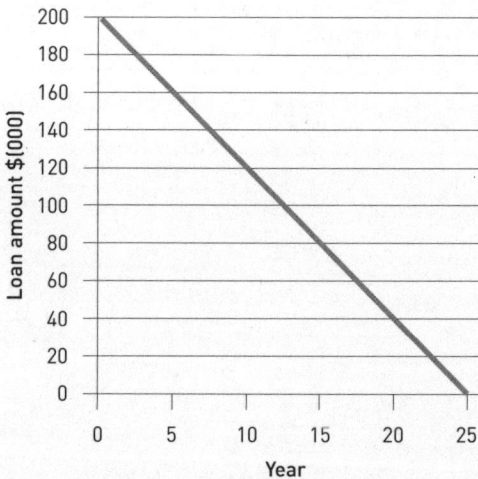

Here's how it works: with a reducing-balance (non-table) home loan, you repay the same amount of principal each period and pay the interest as a separate payment. As the principal amount you owe reduces, so does the amount of interest you pay each time. Your regular repayments of principal and interest are initially higher than for other types of loans. This type of loan is very rarely used for property as the initial costs are significantly higher than for a table loan. These types of loans are even rarer for investment-property purchases.

Pros:

○ Over the life of your loan you'll pay less interest than you would with a table loan.

○ A reducing balance (non-table) home loan can be a good idea if your income is expected to decrease; for example, if you or your partner plan to stop working in a few years' time.

○ Your principal payments and interest charges can also be paid from two separate and different accounts.

Cons:

○ Higher initial repayments on a reducing balance (non-table) home loan make this type of loan more expensive in the short–medium term.

○ It may be more affordable for you to make regular payments of the same amount under a table loan.

Loan products and structures

Type of loan	Interest only	Principal and interest	Fixed interest rate	Floating interest rate	Offsetting
Offsetting	Y	Y	N	Y	N/A
Revolving credit	Y	Y	N	Y	N
Table	Y	Y	Y	Y	Y
Accelerated repayment	Y	Y	Y	Y	Y
Reducing balance	Y	Y	Y	Y	Y

Note that not all lenders have these products, particularly offsetting loans where BNZ has been the market leader with their TotalMoney product.

19 | How to structure your loan

It is important to have the right loan structure from the outset, as changes later on can be costly — risking inefficient tax treatment, potentially extra interest and not getting the best return on investment. If you have a loan on your own home and investment property loans, it generally makes sense (and cents) to pay down the principal on your own home loan as quickly as possible, while having your investment properties on interest-only loans. This is because the interest on your own home is generally not tax-deductible, whereas on investment properties it is.

There are some exceptions to this statement: if you have a home office, you can deduct the proportion of interest that matches the area available for exclusive use as an office as a proportion of your home. For example, Beryl and Andy have a 100m² home in Invercargill and they have a bedroom exclusively used as a home office which is 12m² in size. They are able to deduct 12% of their loan interest for tax purposes. Also if you have boarders or flatmates, or run a business from your home, some of the interest on your home loan may be deductible, and if you use your own home as security and use that for your property investments, then this interest may be tax deductible too. Be aware that this may have some insurance impacts, so always discuss with your insurance provider.

Loan length

One of the most important choices on a loan is its length. While loans range typically from five to 30 years, I believe that where the lender doesn't dictate terms to you, that you should choose the maximum loan length of

30 years. Note that for investors borrowing at over 80% loan-to-value ratio, and also for some homeowners with only 10% deposit or less, you may get a slightly shorter maximum loan length (eg. 25 years).

Now I know that some readers will be thinking: 'Hold on, didn't you say earlier that one of the ways to improve your cash flow from property investing is to pay down your loans?' Yes, by paying down your loans you reduce interest expenses and increase your profitability. However, it is important to have as much exposure to good property as possible. Therefore, by having a shorter loan term, you would have to repay your loan in full faster. But with a longer loan term you have the option to repay your loan faster without penalty in most cases. More importantly as time goes on, if you have invested in property in a halfway decent location (remember that you are buying in cities and not remote single-industry towns or ghost towns) your property will go up in value enormously, as will the rental income, so refinancing it (with the same bank or to another lender with another 30-year loan term) will not be all that difficult.

This is where another important part of loan structuring comes into the equation. That is whether to have an interest-only loan or a principal-and-interest loan.

Interest only vs principal and interest

Firstly I had better define what interest-only and principal-and-interest loans are. The outstanding loan balance incurs interest so this will always be payable to your lender, however every loan has to repaid eventually. To repay loans you need to pay down the loan principal (loan balance) entirely. All loans have the default position of being principal and interest, so you have to specifically request that the loan is interest only.

When you have an interest-only (I/O) loan, you only pay the amount of interest on the loan balance outstanding. For example, if you had a $765,000 interest-only loan with a fixed interest rate of 9.2%, you would have a fortnightly payment of $2,706.92. You can select an interest only period typically from one to five years, although some lenders, such as BNZ, offer up to 10 years, before the loan automatically reverts to principal-and-interest basis. The loan length doesn't change with I/O loans as some investors erroneously think. So if you had a $200,000 loan for a 25-year term and had the first 21 years of it from drawdown date on the interest-only basis, you would technically be left with just 4 years in which to repay the $200,000 loan principal to the bank. In 21 years' time your property is likely to have more than doubled if not tripled if history proves correct, and extending the loan term should be a 'no brainer' and easy to do.

With this amount on a principal-and-interest (P&I) loan, I like to establish what I am paying so I use the figures on the interest.co.nz mortgage calculator (entering in 100 years as the loan term). You can also calculate these figures by using Microsoft Excel's PMT function, or by using financial calculators or numerous other software products. If you had the same amount on a 25-year P&I loan, it would be a fortnightly payment of $3,010. This represents an additional $303 every fortnight.

A good way to explain principal-and-interest versus interest-only loans is by showing you a graph with a loan on interest only for the first five years, and principal and interest thereafter. Let's say Kath has a loan of $250,000 for 20 years, and she applies for and is granted an interest-only period of five years by her bank. As a result she doesn't reduce the loan principal at all, as she is only paying the interest in this timeframe. However after that she is making both payments of principal and interest and her loan balance reduces slowly initially after the interest-only period, then fairly rapidly in the later part of the graph as the percentage of principal repaid goes up as time progresses.

Comparison between interest-only loan and table loan

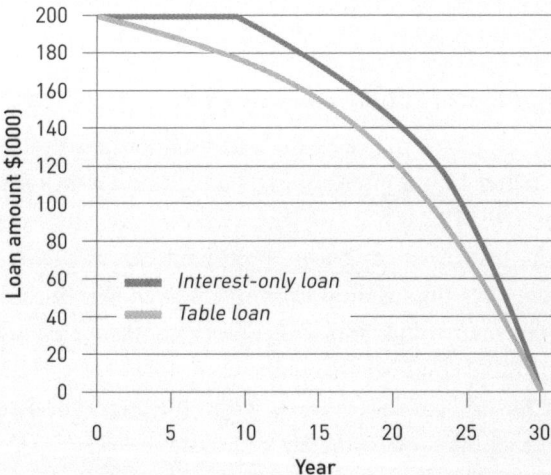

Here's another example of the impact between principal-and-interest loans on varying terms, and an interest-only loan. Bob has a loan of $320,000 and is deciding whether to have a 20-year P&I loan, 25-year P&I loan, 30-year P&I loan or a 5-year I/O loan (which is technically described as a

30-year P&I loan with an interest-only period of X years, where X is from 1–10 years, and most typically five years).

So you can see that you can pay off your loans faster with P&I loans. This has the effect of reducing your interest cost. However this can take up money that you need to buy more property, and you may miss out on that hot property deal 20% below valuation if you don't have the money to contribute at the time. The fact of the matter is your lender may force you to be on P&I and in downturn phases of property cycles this is increasingly common, with separate applications required to stay on an I/O basis. During property booms lenders barely bat an eye when you ask to rollover your I/O loan, even for a longer term like 5 years. Property booms are also the best time to increase the lifetime of those loans you have had for a number of years or couple of decades!

Got a loan on your own home?

If you have investment properties as well as your own home, I highly recommend that you have all your investment properties on an I/O basis, and repay as much debt as possible off your own home on the P&I basis. This is because the debt on your principal place of residence is not tax deductible (barring any portion for your home office, boarders or flatmates). Therefore it is most tax-efficient to retire debt from your own home first. Isn't it nice to have a rental property portfolio to assist you in getting a freehold home as well as other financial goals?

Freehold home or renting

If you are taking a true management accountant's perspective you would generally be better off on interest-only loans from a return on investment (ROI) perspective. This is because you are putting less money down when measuring the performance of a property and can as such acquire more properties that over time should exhibit strong growth in both cash flow and equity. For many older and also conservative property investors of all ages, P&I sits more comfortably for them.

However for other older investors with only a few good years of work left in them, and investors with low cash flow but significant amounts of equity, I/O may be the better choice. You can also change between I/O and P&I loans too. Just remember that you need to repay your loans eventually and that your credit history improves as you prove your ability to clear debt. In these situations this is very much a personal choice that needs to be made on a case by case basis.

Interest rates

Now you have decided the type of loan you want from this and the previous chapter, you need to work on the strategy that you believe will pay the least interest possible over time. You can do this by floating all of your debt, fixing your debt or mixing it up in various portions. Alternatively, you could use an interest-rate averaging strategy, as I discussed at length in Chapter 16.

In a nutshell the choice you have is between fixed or floating. You do have a number of sub-choices within fixed rates (6 months, 1 year, 18 months, 2 years, 3 years, 4 years, 5 years, 7 years), but I shall leave these to you as interest-rate choices are subjective and require a lot of crystal-ball gazing. Chapter 16 covered how these rates work and the pros and cons of each.

Here is an easy table to help you compare different options. In this example, an 8% per annum rate has been used for all calculation throughout the term of the loan (8% is the approximate 10-year average variable rate over time). The example below assumes a loan with an initial balance of $200,000:

Structure	Fortnightly repayments	Fortnightly interest only	Total interest over life of loan	Length of loan
25 years P&I	$710	N/A	$263,420	25 years
30 years P&I	$675	N/A	$328,516	30 years
5 years interest only + 25 years P& I	$710	$615	$343,420	30 years
10 years interest only + 20 years P&I	$769	$615	$361,462	30 years
25 years accelerated repayment	$769–$1,163	N/A	$147,344	14.2 years
25 years reducing balance	$920–$242	N/A	$200,307	25 years

20 | What do I need to know about accounting and taxation?

It is important that you are aware of your taxation obligations, as property investment is a business. Since you are planning to profit from property, you need to treat your investments like a business. Property investors have to file annual income tax returns declaring all rental income. This includes income received in cash from tenants. You should also be claiming all tax-deductible expenses against this income.

Accounting system

Running a business requires setting up an accounting system. You will need to ensure that you can record all income you receive. This is mainly rental income but may also include interest income, and perhaps even insurance income from a policy paying out compensation for lost rent. I know some investors use a ledger-book system and a folder with clear pockets to put their receipts in. Another investor uses Microsoft Excel to manage her 10 tenancies, and a younger client uses Google spreadsheets (a Google documents cloud computing feature) for his rental portfolio. Others use excellent software packages like Xero (cloud computing again) and MYOB.

When you run a business you should expect to be audited at some stage by the Inland Revenue Department. If you have very high expenses and large tax deductions, the risk of an audit is reportedly higher. This makes sense from Inland Revenue's perspective as they have a lot of information at their fingertips. They have sophisticated systems to put similar businesses' accounts together (for instance, analysing all property investors' tax returns), and then they can pay particular attention to the anomalies, as well as selecting a number of people at random.

Setting up a good book-keeping system to keep all of your financial information and records together is vital. This will also make life easier for you or your accountant when it comes time to preparing your annual accounts — that way you have all the information required to complete your income tax return at your fingertips.

Types of accounts

The two most common types of accounts are the balance sheet and the profit and loss statement. The balance sheet records the assets, liabilities and owner's equity. While this is important, it is nowhere near as important for preparing an income tax return as the profit and loss statement, which records the income and expenses in a given period — and for tax purposes, this period will be one year. Let's focus on the profit and loss statement. Below is an example of a typical investor's profit and loss statement.

Sample profit and loss statement for a property investor

	$
Income	
Rental income	29,400
Total income	29,400
Expenses	
Accounting fees	1,723
Bank fees	353
General expenses	850
Insurance	1,025
Interest	13,783
Management fees	2,287
Legal fees	1,230
Mileage	672
Office expenses	1,878
Rates	2,645
Repairs and maintenance	2,480
Total expenses	28,926
Net profit/(loss) before tax	474

Income

The best set-up is to have your tenants paying rent weekly (or fortnightly) into your bank account by way of automatic payment. You can then take the rent information from your bank statements (most banks in New Zealand offer excellent customer service and store your data online for years). Then you can add any rental income that you have received in cash, or the value of contra payments (I know a tenant who paid their rent to their landlord in the form of panel-beating services, for example).

You can record your interest income from bank statements or the annual statement your bank sends you setting out gross interest earned and resident withholding tax (RWT) deducted. If you have received any other income, record that too.

Expenses

There are a number of tax-deductible expenses that a property investor may claim. These include but are by no means limited to:

- loan interest
- repairs and maintenance
- mileage
- tenancy tribunal application fees
- cleaning
- installing a smoke alarm
- due diligence costs (eg. a LIM report)
- accounting and book-keeping fees
- property mentoring fees or event tickets
- water rates
- your local property investors' association membership
- loan application and fixed-rate rollover fees
- council rates
- property management fees
- advertising to find tenants
- depreciation
- legal fees

- ○ electricity
- ○ business cards
- ○ *NZ Property Investor* magazine subscription
- ○ bank fees (on the account where the rent is banked).

Let's look at some specific categories of expenses:

Mileage

If you drive your car when carrying out investment-related activites, such as collecting rent, performing inspections, showing your house to prospective tenants and project managing or doing repairs and maintenance, you can claim a mileage allowance. The Inland Revenue Department website (www.ird.govt.nz) has the latest rates (search under 'mileage').

Loan interest

Only the interest component of your loan is tax deductible. The principal component is not tax deductible as it is the repayment of debt.

Break fees

Since interest rates have started heading down sharply from late 2008, some property investors have refinanced to fixed-rate terms with much lower interest rates. Inland Revenue has made two public rulings since then to determine the deductibility of break fees. Firstly, they ruled that any costs for breaking a fixed-interest-rate loan (by either terminating an existing loan due to the sale of the property or because you have refinanced with another lender) is fully tax deductible in the year the cost is incurred, provided of course that the loan was borrowed to purchase property for deriving rental income.

Secondly, they ruled that where you pay a break fee simply to change the rate of an existing loan (changing to a different interest rate but staying with the same lender), deductibility is based on whether you are defined as a 'cash basis person' under the Income Tax Act 2007 or not. Seek professional tax advice in this regard. Trusts and companies can be cash basis persons now too, as of 1 April 2009. If you are a cash basis person you can claim a full deduction of the break fee to your lender in the year the cost was incurred.

If you do not meet the definition of a cash basis person, the deduction of the break fee needs to be spread over the remaining term of the loan.

Therefore if you are considering refinancing and there is a break fee payable, ensure that your bank terminates the existing loan and starts a new one to get a full deduction under early repayment provision, or refinance. Again, the loan must be borrowed to purchase property used in deriving rental income.

Repairs and maintenance

Repairs and maintenance include any items of expenditure needed to maintain your asset, such as painting the exterior, installing new cupboard hinges, repairing cracked mortar on roof tiles, replacing a hot water cylinder, fixing a burnt-out electrical plug and so on. These are all items of expenditure that are necessarily incurred in earning rental income. If you don't maintain your property and keep it looking good your rental income goes down. Also, you get longer vacancy periods, and you can't put your rent up as much as if you regularly maintained your property.

Note that it is critical to draw the line between capital and revenue expenditure. I have heard this firsthand from two Inland Revenue auditors I know — one ex-auditor and one currently auditing. Both auditors have told me that too many investors make the mistake of claiming large amounts of money as repairs and maintenance expenditure in the first year that they own their property.

Investors claim many thousands of dollars for repairing a new kitchen, re-roofing, rewiring and redoing the plumbing. Inland Revenue can make a strong argument that you are doing these things in exchange for a reduced purchase price, and that these are improvements and not repairs. After all, you haven't even started receiving rental income on the property.

The result is that, upon inspection, some investors get caught out. They then face penalties on the core amount of tax they should have been paying but for these expense claims being denied: 20% for an 'unacceptable interpretation' penalty and 40% for a 'gross carelessness' penalty. My recommendation is that you seek skilled professional advice (generally from a tax accountant) if you are in doubt on whether or not to claim. The New Zealand Property Investors' Federation, the Inland Revenue Department and the Department of Building and Housing run seminars that cover topics like this too, so make sure you are a member of your local property investors' association (branch of NZPIF) to ensure you are up-to-date with all legislation and changes.

You have to submit your annual profit and loss statement or do a summary of your financials on the IR10 form every year. You will likely have a line item for repairs and maintenance, or general expenses. If this is too large, it will stand out like a sore thumb, and you will face a vastly increased chance of being investigated. It is not smart to get Inland Revenue's back up and in effect be blacklisted by them — this will cost you a lot of time and money, including opportunity cost and lost sleep. Ensure that you follow the tax laws and don't be greedy!

Repairs and maintenance claims are far simpler after tenants have been in the property and the curtains get worn and need replacing after a few years, the sewer macerating pump fails after too many uses, or the walls need to be painted and kitchen cabinetry upgraded over time. These are clear-cut cases of tax deductions. Don't worry about getting an audit because bad luck struck you on one year where you had to replace roofs on two properties, resulting in an unusually large figure. This in itself will not trigger an audit.

A quick question for you: if you have a steel roof and replace it with a concrete-tile roof, is this tax deductible as repairs and maintenance, or something that needs to be capitalised and depreciated?

The answer is that this is something to be capitalised and depreciated as you are not replacing like with like and this is said to be an improvement. Again a note to property investors to seek professional advice! This is borne out by cases like *Auckland Trotting Club (Inc) v CIR* [1968] NZLR 967, in which the Auckland Trotting Club was denied a tax deduction for repairs and maintenance. The club had reconstructed a trotting track, taking it out and re-laying another one. The court held that this was an item of capital expenditure and not repairs to the old track.

The current approach adopted to determine whether an item is classified as repairs and maintenance expenditure (to be deducted) or a capital item (to add to your fixed asset register) is a two-stage test as follows:

○ Identify the relevant asset to which the test of repair or replacement is being applied. Is the item that is being repaired or replaced part of a larger asset, or is it a single asset?

○ Ascertain the nature, extent and cost of work undertaken. This will involve determining whether the work remedied wear and tear, which is generally deductible, or whether the asset has been improved or otherwise substantially changed (generally non-deductible).

Depreciation

This is an allowance for the wear and tear on fixed assets. For example, putting new carpets in a fairly standard rental property may cost you $3,000. However over time (let's say five years) they wear out and you have to throw the heavily worn carpet out and replace it. The goal is to write down the value of the carpets each year to match their expected economic life. There's more information on depreciation in the next chapter.

Preparing your accounts for year end

Whether you are one of the many investors doing your own accounts and tax returns, or you have an accountant, you need to do a number of things to prepare for the end of the tax year. Apart from having access to your bank statements, you will need to keep all records for your rents received, and all expenses (including keeping invoices for all items of expenditure over $50). With just one property this may be quite easy; it is very common with just one property to do your annual accounts and income tax return yourself, perhaps calling Inland Revenue's 0800 number for free assistance when needed.

The standard and default balance date is 31 March for investors, meaning the year runs from 1 April to 31 March. The 2012 financial year therefore runs from 1 April 2011 to 31 March 2012. You can prepare for the end of the financial year and get yourself a small timing advantage by pre-paying your insurance in March — you get a full deduction for pre-paying a premium up to 12 months prior (if you don't exceed $12,000), and on some other expenses such as stationery and postage.

Actions to consider before the end of the financial year

Are you going to sell your property (fixed assets)?	Consider delaying the sale (unless you are expecting a loss on sale) until after balance date to defer any possible depreciation recovery. Note that you should write off any obsolete assets not working (for example, broken old rangehoods) by physically disposing of them.
Thinking of spending money on your rental properties soon?	Consider doing any repairs and maintenance, and buying the new business assets in March to get the deduction in the financial year or to claim a whole month's depreciation.

Leaving New Zealand permanently or for an extended period of time?	If you have a look-through company and you intend to leave New Zealand in the next 12 months, then the company could lose its LTC status, so you need to plan for this.
Making any donations?	Companies and individuals can claim a tax deduction on donations made to registered charities (like other expenses).

Let me tell you how I feel about profitability: it is important to run your property investments like a business, and create positive cash flow. Initially, like many larger companies, it may be acceptable to make tax losses. But you can't keep doing this! It is not a long-term strategy if you want to get finance to assist you to grow a portfolio.

Sadly, the accounting fundamentals were seemingly forgotten in the credit-fuelled property boom of 2003 to 2007. This is slowly changing, as the ability to claim depreciation on building structures has been removed with effect from 1 April 2011 onwards. Investors have returned to becoming net taxpayers, with the extremely high interest rates of 2006 to 2008 having reversed and gone to below 10-year average levels, and Auckland and Christchurch in particular have benefited from rental increases.

Tax legislation for the future — future tax reform?

We have seen changes to the legislation with building structure depreciation being removed and LAQCs becoming LTCs. I predict further changes in the years ahead, particularly if a Labour-led coalition government is elected on Saturday 26 November 2011. Labour's shadow Minister of Finance, David Cunliffe, has told the media how he would like to ring-fence tax losses for property investors. This means that tax losses from rental properties would be quarantined and not able to be used to offset personal salary or wage income. Green party leader Dr Russel Norman has long said the Greens would like to impose a capital gains tax (CGT) on the sale proceeds of all properties but the family home. Then, in July 2011, Labour announced their tax policy where they would introduce a CGT at 15% on all property but the family home. It strangely exempted things like jewellery, luxury boats and profits from gambling.

There is a real risk of the ring-fencing of tax losses being introduced. In Australia, when Bob Hawke's Labor Government introduced ring-fencing in 1985, it was scrapped again in 1987. Rents had skyrocketed and Labor's voters were hit directly in the pocket. Many landlords sold out of their investments, which meant there was a massive undersupply of houses available for rent, so landlords put their rents up as hordes of tenants attended open homes, house overcrowding occurred and protests ensued before the calls from tenants and property investors were heeded and ring-fencing of tax losses was abolished.

For those reasons, I don't envisage ring-fencing legislation lasting more than one three-year election cycle in New Zealand if it is introduced. I would predict tightening of the LTC's loss limitation rule. Possibly loans personally guaranteed will not be included as part of the shareholders' contribution, so the effect will be that LTC shareholders will only be able to claim a tax deduction against their salary or waged income up to the amounts of money they have actually put down.

Other tax reform could include reintroduction of estate and death duties. While I don't like these taxes that erode individual property rights, there are some that think these are a good idea. They believe if the value of your assets is above a certain threshold when you die, you should be taxed on the amounts above these thresholds even if it means having to sell assets to raise funds to pay the taxes. If this is to come in, it will probably start with a high threshold to be politically palatable, and then come down over time and not be adjusted for inflation.

Imposing a capital gains tax is a bad idea

I am on record with numerous media as thinking introducing a CGT in New Zealand is totally unnecessary. In my view the focus instead must be on improving the quality of government expenditure and cutting it. It is not a sustainable situation to overspend over $300 million per week, and fund this by borrowings. The government is mindful of this and will return to surpluses soon.

CGT is an envy tax on those who hold assets. It is not aspirational to tax and therefore penalise those who don't want to be a burden on their fellow taxpayers. In addition, proponents of a CGT suggest it will stop housing booms. Unfortunately, in every country in the world with a CGT, this has been proven not to be the case.

The Savings Working Group produced a report recently which omitted to analyse the impact of 2008 on the housing market, which was the single worst year for house prices in New Zealand history (real falls were around -11% in NZ for that single year). Instead they worked on the 2001–2007 period, mostly a 'boom' period in the housing market. They used flawed data, as it is not fair to only include the boom years and ignore downturn years. We need to also remember that New Zealand from 1990–2007 had the third largest population growth rate in the OECD, and migration is one of the major factors in the housing market. Andrew Coleman and John Landon-Lane in September 2007 produced a report for the Reserve Bank entitled 'Housing Markets and Migration in New Zealand, 1962–2006'. Their research showed that a net immigration flow of 1% is equivalent to a 10% increase in house prices. So if our net immigration went up by 10%, could this one factor alone explain the movement in house prices?

I would argue that proponents of a CGT need to look at the full picture and not just the portion of the statistics that suits their arguments. For example, Russel Norman, leader of the Green party, stated that 'the tax system is the cause of half the increase in house prices in the last decade — clearly the thing that's missing is the capital gains tax, excluding the family home'. With all due respect to Russel this is not correct, and in fact imposing a CGT would be a disaster for our country — there would be reductions in investment, competition, fairness, privacy and employment as a result of imposing a CGT.

Imposing a CGT would also mean fewer investors. Even if this envy tax were imposed, I still think that it is a good idea to invest and prosper with property. If you are buying based on the fundamentals with positive cash flow and great growth, then why can't you park this asset in a modern flexible trust to provide for your needs in retirement and perhaps even those of your children and grandchildren? Just because one government imposes a CGT doesn't mean another will not repeal it. I'd strongly consider standing for Parliament on this platform to repeal a tax like this.

We investors risk our capital, personally guaranteeing — at a minimum — many hundreds of thousands of dollars. We have our assets let out to other people; we are responsible for repairs and maintenance costs; we face interest-rate spikes; increasing council rates; provide the basic good of accommodation and collectively pay billions of dollars every year to tradespeople and companies in the construction sector. We even wear the impact of GST (we cannot charge GST on residential rentals). A CGT may see many investors sell, driving supply down and potentially forcing rents to skyrocket. Does the government want to impose large rental price increases on all the New Zealanders (over one-third of our country) who are tenants?

21 | Depreciation: making it as simple as possible

Heavy reading alert: employ a great tax accountant
and you can skip this chapter.

Depreciation is an allowance provided in the Income Tax Act 2007 for the wear and tear of fixed assets over their estimated useful life. For items under $500 you can 'expense' them as repairs and maintenance. However, capital items worth over $500 must be capitalised and depreciated — if you are allowed to depreciate them. Since a depreciable asset is expected to last more than one financial year the depreciation rate allocated to it is meant to reflect its loss in economic value every year.

What is depreciable?

Now getting more technically correct, 'depreciable property' means any property which might reasonably be expected to decline in value while used or available for use by taxpayers in deriving gross income, or carrying on a business for the purpose of deriving gross income. Depreciable property includes buildings, fixtures on land and certain land improvements. Depreciable property does not include trading stock (for instance, if you are a property trader holding the property that you have purchased on revenue account — where you have bought the property with an intention or purpose of resale) or land.

Interestingly, after the Tax Working Group's recommendations for tax reform were announced, there seemed to be a clear goal of refocusing investors away from property as it is clearly New Zealanders' favourite investment choice. The group neglected to say this is because of its proven long-term track record in delivering great cash flow and equity gains to property investors, and also neglected to go through the performance of the other asset classes.

Two depreciation rate methods

Under the tax depreciation rules, taxpayers can elect to use either the diminishing value (DV) or straight line (SL) method to depreciate capital assets:

○ Under the straight line method, a constant percentage of the cost of the asset to a taxpayer is deducted from the property's adjusted tax book value.

○ Under the diminishing value method, a constant percentage of the adjusted tax book value is deducted each year.

The IRD prescribes depreciation rates for both of these methods. The straight line rates are lower than the diminishing value ones. As a result you would have lower book values for your asset in the earlier years of its life under the diminishing value depreciation method.

The best way to show this is graphically:

Book value of an asset under different depreciation methods

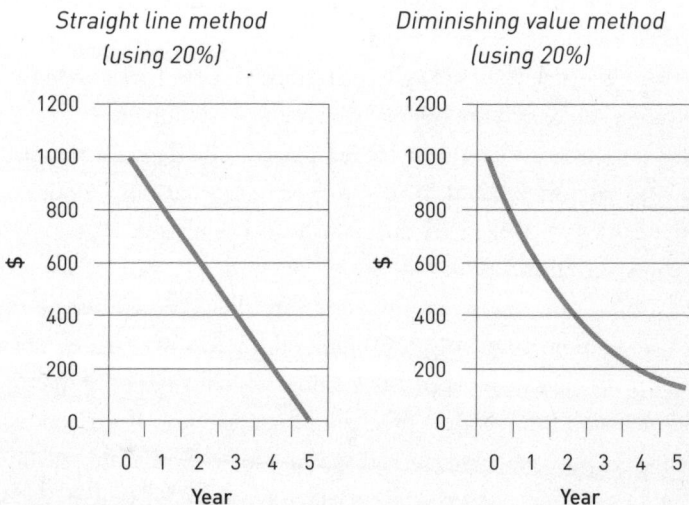

Straight line method
(using 20%)

Diminishing value method
(using 20%)

Claiming for a part year

Depreciation is also adjusted for the proportion of the income year the property is owned and used or is available for use in business. So, for example, if an asset becomes available for use in a taxpayer's business halfway through the income year, the depreciation deduction in that year will be apportioned to reflect the fact that the asset was available for use for only half the year.

The formula to show this is:

$A \times B \times C / 12$

A is the annual depreciation rate

B is the adjusted tax value or cost of the asset

C is the number of months in the income year the asset was used or was available for use

The number of months includes part months, so even if you purchased an item on the final day of the month, for example 31 January, you could still claim for three full months' depreciation (1 January to 31 March).

Disposal of fixed assets

If you dispose of a depreciable item inside a financial year which runs from 1 April to 31 March of the following year, you cannot claim depreciation in respect of that item in that financial year.

For example, if you owned light fittings and disposed of them in February for no value, you would not be able to claim depreciation on them in respect of that year, despite 11 months having passed. The depreciation claim for the year is therefore $0, and the disposal value is what is important.

On disposal you need to do a wash-up calculation to see which of these three scenarios applies — have you underclaimed or overclaimed depreciation, or are you in fact all square with the depreciation you claimed being just right in matching the book value? You need to compare the asset's disposal value against its book value, which is typically the value on 31 March of the immediately preceding financial year. If this value is also $0 then there is no gain or loss on disposal. However, if in this example the book value was $200 then you would have a loss on disposal of $200. This is because you have only been able to claim depreciation for an expense at a specified rate over the years, and it has worked out that the depreciation rate didn't match the actual useful life of the asset.

Chattels appraisals

A chattels appraisal is a report that splits the purchase price of your investment property into its component assets and asset classes. It has the effect of greatly increasing your cash flow. The chattels appraisal firstly looks at land and buildings, where land cannot be depreciated. Then buildings are split into the three main asset classes: building structure, which cannot be depreciated with effect from 1 April 2011, building fit-out and chattels.

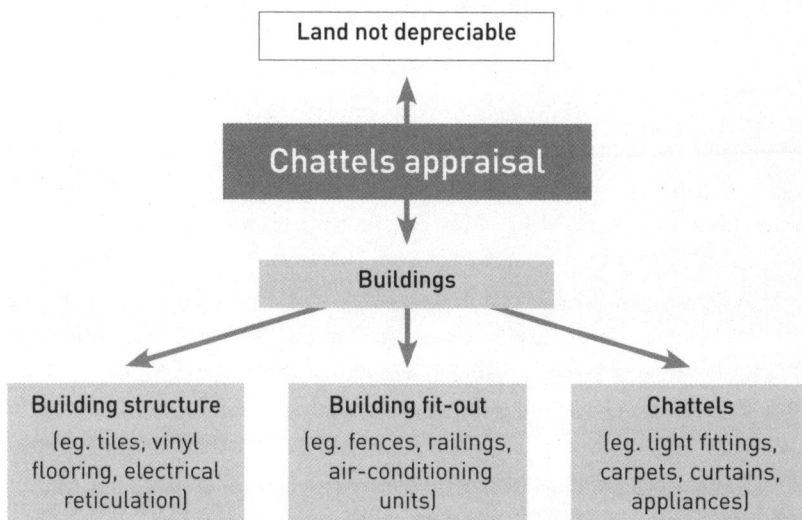

```
                    ┌──────────────────────────┐
                    │  Land not depreciable    │
                    └──────────────────────────┘
                              ▲
                              │
              ┌───────────────────────────────┐
              │     Chattels appraisal        │
              └───────────────────────────────┘
                              │
                              ▼
                    ┌──────────────────┐
              ┌─────│    Buildings     │─────┐
              ▼     └──────────────────┘     ▼
                            │
                            ▼
```

Building structure	Building fit-out	Chattels
(eg. tiles, vinyl flooring, electrical reticulation)	(eg. fences, railings, air-conditioning units)	(eg. light fittings, carpets, curtains, appliances)

Why not just use a registered valuation as that splits out 'chattels'?

Many investors claim minimal depreciation based on the value of chattels given in a registered valuation report that is assessed by a registered land and buildings valuer. This value is purely assessed for finance purposes or otherwise to provide assistance in determining a sale or purchase price. It certainly will not maximise your depreciation claim.

The market leader in New Zealand and to the best of my knowledge the only company specialising in chattels appraisals is a company called Valuit Asset Appraisals (www.valuit.co.nz). For a little over $400 you will get a professional report designed to maximise your depreciation. The report complies with Inland Revenue rulings and requirements, and provides a reduced risk of penalties while maximising your allowable depreciation expense and increasing cash flow (through a reduced tax bill).

2010 — the year for big changes

Treasury and Inland Revenue were concerned throughout most of the noughties decade about the growing practice of allocating the cost of buildings into separate depreciable parts. This enabled property investors to claim higher depreciation deductions than the deduction available for depreciating the building as a whole.

The previous legislative framework was unclear and ambiguous on this point, which created both a compliance risk for property investors as well as increased administrative costs for Inland Revenue. This uncertainty also created the potential for misuse and led to depreciation claims varying massively among different investors. Some investors elected not to depreciate at all, others claimed based on the typical minimal figure provided in a registered valuation report, and many others opted for a Valuit or similar report where the costs of the building would be broken down into a schedule of fixed assets as permitted by the Inland Revenue guidebook IR260 Depreciation.

For years, Inland Revenue's operational view was that the building depreciation rate is inclusive of structural items like electrical wiring and plumbing. Inland Revenue's Tax Information Bulletin, Volume 5, No. 9 (February 1994) set out the following view of what is an asset:

> 'Inland Revenue considers that a distinct physical unit which can function on its own is a unit against which the extent of any expenditure will be measured. So, if a building is part of a larger complex, the particular building (and not the wider complex) will be the unit if it is a stand-alone building. However, each situation will depend on its own facts.'

The issue was that many investors were separately depreciating items like internal walls, built-in cupboards, pipes, vents and wiring, which really were part of the building structure. Some taxpayers were investigated by Inland Revenue and lost the ability to claim depreciation at a higher rate. Confusion reigned until April 2010 when Inland Revenue released an interpretation statement (IS10/01) on this, and then the government Budget announced on 20 May 2010 that building structure depreciation was to be removed, with the depreciation rate to be legislated as being 0%.

Certainty at last

In April 2010 we finally had some certainty with the Inland Revenue publishing Interpretation Statement IS10/01 Residential Rental Properties — Depreciation of Items of Depreciable Property. This interpretation statement sets out the Inland Revenue's view of just what is a separately identifiable item of depreciable property and what is part of the building structure. This is important as if an item in a residential rental property is distinct from the building and it meets the definition of 'depreciable property', then it may be separately depreciated. However if an item is part of the building, it cannot be separately depreciated, and is depreciated with the building (at 0% as of 1 April 2011).

A residential rental property comprises several different items. It is important to know whether an item in a residential rental property forms a part of the building, or is separately identifiable because this affects the depreciation rate to be applied and also the tax treatment of expenditure on repairs. For many people this will be heavy reading, so you may want to skip to the next chapter and make the decision to get a skilled property investment accountant (they should ideally be a property investor themselves) to manage your fixed-asset register and depreciation expense claims, particularly in light of the new legislation.

There is now a three-step test to determine whether a particular item is part of or separate from the building:

Step 1

Determine whether the item is in some way attached or connected to the building. If the item is completely unattached, then it will not form a part of the building. An item will not be considered attached for these purposes if its only means of attachment is being plugged or wired into an electrical outlet (such as a freestanding oven), or attached to a water or gas outlet. If the item is attached to the building, go to step 2.

Step 2

Determine whether the item is an integral part of the residential rental property such that a residential rental property would be considered incomplete or unable to function without the item. If the item is an integral part of the residential rental property, then the item will be a part of the building. If the item is not an integral part of the residential rental property, go to step 3.

Step 3

Determine whether the item is built-in or attached or connected to the building in such a way that it is part of the 'fabric' of the building. Consider factors such as the nature and degree of attachment, the difficulty involved in the item's removal, and whether there would be any significant damage to the item or the building if the item were removed. If the item is part of the fabric of the building, then it is part of the building for depreciation purposes.

Here's a flow chart of this new three-step test:

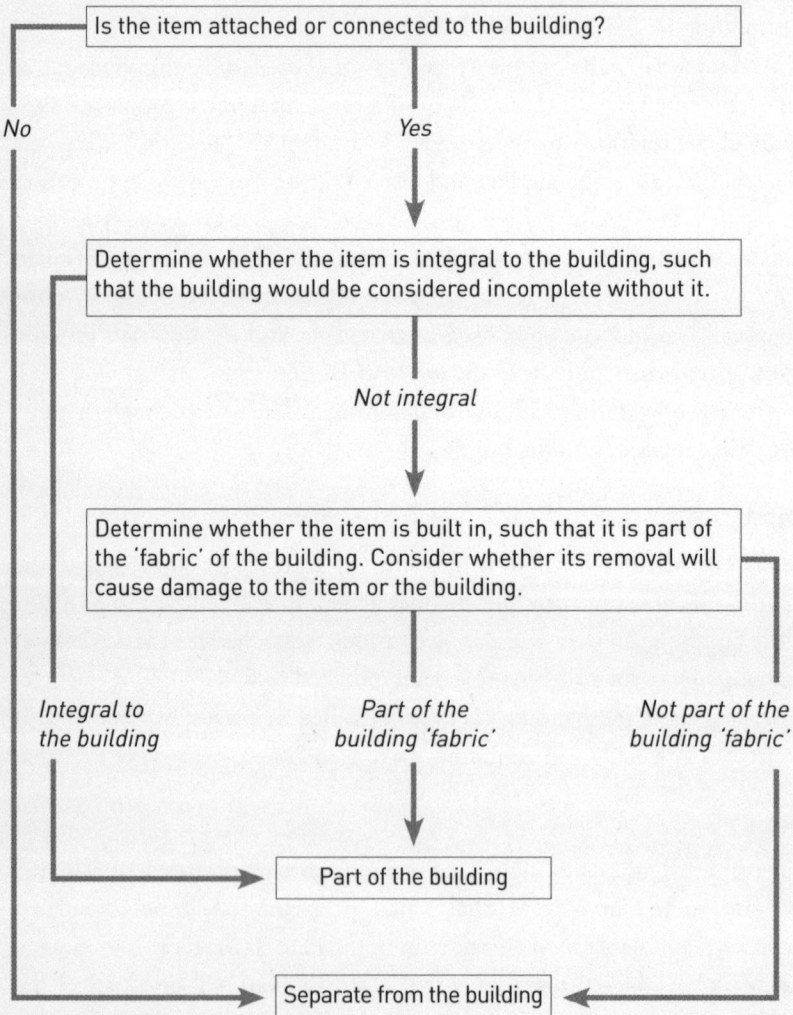

```
       ┌─── Is the item attached or connected to the building? ──────┐
       │                                                              
  No   │                         Yes                                  
       │                          │                                   
       │                          ▼                                   
       │    ┌─── Determine whether the item is integral to the building, such
       │    │    that the building would be considered incomplete without it.
       │    │                                                         
       │    │              Not integral                               
       │    │                   │                                     
       │    │                   ▼                                     
       │    │    Determine whether the item is built in, such that it is part of
       │    │    the 'fabric' of the building. Consider whether its removal will ──┐
       │    │    cause damage to the item or the building.                         
       │    │                                                                      
   Integral to          Part of the           Not part of the                      
   the building         building 'fabric'     building 'fabric'                     
       │    │                   │                                     │            
       │    └───────────► Part of the building                        │            
       │                                                              │            
       └──────────────► Separate from the building ◄─────────────────┘            
```

Source: Inland Revenue Department

The effect of this interpretation statement means that some items widely depreciated are now no longer able to be depreciated separately. This is of concern to investors as shortly after the April 2010 release date of this interpretation statement, the Minister of Finance Bill English (on 20 May 2010 during that year's Budget) said that building structures will have depreciation removed from 3% DV and 2% SL from 1 April 2011 onwards. This means that items which are part of the building structure are no longer able to be depreciated at all.

The following table shows a list of some items of building structure in the left column and items of building fit-out and chattels on the right column that are able to be depreciated separately:

Building structure items (depreciated at 0% as part of the building structure)	Separately identifiable items (separately depreciated at between 4% and 60%)
plumbing and piping	carpets and rugs
roof	curtains
stairs	blinds
plasterboard (GIB)	water-heaters/hot water cylinders
cladding	light fittings
internal timber and steel framing	fences
windows	letterboxes
electrical wiring	air-conditioning systems (some not)
internal walls (including non-load-bearing walls)	free-standing ovens
internal and external doors	microwaves
garage doors (when the garage is part of the residential rental building)	rangehoods
fitted furniture (wardrobes and cupboards built into the wall)	electric hobs
kitchen cupboards	dishwashers
bathroom fittings and furniture	refrigerators
linoleum	washing machines
tiles (wall and floor)	heat pumps (some not)
some decks	log burners
	fans
	waste-disposal units
	loose furniture
	TV aerials
	paths and driveways
	pavers
	some decks
	wardrobes and cupboards not built into the wall

20 May 2010 Budget changes

Building structure depreciation rate to be 0%

Hot on the heels of the interpretation statement IS10/01, the government announced that building structure for all property types (residential and commercial) attracts a depreciation rate of 0%, so that it is not able to be depreciated. The rationale is that the overwhelming majority of properties go up in value and this is part of rebalancing the economy. This has a massive cash flow impact on many investors who were previously depreciating their building structure at 3% DV or 2% SL. When I started investing in 2002 the rates were 4% DV and 3% SL.

There is going to be a reduction in the depreciation expenditure of most property investors in the magnitude of 65 to 80% as a result of the changes made in IS10/01 and abolishing building structure depreciation. For those investors who didn't break their buildings down into their components and only claimed building structure depreciation, they lost 100% of their depreciation claim with effect from the first day of the 2012 financial year, 1 April 2011.

Loading on economic depreciation rates

The second change to depreciation in the budget was the 20% loading which used to be applied on top of the depreciation rates for most new depreciable property (that is, property that had not previously been used or available for use in New Zealand by any other owner). The major exception to this loading was building structure — only items of building fit-out and chattels attracted the loading. This was popular with property investors as loading allowed depreciation rates to be set at 120% of estimated economic depreciation.

This is now largely academic as the loading got scrapped in the May 2010 Budget. Property investors and business owners (building or replacing assets) will no longer be able to claim this 20% new asset loading on new plant and equipment. This change took effect for all assets purchased after 20 May 2010 (which was Budget day). Note that the old rules will continue to apply for assets purchased before this date.

Pooling assets together

The pooling method of depreciation allows assets below a certain value to be combined and depreciated at a single rate, thereby reducing the compliance costs associated with depreciating each individual item separately (and maintaining an asset register in respect of them). In some circumstances it is a good idea to pool your assets for administrative ease. Assets valued at $2,000 or less (either costing this amount or having been depreciated individually to an adjusted-tax-book value equal to or less than $2,000) can be pooled and depreciated as a single asset. You can apply to Inland Revenue to increase this maximum pooling value and can also maintain multiple pools. The depreciation rate to be used in respect of a pool is the lowest single rate applying to any asset in the pool.

Depreciation for commercial property owners

Just like residential property owners, commercial property owners cannot claim depreciation in respect of their building structure.

However, for commercial property fit-out and chattels there is a different approach, as this interpretation statement IS10/01 only applies to residential property. This was highlighted in the 20 May 2010 budget, with a review to what defines the term 'buildings' in the commercial property context, and what can be separately depreciated.

Commercial investors can depreciate any item on the schedule of the building fit-out asset category list of 90 items as seen in appendix A of the August 2010 Inland Revenue publication called Post Budget Depreciation Issues. It is available online at http://taxpolicy.ird.govt.nz/publications/2010-ip-post-budget-depreciation/appendix

This list is rather broad, and includes items like walls, partitions, electrical reticulation, plumbing and plumbing fittings, ceilings, roller doors, escalators, lifts, carpets, fitted furniture, air-conditioning systems and vinyl flooring to name just a few.

Interestingly there is also a proposal to allow a once-only 'carve out' of 15% of the building's total depreciated book value at 1 April 2011, to create a 'building fit-out pool'. This bonus deduction is only available to commercial investors who have never previously separated out their fit-out items. This building fit-out pool will be depreciable at 2% straight line, and (for some kind but unusual reason) will not be subject to recovery on disposal of the building.

22 Renovate, redecorate and revalue

When it comes to property there are a number of things you can do to rapidly increase its value. This is an important part of active investment and one of the secrets to my success in property investment. I buy properties that are run down and do them up to a high standard. This changes the nature of the property, improving both the rent and the capital value of the property. It is yet another reason why I consider property investment to be superior to other asset classes. How can you personally add value to a gold bar, term deposits or your shares?

Types of renovations

There are all sorts of projects that you can tackle, starting with a simple redecoration like waterblasting your path and upgrading the letterbox. That's the easy end of the scale. Medium-scale renovation projects might include moving walls to make an open-plan kitchen, living and dining area. At the complex end of the scale, renovations could include completely gutting a house back to the frames, then putting in insulation, new wiring, plumbing and GIB (plasterboard), gib-stopping (plastering), painting, installing new curtains, light fittings, plumbing fittings, new kitchen cabinetry, new tiles, new carpets, exterior repainting, re-roofing — the works. And if you're talking about restoration on a heritage building, you can notch it up yet another level.

There are all sorts of renovations along this spectrum. It's important that you only tackle projects within your comfort zone. Larger projects take more time and more skill — and more things can go wrong.

Before

After

Villa in Grey Lynn, Auckland.

Simple landscaping can add a lot of value.

Before

After

Bathroom modernisation with vanity repositioned to take a hip 1970s bathroom into the new millennium.

Before and after shots of a small outdoor area in Auckland's eastern suburbs.
Cost $6,000, giving a gain in value of $25,000!

Budgeting and project planning

It is absolutely critical to accurately budget for your renovation projects. Until you are very experienced at them, you need to include a contingency fee of at least 5% of your project cost. There's an old saying that doing up a house takes twice as much time and three times as much money as you think — and there's definitely a grain of truth in that. So to reduce those alarming increases, you need to start with realistic and well-researched budgets for both timing and costs.

I recommend making a list that includes both the exterior and interior improvements you plan to undertake. The interior list of things to do can also be broken down room by room.

Don't overcapitalise

You need to match your expenditure to the market for the area. I like to aim for the upper quartile in my buy-and-hold rentals, but I am not trying to have the best rental property of the suburb. It simply costs too much to achieve this standard and doesn't generally pay for itself in the extra rent gained.

Brett's so clever at property he overcapitalised! That was Kim's proud explanation to her mother in the Australian comedy *Kath and Kim*, to which her mother replied, 'Frankly, these days a spa pool is essential if you're going to overcapitalise.' Naturally, *Kath and Kim* is an example of what not to do — all the features Kath wants to see in a house are the features you don't want to put into your rental property, like that spa pool, swimming pool, gym and mezzanine (mezza-noyne).

Spending too much on renovating your property is simply wasting money. I know of investors who bought a property in a state housing-dominated street in South Auckland. The investors lived in an upmarket suburb in East Auckland, and wanted to have a nice-looking rental property like their own home. They put in $3,600 worth of curtains, top-of-the-line $13,000 Godfrey Hirst wool carpets, and pricy DeLonghi cooking appliances. The issue was that this three-bedroom 80m² house had been purchased for around $180,000. The year later I heard that the curtains had to be replaced for the next set of tenants, as the previous tenants had been swinging off them and the kids had used them to wipe their faces. The designer rangehood had large dents in it and looked well below average. But at least the fancy kitchen appliances still worked. The carpets had to be replaced from dirt and grime being ground into them. The outlay of almost $20,000 on these items was wasted; I would have spent under $6,000 on these items for this kind of property and area.

Now, if the investors had purchased a rental property and let it to a family in an upmarket suburb, they may have been able to charge higher rent for the quality fittings. But even then, the higher rent could probably have been achieved by spending just $10,000 on these items.

Risks

The main risks of any renovation project are financial risks, resulting from underbudgeting and going over the top (overcapitalising) in your renovation. Sometimes starting one job opens a Pandora's box of expenses — particularly on older houses like villas and bungalows. For example, you might take out a wall, then find out it was load-bearing and the ceiling has started to sag.

Best areas to focus on

The best areas to focus upon are undoubtedly the kitchens and bathrooms. The kitchens are where we entertain and we spend a lot of time there making breakfast, lunch, dinner, cups of tea and coffee, snacks and so on. Having a smart-looking kitchen with enough pantry, cupboard and bench space can be critical to maximising your rental return. You need to match the kitchen to the area; for example if you own a villa in an upmarket suburb, a second-hand kitchen from TradeMe with refurbished 1980s appliances and cheap vinyl flooring is not going to maximise your rentals. However in a more typical rental property in the suburbs this would often be absolutely fine.

Bathrooms are important too; features like a vanity cabinet to store medicines, toiletries and such like are very useful. Families prefer houses with baths for their children as they are less dangerous than showers. If there isn't a bath in a free-standing three- or four-bedroom house, consider putting one in. However, in city apartments putting a bath in is more likely to be a waste of time and money as they are typically for professionals living near work and students studying in the city. Big mirrors can make the bathroom look much bigger. I also make the bathroom look bigger by using transparent shower curtains instead of having coloured curtains for showers over baths.

Street appeal is important and often easy to fix. This often only involves waterblasting the front fence and path, decluttering the letterbox, and perhaps painting that tired-looking front door and front door frame. It is imperative to have your property looking good. First impressions count. I know this as in earlier years I used to do renovation work myself. I would often see tenants come down driveways to my properties 30 minutes to two hours prior to appointments with me, then they would not show up at all for their appointment. When I called their cellphones they would lie and say they were stuck at work.

We had two three-bedroom properties on the go at the same time in Massey only a couple of hundred metres away from another. The three-bedroom property down a long drive with a freshly painted exterior, new solid panel front door and painted fences was up against a tired old property that we had just purchased and made the mistake (but great learning experience) of advertising for rentals before the renovation was complete. The fence had palings missing, the glass-panelled front door hadn't been painted in decades and the sills and scribers around the windows were rotting with moss and lichens accentuating the dull, light-green tone of the weatherboards. Tenants that came to the unrenovated property came to look at the house around an hour early and then drove away. I met them two days later at the other property just a couple of hundred metres away. I was no longer in my painting and renovation gear, but was formally dressed, and they didn't recognise me. When they had signed up and paid their bond I asked them about the other property and why they didn't take it despite it being cheaper. Their response? 'It looked like a dog's breakfast' and 'How could I be proud to show my parents and friends that property?' Leading property managers from all around the country also tell me street appeal is important.

Pleasant living areas and creating outdoor space like decks are also important. However, I have found bedrooms to be the least important, and on typical suburban rental properties a couple of coats of paint and new carpet makes these look like new. Consider modernising light fittings and curtains in some bedrooms and living areas as these are relatively inexpensive but can make a big difference.

At the end of the day, whether you are trying to get the best rents to secure your cash flow, or the best sale price on your property, presentation is a vital element.

Use your head

Too many investors destroy value in their properties. I heard of one investor who knocked out a wall to turn a three-bedroom home into a two-bedroom home. A real-estate agent said this took the rent down from $330 a week to $260 a week — but at least the bedroom was bigger for their tenants, so they could have a desk inside the bedroom for their computer, when they would've preferred a third bedroom for a dedicated home office!

Other things investors do is simply waste money by buying expensive fittings and appliances that would look nice their own homes but generally don't add any extra rent or value. While there is little point in going cheap and nasty, it brings me to another one of my golden rules:

> **Do not overcapitalise!**

23 | What do I need to know about valuations?

Firstly, what is a valuation? It is the worth of a property. There are several different types of valuations and a raft of acronyms in relation to them. A number of different methods are used to value properties, and they have different purposes.

Registered valuations

A registered valuation is a report prepared by a registered valuer. It gives a figure that a property is expected to sell for on the open market, if sold by a willing seller to a willing buyer. Registered valuation figures can vary wildly, as I found out in 2004 when a client had his three-bedroom home and three-bedroom 65m² minor dwelling valued in New Lynn, Auckland. The valuer put $410,000 and it sold the next day for $462,000 with a back-up offer of $460,000. In an even more dramatic example, I know a couple who were hoping to invest in a commercial property in central Christchurch, and wanted to use the equity in their home to purchase the commercial property, which they had a conditional agreement on at a price of $1.1 million. They had a registered valuer visit their family home in Fendalton, who valued it at $1.2 million. The husband thought this was a bit on the low side, so he got a second opinion. The second registered valuation came back with a figure of $1.45 million — a difference of quarter of a million dollars, or 20% of the lower valuation!

This alerted me to the fact that I may need to get a second opinion and registered valuation report on a four-bedroom home and three-bedroom minor dwelling we have in West Harbour, Auckland. The figure then was

$420,000 from one valuer, yet the other firm I obtained gave $505,000. Both were registered valuers. I became confused about the difference and on talking to the head of a real-estate agency with 30 years of experience operating in the area, looking at RPNZ data on comparable sales, we felt that the market was probably in the range of $475,000 to $485,000 at that time (2004). That is still quite a range, of $55,000 from the low end of one valuation, to $20,000 off the high end of the other. I never sold that property, so I don't know what it was really worth.

At the end of the day, a registered valuation report is a piece of paper, and its value is a perceived one, in that lenders rely on them (assuming the valuer is acceptable to them, or on their panel) and they will lend on them, basing their lending policies and levels on them for refinancing and also as a check on initial purchases.

Banks often require a registered valuation if you are borrowing more than 80% of the property's value. This is because for stand-alone properties, banks generally have a policy to obtain lender's mortgage insurance for borrowings above 80% of the purchase price or registered valuation (whichever is the lesser). Note that if you are borrowing 80% or less, you should not require one, even if you have to negotiate out of one, or otherwise ask for a subsidy towards valuation fees. Banks make a sizeable amount from having your business so you might as well get some initial subsidies for having your business with them.

If you are buying a property deemed a special risk, like a leasehold apartment, leaky building, terraced house or a small freehold apartment, then you may need a registered valuation to support borrowings at much lower levels like 50% or 60% of the property's value. It may even be your lender's policy to require a registered valuation on all such special-risk properties.

Becoming a registered valuer is not easy. It is a professional qualification just like law, dentistry or engineering. A registered valuer has to have an appropriate university degree, at least three years of valuation experience, have submitted 20 valuation reports to the Valuers' Registration Board (VRB), as well as having a good character and being competent, as assessed by the VRB. Registered property valuers also become members of the Property Institute of New Zealand and must undergo a minimum of 20 hours per year of professional development.

Council valuations

Councils and territorial authorities need to value properties to levy rates on them. These valuations are called council valuations (CV), government valuations (GV) or occasionally rateable valuations. These valuations are based on the most recent sale of the property (if it was sold recently between a willing buyer and a willing seller), as well as recent sales in the area.

The councils often outsource compiling their valuation listings to a registered valuation firm in their area, and in particular to deal with challenges to valuation figures. Many people are not happy paying the level of rates, so they write in to councils complaining that their valuation is too high. Sometimes it works, but often the appeal falls on deaf ears! Similarly if you are selling your property, some savvy homeowners and investors try to get your rates as high as possible in the rating assessment just before they sell their property. They write in complaining about how much money they have invested in their property, giving examples of houses in the neighbourhood selling for higher amounts in the area. Councils are usually keen to oblige by increasing your rates within reason.

Use of valuations

One use of registered valuations is as a tool to check your purchase price under a due-diligence period or prior to an auction. As time goes on you become an area expert for your chosen style of house, and a registered valuation becomes of less use. I implore you to never pay more than a registered valuation on a property. Besides, the banks will punish you as they only lend on the lesser of purchase price and registered valuation report. Legendary British property investor Kevin Green states that the 'easiest dollar made is the dollar saved' in property deals.

A registered valuation can be very useful if you want to know what price you would likely get if you were to sell your property, or perhaps in setting a listing price or minimum price that you would accept.

My favourite use of a registered valuation is to do the 'revalue and extract my money out' strategy. I take my borrowings to between 70% and 80% of the property's new value, which allows me to extract my equity (from buying below value and adding value from doing a good renovation). Here's a recent example of mine:

Purchase price	$265,000
Loan (80% of the purchase price)	$212,000
My money put in (20% x $265,000)	$53,000
Renovations (my money)	$22,000
Total price	$287,000
Valuation after renovations	$345,000
Top-up lending (80% loan-to-value ratio = 80% x $345,000)	$276,000
My money invested in the deal after the top-up	$11,000

So for $11,000 of my own money down I had purchased a $345,000 house. The house was cash flow neutral just after the top-up, and will serve me well as regards rental growth and capital growth.

Historical abuse of valuations

After the Blue Chip property financing debacle — which cost many trusting investors a lot of money — a couple of Auckland-based valuers got into trouble for jacking valuations (overvaluing property). This was a big part of the problem with the Blue Chip apartment investments.

When valuing things off the plan, particularly apartments, a registered valuation is vital as that will often determine the selling price. From 2002 to 2007 in Auckland, we had the rather strange situation of having two markets for CBD apartments. One market was for new buildings, with prices set by registered valuations (that Blue Chip played a major part in) and sold by developers. The other market was for non-new dwellings sold on the open market through real estate agencies. As a result of the global financial crisis hitting in 2008, and the consequent downturn of the property cycle, supply of new apartments and demand both dried up. Finance for new apartments and their pricing collapsed, so there is only one market for them now (just like for stand-alone houses).

What can I do to get the best possible valuation on my property?

Rene McLean of Property InDepth Valuers has compiled this list of the top 10 ways to help your property achieve the highest possible valuation. Rene has completed thousands of valuations. Here's what he has to say about how vendors can make the process work as much in their favour as possible:

A good valuation is one that takes an accurate account of both the attributes and detriments of the property at the date of inspection, and logically compares them with recent, relevant sales in that locality. While some investors and developers might disagree, a good valuation is not one which is 20% overvalued!

1. Mowing the lawn helps with a first impression but to look good a lawn needs to be regularly mowed. If you are thinking of selling or maximising value, consider getting the grounds professionally cared for in the four months leading up to sale. If a regularly mowed lawn is slightly long, this should not have much impact on value. Uncared-for lawns and grounds, however, certainly have a negative impact. (If a dog lives at the property you are pushing doggie doo doo uphill if you hope to have a tidy lawn!)

2. Landscaping can help immensely with first impressions and can certainly maximise the value of your property. Simply weeding the gardens is a good start and some well-placed bark and weedmat can enhance the property and value somewhat. Don't necessarily expect tens of thousands to be added on though.

3. Established and well-placed trees, shrubs and plants can consistently improve the value of your property and make it look more 'owner occupied'. Bear in mind though that overbearing trees which are untrimmed and blocking light can have a negative effect.

4. If tenanted, make sure the tenants are advised of the valuer's visit (by phone preferably). You need to ensure that the person you speak to will either be there (or inform whoever will be home that the valuer is coming). Especially if you are intending to do repairs, you could mention you need to get a bank valuation first and please could they have the place looking tidy for the valuer.

While there is no need for the owner (or purchaser) to be at the property, it is always a good opportunity to inspect the property when the valuer goes through. Though the valuer should largely ignore tenants' possessions, as they do not form part of the valuation as such, it certainly helps if the tenants have the place looking reasonable and in reality can it have an impact on the price a purchaser will pay. Remember though that the tenant has the right to live there. So don't fuss if every toy and bit of clothing isn't put away. If the tenant is good enough to give you frequent access, don't moan or comment if it is a bit of a shambles from time to time.

5. There are always bits and pieces to repair at a property and one or two minor things won't impact the value much. However if the valuer walks around and finds deferred maintenance in every room, a little thought bubble will appear over their head with the words 'do-up' inside it.

6. Be helpful to the valuer: let the valuer do his or her job properly. Don't impersonate a real estate agent and point out the double wardrobe (which is probably a single), while staring the valuer in the face as they walk in the room. Don't 'ghost' the valuer; ghosting is following a person as closely as possible without actual physical contact. Don't rush the valuer around, giving them a tour of the house after which the valuer will need to revisit every room to take proper notes. However, do advise the valuer if someone is sleeping in or occupying a room in the house. Do advise the valuer of unseen work such as internal plumbing and electrical work and items that add value but may not be immediately obvious, such as an induction hob or new ceiling insulation.

7. After the valuer has completed their inspection, mention and discuss any recent sales you are aware of that have some relevance to the subject property. Check if they have access to the real estate statistics, and look suitably horrified if they do not, as their sales information is likely to be several months old.

8. Mention any initiatives or projects planned to occur in the local area which could impact on the desirability of the property.

9. Mention relevant circumstances surrounding the current or

historic sale of the property — the bank likes to know this especially if a property has been purchased under market value (for example in a mortgagee sale or during a matrimonial settlement). Likewise, the bank likes to know how much work has been completed on a property (and likes the valuer to mention this).

10. Naturally, redecoration or refurbishment is going to increase the value of your home. Perhaps the best bang for your buck is exterior painting as it helps improve the initial first impression, so do this first if weather allows. Obviously complete as much as possible before you get the valuer in and don't expect the valuer to imagine and include a whole lot of stuff you haven't done unless the report is specifically on an 'as if complete' basis. Be aware of over- and undercapitalising as dollars spent don't always equate to value. Things that are necessary for an investment property may not be so important to an owner-occupied property and vice versa.

24 | Keeping your investment safe

You have worked hard to own an investment property; the last thing you want is to lose your money if your house burns down. You would have no income coming in and be left to fork out for an expensive rebuild. For the vast majority of investors it is important to insure your properties. In addition, most lenders' loan agreements require you to have house insurance. There are also traps to be aware of that might result in claims being scaled back or denied.

What is insurance?

Insurance is a special type of contract between an insurance company and you as its client. It is an arrangement whereby if an event happens, the insurance company will make payment to you or provide you with a similar replacement item. It is in many ways like a bet, in that you are taking a small guaranteed amount of loss, in exchange for a big pay-out if the event you bet on happens. The reason why I call insurance a special type of contract is because it has a feature that other contracts don't have. There is a duty of utmost good faith (or as I was trained at the University of Auckland Law School in Insurance Law 431, *uberrimae fidei*) in insurance contracts. This means that there is both a duty of disclosure as well as a duty not to make any false statements in relation to a claim. Insurance companies can and do refuse to pay claims for breaches of this duty of good faith. For example, if you have not told the insurance company all material information when you applied for or renewed the insurance, they may decline your claim.

An insurance policy is a contract, with terms and conditions including obligations on both the insurance company and yourself. The common law (case law) and statute law provide further obligations on both parties and guide both interpretation and administration of insurance policies.

Elements of an insurance contract

You need to have an insurable interest in the subject matter that you wish to insure at the time of the loss. This means that you have to suffer a financial loss. Basically insurance companies are testing whether you stand to lose if an event that is insured against happens.

Duties

Insurance is all about honesty. This is both in a duty of disclosure and the duty to act in utmost good faith. You must disclose to the insurance company all material facts so that they can assess the risks, price the premium and draft the insurance policy appropriately. You also must not make any misstatements (materially incorrect statements) to the insurance company. If you have breached any of these duties your insurance company could void the policy and not have to pay out on your claim. Even worse, you are likely to be unable to recoup your premium and in future you will need to disclose on all insurance policies that you have had a claim declined and the reason why. You may be rendered uninsurable for at least a period of time.

Don't lie, and if you don't know, say so!

When you want to get insurance it is important to disclose all information, and if you are unsure about its relevance ask the insurance company or your insurance broker. For example, you should always disclose that you have a home office as a rental-property investor. This will generally not give rise to an additional premium.

Likewise don't lie about what you have lost by putting extra things on the claim. If you have a claim you can be asked to prove ownership of items (for example, various items in your claim under a contents policy might include loose tools, computers, DVD players, sunglasses, watches and so on). It is better to say, 'I don't know when I purchased the item,' or, 'I think I purchased it roughly . . .', or, 'I bought this for approximately . . .' That way you are not lying and breaching your duty of utmost good faith. It is OK not to know something, but it is never OK to lie.

Importance of insurance — the fire in my house

In mid-2009, one of my rental properties in Te Atatu South, West Auckland, caught fire. The blaze was started by my tenant lighting a candle; unfortunately he didn't put it out before he went to sleep. The problem was the wax dripped onto the book the candle was sitting on and as the candle burned down the book caught fire, and so did the bedside table. The flames then quietly spread onto the curtains, the windowsills and Gib. Fortunately the noise woke up the tenant, who then shouted and woke up the tenants in the other two bedrooms.

The fire continued to spread throughout the house. The tenants escaped in time, taking what little they could as the fire had intensified. Unfortunately the tenant who inadvertently and accidentally started the fire had to go into hospital. This was because he had suffered minor burns (as he tried to put the fire out in his room) and also smoke inhalation, as he went back into the house to get his uninsured CD and DVD collections. That's another good reason to have insurance on all your possessions — so you never have to go into a burning house to rescue them!

The fire service was contacted by both a tenant and the neighbours, which I really appreciated. (Interestingly TV3 arrived at the site just before the firemen arrived, but the funding and resourcing of our fire service is another subject.)

This was a property that was under management, so it was a surprise to get a call from my property manager, but I was glad to hear nobody had any serious injuries. The minor burns and smoke inhalation were swiftly treated and the tenant discharged from hospital the following day. The fire was also covered in the *New Zealand Herald* the following day. That day was a nightmare: making an insurance claim, and liaising with the fire-service investigators, the claims investigator, the property manager and making numerous calls to the insurance company.

The property was ruined by the fire. The temperature reached more than 1000°C, causing the roof to buckle. The ceiling trusses and framing were almost entirely unusable due to charring. In addition, all the flooring was ruined — not just from the fire but also from the water from the firemen's hoses as they extinguished the flames. The electrical cabling, light fittings, plumbing and plumbing fittings were all destroyed, as were the kitchen, the floor coverings and curtains.

State Insurance accepted the claim after investigating it and finding the fault to be attributable to the tenant. He didn't have contents insurance, and unfortunately for him they decided to investigate him for lack of reasonable care in starting the fire. Then State got three quotes for rebuilding the property. (I had no say and State didn't select the cheapest — it chose the middle one at $137,000 plus GST to rebuild.)

This was a rather sorry incident, but ultimately no lives were lost and no one had any lasting injuries as a result of the fire. I got a brand-new house with a new code of compliance certificate and my insurer paid me the same weekly rental that the tenants were paying in the meantime. The builders were exceptionally slow. Having had minor dwellings built for me in four months, it seemed very slow when this build took over seven months, a fair amount of that time waiting for council. That might have caused me a major problem, but my policy covered loss of income. As a result I had found the best tenant I have ever had: State Insurance. These tenants were amazing. They returned the property to me in a condition far superior to what it had been. They cleaned the property and did absolutely no damage. They were twice a bit slow in paying rent though, so I had to write a few letters flashing my legal qualifications, which got action within a couple of working days!

The only thing was that I didn't have landlord's insurance, so as a result I had to pay $940 for heavy-duty tracks and curtains from The Warehouse and I wasted half a day putting them up. I also had to pay about $2,400 for floor coverings (carpets) and $90 for bathroom hardware. Hopefully the previous tenants didn't suffer too much grief from State. I am aware of cases where the insurance company has sued the tenant for their total costs in the landlord's name (they have this right of subrogation in virtually all insurance policies).

The moral of the story is to have contents insurance if you are a tenant (or otherwise go to the rather impractical step of getting your landlord to note your interest as tenant on the policy), and to insure your assets if you are a property investor. Total replacement policies are best as they cover a replacement building to the square-metre size of your building, and importantly they are built to the current building code. It is only when you have an enormous portfolio and a very conservative level of gearing that you can contemplate self-insuring your properties.

Claiming after an earthquake

The Canterbury earthquakes really underlined the importance of insurance for landlords. For residential-property owners who have suffered a loss from an earthquake, the first port of call is the Earthquake Commission (EQC). The EQC covers any residential dwelling, contents or land that has suffered damage caused by an earthquake. Importantly you must, however, have had a current valid house or contents insurance policy (which some insurers refer to as a fire and general policy).

Note that the EQC will meet claims for damage to dwellings up to $100,000. For your own home, and your tenants' contents policies, the EQC covers certain contents of up to $20,000 and land on which the house is situated. Not all of a section may be covered. There is also an excess of 1% of the amount claimed, with a minimum excess amount of $200. There is also an excess of 10% of the amount of a claim on land with a minimum excess of $400 and a maximum excess of $5,000.

Many buildings incurred massive damage requiring repiling, partial recladding, fixing twisted frames, door jambs, warped window frames, broken glass, replacing cracked tiles, plasterboard, plaster and paint work. As a result homeowners may have several claims over and above $100,000. These must be topped up by your insurer. Hopefully the homeowner will have a replacement sum insured policy, as opposed to a specified sum (agreed amount) insured. These policies may not apply to land.

Commercial investors

The EQC doesn't cover commercial, rural or non-residential property. It only covers residential property. Investors therefore need to have insurance from their own insurer — perhaps with an extension to include a business interruption policy. Interestingly, business interruption insurance may provide cover for various financial risks like loss of profits, or expenses incurred due to the interruption to business operations such as wages and rent, or relocation costs. You need to consider whether you take an all-risks insurance cover policy where all risks are covered unless the policy specifically includes them, or the more typical specified insurance policy which only covers specified events like damage from theft, fire and weather damage. With these policies you must specify cover for damage caused by an earthquake. The terms of the insurance policies are absolutely vital and this earthquake has caused some significant arguments, some of which are heading for litigation.

Advice for insured victims of an earthquake

Contact your insurance company immediately and lodge a claim for all damage caused by the earthquake. Don't undertake any demolition or repairs unless your insurance company has approved such action. If, for instance, you have a chimney perilously close to falling through your roof and ceiling, you should take photos of the damage to document for the insurance company and also to protect yourself in the event of a subsequent dispute.

Why claims are declined

I have friends and family members in the insurance industry and with more than 100,000 claims filed every year they have seen a number of claims declined. They tell me that main reasons are:

- Not disclosing all material information when the policy was taken out or renewed. For example, if you have an income protection policy you might make a claim to say you can't work due to your bad back, and you have a doctor's certificate. Yet the insurance company may hire a private investigator and if you are photographed lifting a jukebox and keg of beer into your house for a party, you're busted. The insurance company will decline your claim and cease payments to you, requesting the compensation they have paid to you to be reimbursed. If you then didn't disclose that your insurance claim had been declined to the insurer of your rental property, this would be a material fact.

- Cover is excluded in the policy.

- A claim is made outside the time limits in the policy.

- The premium wasn't paid in time so the policy lapsed.

My insurance tips

- Having insurance cover is important, until your portfolio is large enough with very low levels of gearing for you to put money aside as self-insurance.

- For residential rental properties I recommend total replacement cover policies based on the square metre size of your buildings.

- Remember to renew your policy on time. Some insurers get out of providing cover by citing policy premiums not being paid in time; you get sent a letter from your bank which specifies (in the fine print of your loan agreement) that they require total replacement cover policies with their interests noted as first mortgagee.

O When buying a property, a common reason for late settlements is not having a certificate of currency or cover note in your solicitor's or conveyancer's possession. This letter is evidence that you have a current insurance policy with the lender's interest as first mortgagee noted on the policy. Without this your lender will not advance the funds to complete settlement.

O Get at least three quotes from insurance companies on your properties and check them regularly. Include your car, home and contents in the quote as you may be able to get a bulk or package discount.

O On multiple-income properties, don't forget to call Tower as they have an excellent policy that saves me thousands of dollars a year.

O Have an insurance management system. I use a spreadsheet to record the property address, name of my insurance company, premium charged, size of buildings and any notes on the property.

O Consider paying your premium annually to get a discount from your insurance company (or six-monthly or quarterly if you don't have sufficient funds to pay in advance).

25 | Managing your property

Cash flow is one of the three fundamental pillars in an investor's portfolio. Without steady cash flow you would be unable to obtain or service your property loans. Your portfolio's value would come to a standstill — or worse, crash. Over time you want your cash flow to be large enough that you can give the keys of your properties to an excellent property manager and sit back and relax on tens (if not hundreds!) of thousands of dollars of passive cash flow.

In property investment your cash flow comes from your tenants. It's therefore important to do due diligence on your tenants, as you are entrusting them with a licence to occupy your valuable asset. You want to be confident that your tenants will supply you with a steady stream of income. It's important to know market rents in order to ensure the rent isn't overpriced (which would mean the property would be likely to be vacant), or underpriced (which would mean you might be jeopardising your retirement plans and your family's financial future).

In a perfect world, your tenant will pay their rent on time every time, not argue when you increase the rent every six months, stay for many years, and look after your home and grounds immaculately. Such a dream tenant is pure fantasy, unfortunately. If you waited for this mythical tenant to arrive, it could be a very long wait, and you'll have a long vacancy period with mounting expenses and no income.

As president of the Auckland Property Investors' Association, I am fortunate to have a strong relationship with the Department of Building and Housing (DBH). I acknowledge the DBH for providing me with technical assistance and a review of this chapter, which is designed as an instruction manual with some stories added in for good measure. This chapter covers your obligations as a landlord, your tenants' obligations, how to procure good tenants, forms you need to fill in, managing tenants and what to do when tenants leave. There is a summary of the benefits of a good property manager, plus the changes to the Residential Tenancies Act 1986 that came into effect on 1 October 2010.

Residential Tenancies Act 1986

The legislation that governs the legal rights and obligations when a landlord and tenant agree to a tenancy is the Residential Tenancies Act 1986 (RTA). The Tenancy tab on the DBH website (www.dbh.govt.nz) is a great resource. It has a full copy of the RTA as well as an exhaustive list of your obligations as a landlord and your tenants' obligations. The RTA was amended in 2010 by the Residential Tenancies Amendment Act 2010 to clarify and amend these rights and obligations, and also bring boarding houses under the RTA.

What to do at the start of a tenancy

Sign a tenancy agreement

The RTA requires all new tenancies to have a written tenancy agreement. Both you and your tenant must sign it and you need to give the tenant a copy before the tenancy begins. Since tenancy agreements are easy to complete, I normally prepare two originals that I have downloaded from the DBH website (http://www.dbh.govt.nz/UserFiles/File/Publications/Tenancy/pdf/Residential-Tenancy-Agreement.pdf) with exactly the same wording and terms and give one of them to the tenant. The tenancy agreement is also available from bookshops.

What should be in the tenancy agreement?

A basic tenancy agreement must include the following items:

○ names and contact addresses for you and your tenant

○ property address

○ date the tenancy agreement is signed

○ date the tenancy is to begin

○ date the tenancy will end (if it is a fixed-term tenancy)

○ addresses for service for both you and your tenant

○ whether the tenant is under the age of 18

○ amount of the bond

○ rent amount and frequency of payments (usually weekly)

○ place or bank account number where the rent is to be paid

○ fees (real estate or solicitor's) which are to be paid (if applicable)

○ statement (if applicable) that the tenant is to pay for metered water

○ list of any chattels (like furniture, curtains and other fittings) provided by the landlord.

If something that is inconsistent with the law has been written down in a tenancy agreement, it has no effect. For example, I once saw an investor put a 'special clause' in their tenancy agreement that said the tenant had to leave on two weeks' notice. This is unenforceable because the law says the tenant is entitled to 90 days' notice for any reason, or 42 days' notice if the property has been sold or if you or an immediate family member need to move into it. As another example, some landlords and property managers specify in their tenancy agreements that a tenant must have the carpets commercially cleaned when the property is vacated. However, the Tenancy Tribunal has ruled in past cases that this is beyond what the Act intends by 'reasonably clean', so even if you write this into your agreement, it isn't enforceable.

You can include other clauses in the agreement that are specific to the particular tenancy, such as the maximum number of people living in your house, whether the tenants can sublet and where cars can be parked.

While it's not compulsory, I would strongly advise you to complete and sign a property inspection report, which should be kept with each copy of the tenancy agreement.

Having a written tenancy agreement, with a properly filled-in property inspection form, can be very useful evidence if problems or disputes arise later, or if a Tenancy Tribunal decision is required. Twice I have seen my tenants say, 'We didn't create this hole in the plasterboard walls, a previous tenant must have done it.' Fortunately, I always document the conditions of the property before the tenant moves in. So if the hole in the wall is not on the property inspection form, which is signed and dated by me and the tenant, then the adjudicator will rule in my favour.

I recommend everybody take digital camera photographs of their properties. Digital cameras are tax-deductible items and a vital business tool when photographing conditions of properties. Plus, if you ask your tenant's permission, you can photograph them, their car, car registration and other identification. Photos are also helpful for due diligence when you're looking at properties to buy. These cameras soon pay for themselves. Smartphones are also excellent tools for property investors, because you can use them to take pictures and videos of your properties, as well as receive your email and do your internet banking.

What is an 'address for service'?

You and your tenant need to write down an address for service on the tenancy agreement. This is a physical street address where official notices will be accepted by, or on behalf of, the person concerned. It is especially important where an application to the Tenancy Tribunal has been made. A post office box number is not adequate as an 'address for service', because legal documents cannot be served on a post office box.

Many investors don't want their tenants to know where they live and therefore give their work address, which is absolutely fine. There is another field on the second page of the standard form residential tenancy agreement, called an 'additional address for service', which may be an email, postal address or fax number. If you change address then it is crucial that you tell your tenant, and the Department of Building and Housing's Bond Centre if you have lodged a bond.

The tenancy address may not be a valid address for service for the tenant after the end of the tenancy (as they have left), so I prefer to get the address of the tenant's next of kin or best friend as an address for service.

Types of tenancies

There are two main kinds of tenancies: periodic tenancies and fixed-term tenancies. There are also service tenancies, which are very rare.

Periodic tenancy

Any tenancy that is not for a specific term is called a periodic tenancy. This is the most common form of tenancy. It continues until the landlord or tenant gives the correct notice to end it.

Fixed-term tenancy

A fixed-term tenancy finishes on a specific date set down in the written tenancy agreement. There is no provision for you to give notice to the tenant to quit, and your tenant may only leave if there is severe hardship (for example, their child has an illness and they have to break the tenancy to live near a city hospital).

Service tenancy

A service tenancy occurs when an employee rents a property from their employer as part of their contract or terms of employment. There are special rules that apply to this type of tenancy, but they are covered by the RTA.

Fixed-term tenancies

Since 1 October 2010 there are some important new rules about what happens at the end of a fixed-term tenancy. On the date the fixed-term tenancy ends, the tenancy continues as a periodic tenancy, with the same terms contained in the expired tenancy, unless:

○ the tenant and landlord enter into a new tenancy agreement, or

○ extend the existing tenancy agreement, or

○ either party gives the other party written notice of their intention to end the tenancy.

The period in which a landlord or tenant can give notice to end the tenancy is between 21 and 90 days before the date the tenancy expires. If there is a right in the tenancy agreement to renew or extend the tenancy and the tenant wishes to remain, the tenant must write to you at least 21 days before the tenancy expires, notifying his or her intention to renew or extend the tenancy.

Exceptions to the fixed-term rules

Fixed-term tenancies are fully covered by the RTA. There are two small exceptions:

○ Market rent and notice to quit provisions do not apply to short fixed-term tenancies of less than 120 days, unless the tenancy is renewed. All other provisions of the RTA apply.

○ Fixed-term tenancies of greater than five years may not apply, if the tenancy agreement specifically states that the RTA doesn't apply. You cannot contract out of the RTA for residential tenancies of less than or equal to five years in duration.

Finding tenants

Advertising

Since cash flow is a fundamental pillar of property investment, you must ensure that you advertise and attract the right tenants in the quickest possible time, at the right price. Obviously, prior to advertising, the property needs to be very clean and looking attractive for tenants to view.

You need to tell people that you have a property available for rent, and you can use a variety of media to do this. Hitting the target market is not difficult, but in some areas and at particular times it's not easy either. Consider what prospective tenants are looking for, and highlight these points in your advertising.

There are two main ways to source tenants: via a property manager, or by doing it yourself.

Property manager

Consider if you want to advertise your property yourself or get a property manager to list it for you. Many property investors struggle to determine what the market rent is for their property. Often they haven't realised that the market has moved significantly and they are under-renting their property and subsidising a stranger's living costs. That is a nice thing to do for the tenant, but not the smartest way to achieve retirement goals. My advice is to use a good property manager in the area if you are not actively keeping an eye on the rental market, because their experience comes in handy and their letting fees (often one week's rental) are charged to your tenants.

The advantages of using a property manager are:

○ A good manager knows the rents for the area your property is in, and after inspecting the property to establish its condition, can put an accurate value on the appropriate rent.

○ He or she can do the advertising for you.

○ The property manager does the all-important tenant screening — it's great to have this job done by a professional.

○ Property managers also have weekly or twice-weekly updated lists of properties available for tenancy. Many prospective tenants pick up these lists to do 'drive-bys'.

The disadvantages of using a manager are:

○ It can cost the tenant one week's rent as a letting fee (this could potentially be charged to landlords in the future), and the agents often take your first week of rent as commission. Ask the property manager about the cost to you as the landlord.

○ Less hard-working property managers may under-rent the property. This happens because it is easier to find a tenant for a property with a lower rent, and they still receive the letting fee for a job done. If you are not using the agent to manage your property, they are often less motivated because they miss out on the weekly commission of approximately 8% of the rent.

Doing it yourself

It's not a problem if you want to organise the advertising yourself. However, if you do a half-pie job, this could mean a couple of weeks of no rent and possibly failure to maximise the rental yield or get the best tenants. I recommend using a variety of forms of advertising for maximum exposure.

Websites   A lot has changed since I started investing — back then I basically used the internet to check my email, bank balance and the cricket scores. While I still do these things online, I now also shop online and am a regular user of TradeMe. This site has grown from nothing much to a massive auction and sales portal; you must have your property listed on www.trademe.co.nz to get maximum exposure. This costs $99 including GST per rental you list, so it's not cheap. Watch for competitors to rise in the years ahead as TradeMe's fees climb. Sites like www.sella.co.nz, the Gumtree and NZ Flatmates may become increasingly useful and cost-effective options. TradeMe is your best bet by far right now though.

Word of mouth and signage   Word of mouth may include asking good outgoing tenants if they know anyone interested, as well as talking with your neighbours, real estate agents, tradesmen and friends. In busy street areas, putting up a sign is a fantastic idea. This can be corflute or painted onto wood or metal, stating 'For rent, call (number)'. You can also state the main features of your property.

Print media   Often the local weekly or twice-weekly community newspapers are a good source of advertising. They generally have more readers than the pricier and less targeted major national newspapers. I recommend you make use of the local rag, giving the suburb name first (to make it easy for tenants to find), then point out the main features and benefits of your property. Remember to state the desired rent and give your phone number. For example:

> **KELSTON**, spacious 3-bedroom home, recently refurbished, large deck, carport, lots of OSP. $365 per week. Potential long-term tenants, call Debbie on 123-4567 or 021-123-4567 today.

Viewings

Once your advertising is up and running, it will only be a matter of time before tenants want to look at your place. In fact if you slightly under-price the rent in a sought-after location you could be inundated with phone calls. In March 2011, I did a live interview on TV One's *Close Up* when they profiled a rental property in Mt Eden that attracted over 100 people to an open home! If you are getting too many phone calls from prospective tenants, arrange general viewings at certain times, rather than meeting every single tenant at a time that is convenient for them. Conversely, if the phone is not ringing, you will have to be more flexible.

At viewings, your aim is to make a 'sale' of your property at the rental level you want. You also want to get your tenants' commitment to the property so ask them to fill out a short application form.

Due diligence on prospective tenants

It is important to carry out due diligence on your prospective tenants. Getting them to complete an application form is crucial as it provides you with all their details and their permission for you to run credit checks. You need to decide whether or not you want these people living in your valuable asset, and you also need to check the likelihood of them getting into arrears. If you use a property manager or letting agent this should be done as a matter of course. Otherwise you can do this yourself by asking for written and/or verbal references from previous landlords and employers.

For credit checks, I recommend registering with Tenancy Information New Zealand (TINZ) at the following address: www.tinz.net.nz. TINZ is part of the CIA Debt Recovery Group Limited (CIA), New Zealand's leading residential tenancy debt collection agency, with licensed investigators (former police) and debt collectors on their staff. TINZ discounts are available for Property Investor Association members.

When your due diligence is complete and you have decided to accept a particular tenant, you need to sign them up to a tenancy agreement, collect the bond from them and remove your advertising.

Lodge any bond money with Department of Building and Housing

While you don't have to charge a bond, you would be stupid not to. You can legally charge up to four weeks' rent as a bond. I believe that you should always seek four weeks' rent in bond money from your tenants; if they genuinely don't have it consider three weeks' rent instead. Your tenants will pay this bond money to you, and you have to lodge this within 23 working days with the DBH bond centre using their form (http://dbh.govt.nz/ UserFiles/File/Publications/Tenancy/pdf/bond-lodgement-form.pdf).

Charging a bond gives you some protection if there is rent owing at the end of the tenancy, or if you have to pay to repair or clean the property, dispose of abandoned property or deal with any other breach by your tenant. If you have a claim greater than the bond amount, a tenant may be ordered to pay the extra as well.

As you put the rent up over time you can and should increase your bond amount too. For example, if your rent is $350 per week and you increase it to $380 per week, the $1,400 bond (four weeks' rent) should increase by $120. This top-up would also be forwarded to the DBH bond centre. Free advice and information on bonds is available by calling freephone 0800 TENANCY (0800 83 62 62).

Note that you can't charge key money (a payment for a key to your house or deposit on an item supplied with the tenancy), except with the consent of the Tenancy Tribunal, and this would have to be in an extremely special circumstance.

Rent payments

You may ask for up two weeks' rent paid in advance. However rent is not actually 'in arrears' until the end of the period for which the rent has been paid.

For example: A tenancy agreement is signed to begin on 1 February. The tenant pays two weeks' rent as bond and two weeks' rent in advance. The two weeks' rent in advance pays for the period 1 to 14 February. The tenant does not have to pay rent again until 15 February, when a further two weeks' rent in advance is paid for the period 15 to 28 February.

Ways to pay rent

It is up to you and your tenant to decide how rent will be paid and to write this into the tenancy agreement. It's best to have rent automatically credited into your account. Rent may also be paid by cash or cheque, or by bank transfer. You must issue your tenant a receipt immediately if they pay you by cash or open cheque. Receipts aren't needed for bank transfers or negotiable personal cheques as your tenant's bank statements would show the rent was paid.

Keep all records that allow the tenant and, if required, a mediator or the Tenancy Tribunal, to see the rent due and the rent paid for any period. All receipts and bank statements showing rent payments from tenants should be kept in a safe place throughout the lesser of the duration of their tenancy or for seven years (you need to keep tax records for at least this long anyway).

Managing tenants

Keeping good tenants

Finding and keeping good tenants is vital for cash flow. Without cash flow you cannot service your mortgages and you could resent your forced savings scheme. A good tenant is not someone who looks after the gardens. Most tenants say they will, yet in practice most will not. This is not a big deal. The tenants that I like best are those who pay their rent on time and who look after your valuable asset, their home.

When you regularly inspect your property and are pleased with what you see, praise good tenants and thank them for keeping your property clean and tidy. Consider rewards like a gift for Christmas, such as a bottle of wine, or even just a card to thank them for being excellent tenants.

Benefits of a property manager

There are many situations where you would want to use a property manager (including when you are away on holiday), if you struggle to deal with your tenants, or if you lack the time to manage the property properly.

Good property managers will have:

○ rental collection systems, so they can check the rent daily and follow up rent arrears immediately

○ a network of tradespeople, including plumbers, electricians, tilers, carpetlayers and painters, to deal with any urgent repairs, and also to conduct regular maintenance to protect your cash flow and asset value

○ advertising skills, including a monthly unlimited subscription to TradeMe (saving you the $99 listing fee), and the ability to take good photos and write an excellent description of your property, highlighting its features.

Good property managers will also save you a lot of time. This is critical as many investors will want to focus on their primary career or business, and can in effect outsource property management for as little as 6% to 10% of the weekly rent. It is critical to factor in your time input with regards to property investment. If you are investing in lower socio-economic areas, it is more likely you will have tenants struggling to pay their rent on time all the time, and you are more likely to have higher wear and tear on your properties.

Watch for bad property managers

You must ensure that you do actually have a *good* property manager; unfortunately, many are not good, and there are no regulations or minimum standards imposed. All too often I see the office receptionist at a franchised real estate agency become the agency's property manager, and while this might occasionally work well, that's the exception.

Some managers are very slow to chase rent arrears, and like to manage from the office as much as possible by issuing letters rather than ringing or personally visiting tenants. I have had three appalling property managers in the past. However, unlike most investors, I took the keys off them as soon as their incompetence became apparent. Don't be so keen to avoid confrontation that you keep giving the keys of your very valuable asset — and your financial future — to somebody you don't trust to look after it.

Charge market rent

I do think you need to be a little wary of tenants who stay too long — over three or so years. Ask yourself, why are they really staying on for so long?

It may be perfectly innocent and you are charging fair rent and they love your house. However you need to consider whether you are subsidising them too much by under-renting your place. Get a market rental appraisal done by a property manager in the area and compare that to the property rental statistics grouped by suburb and to the rent you are charging. You can also look at the market rental information available on the DBH website and at the back of the *NZ Property Investor* magazine, and at what similar properties in the area are renting for on TradeMe and other websites. Then adjust the rent correspondingly.

You should always charge market rent to get the maximum value for your investment, and to ensure fairness. Market rent is described (in the Residential Tenancies Act) as what 'a willing landlord might reasonably expect to receive, and a willing tenant might reasonably expect to pay for the tenancy', in comparison with rent levels for similar premises in similar areas.

A tenant may feel that a landlord is asking for too much rent. In this case a Tenancy Tribunal application can be made for a market rent assessment. The Tribunal may make an order to set the rent, if the rent the landlord wants substantially exceeds the market rent. The landlord would not be able to increase the rent again for a period decided by the Tribunal (usually six months). In practice a tenant is highly unlikely to take you to the Tenancy Tribunal for a market rent assessment — they generally just leave. So don't be too greedy, but do charge market rent.

I know of several investors that under-rent their properties. One inferior property manager in Ellerslie, Auckland, had a two-bedroom flat rented at $280 per week, when the neighbouring flat in essentially the same condition was let at $400 per week by a different property manager. They are lucky the tenants didn't talk to one another! This $120 difference represents $6,000 a year. You aren't getting into property investment solely to be charitable, so why sacrifice you and your family's goals by significantly under-renting your properties?

Increasing the rent

You must give 60 days' written notice of any rent increase and cannot increase the rent more than once every six months. Rent can only be increased in a fixed-term tenancy if it is written into the tenancy agreement.

Inspections

Property inspections are an absolutely vital part of your business. You must schedule regular property visits, at least every four months. Some insurance policies require inspections every three months. Since you have many thousands of dollars invested in these assets, you must protect your investments by inspecting them regularly. This also shows your tenants that you care; they will be more likely to keep your property tidy if they know that it will be inspected regularly, and they will also get into a mindset where they quickly fix any damage they cause. The inspection also provides an opportunity to ascertain various maintenance needs for your property.

To undertake a property inspection, you must give your tenants at least 24 hours' notice under the RTA. You will be inspecting the property for any damage caused by the tenants. If you see any damage, point out that they need to remedy it.

Use the property inspection report section of your tenancy agreement to monitor the property and check for any damage done. Notify your tenants of the need to rectify any breach of the agreement (for example, having extra permanent residents in the house, smoking inside, or the presence of pets). You must follow this up promptly to ensure it is done. If the breaches haven't been fixed, then you need to prepare and post the tenants a notice to rectify the breaches of the agreement. Save a template '14 consecutive days' notice letter on your computer (or a system like Google Documents or Dropbox) as you will no doubt have a use for it in the future. If this letter is unsuccessful, use the disputes resolutions measures provided later in this chapter.

Rent arrears

Note that nearly 75% of all claims to the Tenancy Tribunal are for rent arrears. If your tenant gets behind in their rent, give them a phone call immediately to ask why they have got into arrears. Tell the tenant that you will be serving a 14-consecutive-day letter to require them to remedy the situation, no matter what the excuse they provide, as it is your 'policy' to do so. Very few tenants argue against something as official as policy.

14-consecutive-day letter

The 14-consecutive-day letter is currently prescribed under section 56 of the RTA. You will need to serve this on the tenants as soon as possible after the rent arrears have been noted, to best protect your position and to minimise rent arrears.

You can either use the Department of Building and Housing's template (http://www.dbh.govt.nz/UserFiles/File/Publications/Tenancy/pdf/

14-days-notice-all-other-breaches.pdf) or use your own similar letter. Remember to always post these letters to your tenants by registered mail or hand deliver it to them (or their letterbox). Here's an example of an assertive 14-consecutive-day letter:

{date}

{Tenant's name}
{Address of tenanted property}

Dear {tenant}

RE: 14-CONSECUTIVE-DAY NOTICE TO REMEDY — PURSUANT TO SECTION 56 OF THE RESIDENTIAL TENANCIES ACT 1986

I, David Whitburn, being the duly authorised agent of the ABC Trust ('Landlord'), give you 14 consecutive days' notice to remedy the breach of the tenancy agreement as set out below:

ALL RENT ARREARS TO BE PAID IN FULL

TAKE NOTICE THAT IF YOU FAIL OR REFUSE to remedy the breach by payment of all rent arrears by 5 pm on 21 April 2011, the Landlord will be entitled to apply to the Tenancy Tribunal for orders to:

1. Remedy the breach,
2. Request compensation, and,
3. Terminate the tenancy.

We have notified you that you are in breach of the tenancy agreement we have. On 7 April 2011 our records indicate that you will owe us $680.00.

Any rent arrears are totally unacceptable and we are pursuing you for payment of these in full. You have 14 days to make full payment of all arrears (keeping in mind your weekly rent payments are still due), before you will meet with me in the Tenancy Tribunal. We will be seeking initial binding orders from the Tenancy Mediator pursuant to the Residential Tenancies Act 1986 as indicated above.

Our trust has a zero-tolerance policy on rent arrears. We must warn you that if you do not rectify these arrears, there are likely to be a range of consequences for you. These may include, but are not limited to, eviction, forced repayment by mediated order, compensation, debts being lodged against your personal names and damage to your individual credit ratings.

We would also appreciate a good explanation for these arrears, and look forward to hearing from you about these as soon as possible, and to receive payment in full.

In the event that you have paid these arrears before this letter reaches you, please accept our apologies. We trust you understand that issuing these letters is our standard practice as late or non-payment of rent is totally unacceptable and shall not be tolerated again.

Can you please call me as soon as possible on 01 123 4567 or email me at david@abctrust.co.nz, to discuss your arrears, this letter and what will happen to you from here. We look forward to hearing from you as soon as possible.

Yours faithfully
ABC TRUST

David Whitburn
Trustee and duly authorised agent of the landlord

If the 14-consecutive-day letter is not effective at resolving a breach of the tenancy agreement (whether rent arrears or any other breach), then it is time to sort matters out more formally, using the disputes resolutions procedures prescribed in the Residential Tenancies Act 1986, including using the DBH for assistance.

Disputes, mediation and the Tenancy Tribunal

Negotiation with your tenants

While the vast majority of my tenancies run smoothly, some, of course, do not. First, talk to your tenants about the issues. Quite often there has been a simple misunderstanding that can be rectified with a phone call, or soon after a 14-consecutive-day letter has been filed. For example, I had a tenant withhold rent because I was too slow at fixing a leaky tap, which increased their water bill. Another reason for arrears can be that their employer has faced some tough financial times and is late in paying them, and your tenant has absolutely no savings.

If the friendly approach doesn't work, use the DBH's helpful staff by calling 0800 TENANCY (0800 83 62 62) for advice. If the tenant has not rectified the breach of the agreement, you need to apply to the Tenancy Tribunal to get the matter sorted out. You have a number of methods available, all with the standard application fee of $20.44.

Mediation

Many disputes between tenants and landlords can be resolved at the mediation stage. Mediation is arranged by the DBH to help landlords and tenants talk about and solve their problems. A mediator facilitates you discussing the problem, identifying the issues, and coming up with a workable solution together. Mediators know a lot about tenancy issues, but they do not actually decide anything for you. The advantages of this are:

○ It's less formal than going to court. Mediated agreements are made with both the tenant and the landlord being fully informed of all their rights and responsibilities, and there is a clear understanding of what the agreement means. In contrast, Tribunal hearings are conducted by the Ministry of Justice and are more formal than mediation.

○ Speed. A mediation appointment can be set up more quickly than a Tribunal hearing. Straightforward disputes can often be resolved by SWIFT telephone mediation. There have been examples of disputes being resolved within a couple of hours of being lodged with SWIFT telephone mediation.

○ More control in many cases, as you don't get told what to do, but come up with an agreement yourselves.

○ Confidentiality. No one else has to know what is said in mediation, whereas Tenancy Tribunal decisions are publicly available (for a period of time).

○ The result is still legally binding and enforceable through the court system if necessary.

Forms and information on how to pay the $20.44 fee are available from 0800 TENANCY (0800 83 62 62), on the DBH website and from your local Citizens Advice Bureau.

Once an application is lodged, DBH will set up a mediation time with both the tenant and the landlord. This may be a phone conversation or a face-to-face meeting.

Three different streams of mediation

DBH provides a comprehensive mediation service with three streams. These are:

○ SWIFT telephone mediation

○ scheduled telephone mediation

○ face-to-face mediation.

I have often resolved disputes with my tenants before the scheduled mediation appointment, in which case you or your tenant can contact DBH to discuss the details of the settlement and have it formalised as a 'mediator's order'.

Preparation

Have with you anything that might have something to do with the dispute, for example, photos, rent records or receipts for work done. You don't need to convince the mediator of anything, but you do have to convince the other party that what you want is fair and reasonable. (Before the mediation, you need to think about the possible solutions to the problem and what you want out of the mediation. Also be prepared to consider your tenant's suggestions.)

What happens at the mediation?

The mediator will help you talk with and listen to each other, answer any questions about tenancy law, and practice and help you reach a fair agreement. They will:

○ ask each of you to explain your view of the situation and then help you both to work out ways to end the dispute

○ provide information and advice if this is appropriate, for example, about parts of the law if that will help your discussion

○ ensure that everyone has their say and that everyone's behaviour is reasonable.

Despite my best efforts in the past, a mediator will not choose the answer for you or your tenants, even if you ask them. They are there to facilitate fair agreements.

What happens if we reach an agreement?

You should ask the mediator to record the agreement, which is then termed a 'mediated order'. It is legally binding and if you ask for a consequential clause, it will usually say what will happen if the agreement is broken.

If a mediator's order is breached, it is a simple matter to enforce it as a Tribunal Order, through the Collections Unit at the District Court. If either person does not live up to what was agreed, then the mediated order can be enforced as if it were an order of the Tribunal.

Tenancy Tribunal

If mediation has failed, then it is time to go to the Tenancy Tribunal (at the nearest District Court building) for a hearing. An adjudicator will make a final decision for you both. It is a part of the justice system, and if you or your tenant wishes to make an application to the Tenancy Tribunal a fee of $20.44 (including GST) will be charged. It is a public hearing and either party can take support people with them. You and your tenants normally represent yourselves. Lawyers are only allowed in exceptional circumstances.

Like any adjudication both parties are heard, any relevant witnesses are heard, and all evidence is tabled. Then the tenancy adjudicator makes a decision (a binding court order) pursuant to the RTA. Tenancy Tribunal decisions are published on www.tenancytribunal.govt.nz. Typically you will be seeking an order such as a possession order, where you have already given your tenant a 14-consecutive-day letter to get their rent paid up to date. By the time the case is heard the rent is 21 days or more in arrears, which is a serious breach so you want the tenancy terminated and to regain possession of your property. Other orders include monetary orders (such as paying rent arrears, damage, or to reimburse a tenant for urgent repairs), and works orders (such as an order compelling you to fix the slippery rotten front deck).

Enforcement

You need to ask for a sealed mediated order or a Tenancy Tribunal order, as then you can ask the District Court to enforce the order. There is a fee is payable for this service. Look at the enforcement sheet available at www.tenancy.govt.nz or call 0800 83 62 62 (0800 TENANCY).

When tenants leave

Tenants giving you notice

When tenants leave there are a few vital matters to attend to as soon as the tenants give notice that they wish to terminate the tenancy. Ensure these things are done properly so there are no outstanding issues.

Receiving notice from the tenants

Often tenants just ring and tell you that they will be leaving, and are out in a week or so. This is completely unacceptable — if you are given verbal notice, then you must tell them to put it into writing. You could say something along the lines of 'Under the Residential Tenancies Act 1986 and our tenancy agreement I can't legally receive notice over the telephone. To protect both of us you will need to give at least 21 days' notice in writing.'

Check the dates on their letter to ensure that you have been given at least 21 days' written notice from the date of the letter. While it should be common sense for all tenants to give notice in writing, I have had one tenant who tried to tell me 'It's only seven days' notice, bro, so don't stress and let's just catch up next week to hand over the keys and stuff.' Nice try!

How do you sell a property with tenants in it?

You need to tell your tenants that a property is on the market. I have found courtesy, biscuits, drinks and twenty dollars all to have worked in the past. You have a right to bring buyers through, subject to your tenant's reasonable conditions. To keep the access to the property amicable it is important to communicate well with your tenants and to make them feel as good as possible about the fact that their home is no longer necessarily going to be available to them (it may be if an investor purchasing the property keeps the tenancy with the same terms and conditions of the original periodic tenancy in place), and they may have to pack up and find somewhere else to live.

If there is a fixed-term tenancy in place and the property is sold, then your tenants are entitled to stay on until the end of that term under the same conditions. If your tenants wish to move then you should discuss this with the new owners, and ensure that you put any agreement in writing.

If the property is sold when there is a periodic tenancy in place, and the new owner requires vacant possession, the landlord may give the tenants 42 days' written notice to leave, rather than the usual 90 days' written notice required.

Once a property is sold the outgoing landlord must tell the tenants who the new owners are and when they take over. The new owners must let the tenant know their name and contact details, and where the rent is to be paid.

Mortgagee sale

If a property is sold by mortgagee sale and there is an existing tenancy, the existing tenancy is taken over by the mortgagee or the new owner. The rights of the landlord and tenant are the same, except that the mortgagee can only give notice once possession has been taken. A mortgagee sale will also override a fixed-term tenancy, with the mortgagee able to give notice as if the tenancy were periodic.

Terminating a periodic tenancy

Under the Residential Tenancies Act the landlord must give 90 days' written notice to the tenants that they have to evict the property. There can be 42 days' written notice to the tenants if the landlord has unconditionally sold their property or is moving into the property.

Any notice to end a tenancy must:

○ be in writing

○ give the address of the tenancy

○ give the date when the tenancy is to end, and

○ be signed by the person giving the notice.

Notice can be served by mail to the address for service (it doesn't have to be sent by registered mail or delivered in person), but four working days must be added to the notice period to allow for mail delivery time.

In the event the landlord gives notice, the tenant can still give their shorter 21-day written notice. A sample letter is set out below.

{date}

{Tenant's name}
{Address of tenanted property}

Dear {tenant}

TERMINATION OF TENANCY ·

We hereby notify you that we have terminated the tenancy agreement on {date in three months' time}. Until this time you are still bound by all of the terms of our tenancy agreement, therefore you must continue to pay rent and keep the property in the standard it was handed over to you.

Please note that you are obliged to return to us all of sets of keys to our property, and to leave the property in the state in which you found it. This will include mowing the lawns just before you leave and leaving the house as clean as possible. In addition, doing these things mean that you will not have lawn mowing, rubbish disposal and cleaning bills deducted from your bond.

We will be in contact with you closer to the date by which you must leave. If you have any questions about this letter, please contact me on 01 123 4567.

Yours sincerely
ABC TRUST

David Whitburn
Landlord

Terminating a fixed-term tenancy

A fixed-term tenancy does not require further notice in writing because the end-date is in the tenancy agreement. However, it is always a good idea to check with the tenant again nearer the time about what is intended to happen at the end of the fixed term. A fixed-term tenancy cannot be ended before the term is complete, without the written agreement of both parties, or a Tribunal order. If you do nothing, then when the fixed term is up, the tenancy reverts to being a periodic tenancy.

Retaliatory notice

If tenants are given notice to quit because they have approached the landlord or DBH about a problem, they may make an application to the Tenancy Tribunal to ask for an order to say the notice will have no effect. If the Tribunal agrees the notice to quit was given because the tenant used or asked for their rights under the law (that is, that the notice was retaliatory), then the Tribunal will make an order saying that the notice has no effect.

Check the property out quickly

After receiving the letter, go over and look at the property urgently and ascertain whether the property needs any repairs or maintenance, and point out to the tenants what needs to be done to restore the property to the standard it was in when they first started their tenancy, with an allowance for fair wear and tear.

Try not to lose a single day of rent from when the tenants move out. Maybe get the tenants to move on a Friday or a Saturday, and the new tenants to move in on the following day. Methods of advertising and procuring tenants are discussed earlier in this chapter.

Provide tenants with a departure letter

Straight after receiving written notice from the tenants, send them a standard letter that explains some commonsense procedures and their obligations under the Residential Tenancies Act and the tenancy agreement signed. Give them a step-by-step checklist to ensure their departure is hassle-free, and to give the incoming tenants a clean and tidy property at the right time.

In this letter discuss that you wish to show prospective new tenants through the property, mentioning that the Residential Tenancies Act permits reasonable access by the landlord.

Negotiate access to do maintenance and advertise the property

Obviously try to eliminate vacancy periods between tenants. This can be hard, as often a good incoming tenant will need to give 21 days' written notice to their landlord.

However, if the property is vacant between tenants, this gives you a good window to perform repairs and maintenance tasks before prospective tenants are shown through. Presentation is the key to getting good market rents and attracting top tenants.

It is a good idea to discuss this with the outgoing tenant and go over all jobs that should be done. Also make a list of all things to do, such as clean the ceiling, buy a new toilet seat, weed the garden, remove the big oil spots on the drive, repair the fence, etc.

Tenant's obligations upon leaving

There are a number of things that tenants must do when they move out. They must:

○ move out by the date set out in the termination notice (for a periodic tenancy), or the end date in the tenancy agreement (for a fixed-term tenancy)

○ pay the rent up to the last day of the tenancy

○ leave the house reasonably clean and tidy

○ remove any rubbish or arrange for its removal by the last day of the tenancy

○ return all keys, pass cards or security devices to the landlord, and

○ leave any chattels belonging to the landlord at the property.

If a tenant doesn't fulfil any one of these obligations, then the landlord is entitled to claim part or all of the bond for any loss that the failure incurs.

Inspect the property on the last day

Before you give the tenants their bond back you need to look at the condition of your property and see if this is the same as the condition you left it in. This can be gauged better by taking quality digital-camera shots on the day tenants move in, and by undertaking regular inspections.

If there is any damage, or anything left unclean, get it repaired or commercially cleaned and take the cost off the bond. In the event that this costs more than the bond, pursue the tenants for it personally first, then if this fails via the Tenancy Tribunal.

Bond at end of tenancy

Either the tenant or landlord may apply to have the bond refunded by filling out a bond refund form. This form would have been sent with the bond acknowledgement letter and is also available on the DBH website (http://dbh.govt.nz/UserFiles/File/Publications/Tenancy/pdf/bond-refund-form.pdf), or by phoning 0800 TENANCY (0800 83 62 62), or from DBH offices. The form should be signed by both the landlord and the tenant. (Refunds are made by direct credit and the correct bank account numbers must be supplied on the form.)

Both the tenant and landlord should go through the property, using the property inspection report from the tenancy agreement again, and check that nothing is damaged or broken. The tenant is not responsible for normal wear and tear to the property or chattels, but is responsible for any (intentional or careless) damage. Tenants are also held responsible if the property was clean when they moved in but is no longer clean. Bond money can also be claimed for money owed, such as rent arrears.

When the bond refund form is sent to the DBH the signatures are checked against those held on the bond lodgement form. It is important to update the signature held if there is a change to either the landlord or tenant. Without this update, bond refunds will be delayed while checks are made. There are forms on the DBH website so you can advise of any changes to the original tenant(s) or landlord, or to their details.

Full refund (no claim)   If the inspection shows everything is in order, the bond refund form is to be completed and sent to the DBH Bond Centre for the refund of the bond money to the tenant.

Part refund (agreed claim)   If there is some damage or other claim that the tenant agrees to have taken out of the bond, then the refund form is filled out and signed accordingly. The bond is divided, giving the landlord the cost of the repair or other claim, and the tenant the balance. For instance, if a bond is $400 and both parties agree the cost of window repairs is $150 then the bond refund form would say 'Pay tenant $250, Pay landlord $150.'

The DBH Bond Centre will pay the tenant $250 and the landlord $150 by direct credit to their bank accounts. (Note that bond money to be refunded can also be transferred to a new tenancy using a bond transfer form.)

Refund not agreed   If you can't agree on how the bond should be paid out, then the landlord should make an application to the Tenancy Tribunal for the amount claimed to be deducted from the bond, and a mediator will be assigned to help sort it out. It is important to make this application as soon as possible, and to take photos and gather evidence in support of your claim.

Review rents

When tenants move out, you have the opportunity to review the rents for the incoming tenants to ensure that you are getting the right price and not under- (or over-) renting your property. The cycle then repeats to continue the wonderful benefits of property investing. You can only raise your rents every six months, and have to give at least 60 days' written notice of any rental increase. Have a template rental letter similar to this:

{LETTERHEAD}
{Date}

{Tenant's name}
{Address of tenanted property}

Dear {tenant}

<u>NOTICE OF RENTAL INCREASE</u>

The rental price for your home at {address} has not been renewed since you moved into the property in {month and year} OR The rental price for your home was last reviewed on {day, month, year}.

Rental prices in the {rental property suburb} area have increased since this time, as have the costs of maintaining and running your property, such as rates, insurance, {water charges?}, repairs and maintenance.

As you can see from the enclosed information from the Department of Building and Housing rental statistics {print out information on the suburb from the market rental information from DBH}, {x}-bedroom {houses/flats/apartments} in the {rental property suburb} area have a rental price range between ${X} per week and ${X} per week.

However we would also like to take into account the length of time you have been in the property, the excellent condition that you keep your home in and your promptness with your rental payments.

We consider that a rental price increase to ${X} reflects current market conditions and your quality as a tenant.

In accordance with the Residential Tenancies Act 1986, this rent increase will not take effect for at least 60 days from the date of this notice. This means that your new rent will not be payable until the rental payment date of {day, month, year}.

Please contact me as soon as possible if you have any questions.

Yours sincerely

David Whitburn
ABC Trust

The largest changes to the Residential Tenancies Act in 24 years

Since 1986, a lot has changed with new technologies, means of communication, new demographics of tenants, and societal trends with many more people renting property and also a trend for longer-term tenancies.

As a result I believe that the changes reflect a good balance between the needs of tenants to have a decent home, and the needs of landlords to be able to effectively manage their rental properties.

Residential Tenancies Amendment Act 2010

After a lengthy consultation and review process of around eight years, the Residential Tenancies Amendment Act 2010 (RTAA) took effect as the new law from 1 October 2010. Basically the changes are, on the whole, landlord-friendly. I particularly like the ability to charge tenants' penalties for unlawful acts (a new concept brought in). I would advise that you print out both the RTA and the RTAA and put it into a folder or bind it. After all, it is an important document as it sets out the rules for you to manage your property portfolio.

Some of the key amendments include:

○ letting fees — all property managers can charge a letting fee.

○ fixed-term tenancies — fixed-term tenancies revert to periodic tenancies on the tenancy expiry date, unless the tenant or landlord gives notice.

○ addresses for service — landlords and tenants will be able to use an email address, PO Box or fax number as an alternate address for service.

○ agent for landlords overseas — if a landlord is going to be overseas for more than 21 consecutive days, a New Zealand-based agent must be appointed and DBH's bond centre notified (or face up to a $1,000 fine).

○ body corporate rules — rules will be required to be attached to tenancy agreements when a property is part of a unit title complex.

○ notices to remedy — previously 10 working days' notice, this changed to 14 consecutive days' notice.

- terminating a tenancy — new rules have been added for termination of tenancy by notice. For example, landlords will be required to set out the reason(s) when giving fewer than 90 days' notice of termination.

- unlawful acts — a number of unlawful acts have been added with fines possible against both landlords, for things like interference with the supply of services (such as water, electricity, gas), and tenants for things like having more inhabitants than the maximum number of persons the tenancy agreement prescribes.

- abandoned goods — new rules have been added for landlords dealing with abandoned goods.

Search my blogs on www.davidwhitburn.com under RTAA if you want to learn about these changes in detail.

Boarding houses

Boarding houses are residential premises with at least one boarding room that the tenant has an exclusive right to occupy and facilities with shared use by the tenants (eg. living area, kitchen, bathroom). Since 1 October 2010 most boarding-house tenancies were brought under the RTA. However, the RTA doesn't apply to boarding-house tenancies where there are five or fewer tenants at any one time, or to tenancies of under 28 days.

As a boarding-house landlord you can have a bond of up to four weeks' rent from your tenant, which again has to be lodged with DBH within 23 working days. Bonds of one week's rent or less don't have to be lodged with the DBH. Boarding-house tenancies need to have a written tenancy agreement which, in addition to the standard details listed previously, must include these specific details:

- whether the tenancy will last more than 28 days

- telephone numbers for the landlord

- boarding room number (eg. room 7)

- number of other tenants in the room (if any)

- services to be provided by the landlord that are included in rent (if any)

- fire evacuation procedures (I think this is a great move, as sadly too many New Zealanders die or get hurt from fires every year in boarding houses)

○ house rules for the provision of services by the landlord, and the enjoyment and use of the premises (if any).

Many investors I know who own boarding houses (or houses which are rented by the room, with four or five rooms, and don't come under the RTA) note that their premises attract a certain kind of tenant. They tell me they are more likely to attract students, people from different cultures and ways of life, recent ex-prisoners making a new start in the community, separated people, rent-sensitive people and hard-core computer-gaming addicts, and they believe they are at greater risk of attracting tenants with addictions or social problems. They say being a boarding-house landlord can open your mind to the various lifestyle choices people have and it makes for excellent work stories! But of course it can also make for complications, which is why some property managers refuse to take them on, and some others charge 15% or more as a management fee for them. Having house rules set down in the tenancy agreement is a great idea too.

You want to maximise your cash flow as a boarding-house investor and therefore you want your property fully occupied as often as possible. Since your tenants are living in close proximity, the risk factors are magnified. These run from the benign, like leaving the toilet seat up, to the seriously unpleasant, like violence against other tenants.

As a result, I would insist that you carefully devise a set of house rules relevant to your boarding house. The RTA requires that a copy of the house rules must be provided to the tenant at the start of the tenancy and a copy must also be on display in the premises at all times. If you want to change the house rules, you must give seven days' written notice. A tenant in a boarding house tenancy may apply to the Tribunal for an order to set aside a house rule as unlawful, or to vary it, so you need to make sure that your rules are fair, reasonable and, of course, legal.

26 | How to minimise the risks

There are a number of risks when it comes to property investments. These can be mitigated by adopting various techniques. The risks include:

Not being able to pay your loan

This is a considerable risk for many. Sadly, the banks and lenders towards the end of the boom and into the downturn of the property cycle had rather easy-to-satisfy lending policies. This means that you have to be responsible with leverage and know when to put the brakes on yourself.

Certain apartments

Inner-city apartments can be an interesting proposition. In Auckland, and to a lesser extent Wellington, the central business district offers plenty of opportunities to bowl over sub-six-storey buildings and replace them with 30-storey-plus apartment towers. This is not the same in Sydney and Melbourne. As a result, our apartment markets have an issue: if there is more demand another tower can be built. In other major cities, increasing demand simply pushes up prices, because the built-up CBD has no room to meet the squeezed supply. The result of New Zealand's propensity to build more apartments means that the apartment market is not renowned for its capital growth. Sure, apartments may well get some capital growth, and they will exhibit price movement throughout their own property cycles, but in general they will not go up as much as stand-alone houses.

Many of the apartments in Auckland's CBD have been hit very hard by the changing financial conditions and the downturn of the property market since the end of 2007. As a result, many apartments are selling for around half replacement cost. Financing apartments can be an issue. I have been told by senior people in the lending departments of two of the country's largest banks that lenders in New Zealand have been a little bit burnt by apartments. The lenders have found that in recent times they are unable to sell apartments at a price which allows them to recoup their investment. One of the reasons has been that there are some extremely small apartments constructed. But the major problem is that many large apartment buildings were erected in a shoddy fashion and have turned out to be leaky buildings. Of course, there are many, many well-constructed apartments which don't leak, but unfortunately they have all been tarred with the same brush. This has frightened off both buyers and lenders.

Having said all that, apartments can provide outstanding net yields of 7% to 10% at the time of writing. That is very good cash flow in anyone's books. I have a student who is making over $5,000 per year from his investment of just over $30,000 (which was 20% of the purchase price) for a two-bedroom medium-sized Auckland CBD apartment, with the safety of a four-year fixed interest rate (fixed at 8.00% in early 2011).

I know the Auckland CBD market very well, and I can assure you that the vacancy rates are generally extremely low. This is partly because of the strength of Auckland University (the only university in the country that has been accepted into the Universitas 21 network and our nation's top-ranked university), Auckland University of Technology (AUT), many businesses employing large numbers of people all within close walking distance, and let's not forget a number of outstanding language schools that educate a huge number of foreign students wanting to learn English. These schools host many thousands of predominantly east and south-east Asian students, who mostly reside in apartments nearby.

So if you are looking for equity, apartments are not in general going to be the best investment for you. However if you just want cash flow, you should give apartments a very serious look.

Leasehold apartments

My advice is to stay clear of these.

Leasehold apartments that are leaky buildings really take the cake. The Auckland Railway Station is one such example. An apartment sold in that building for just under $15,000, which didn't leave much for the owner after commission was paid. That building is a prominent leaky building, and needs millions to be spent on it to bring it back up to a good state of repair. The other bad news is that the freehold land owner (Ngati Whatua o Orakei) is set to review the ground rent for the land, and this is likely to skyrocket to an average of over $6,000 per apartment per year.

There will be all sorts of carnage next year when this ground rent review happens, particularly with the poor Blue Chip victims still struggling to hold onto their properties. In early November 2010, I featured on the cover page of the *Sunday Star Times* business section and mentioned my concern about leasehold apartments and I wasn't alone. My comments were corroborated by a very reliable source: Martin Dunn, the managing director of City Sales, Auckland's largest apartment sales company. It is hardly in his interests to be quoted as steering people away from apartments, so that gives you an indication that these are at present a massively risky investment.

Stupidity

I have learned in property investment to never underestimate the stupidity of humankind. I have seen some startling examples of poor decisions when it comes to property:

○ Renovations by fearless DIY investors (mainly males); one memorable instance when an investor gave himself a severe electric shock as he attempted to install light fittings without turning off the power.

○ An investor who hired a post-hole borer and dug deep to put in a fence pole, only to short the neighbours' power as he drilled down and tore through the conduit and mains cabling (he was extremely lucky not to receive more than a sizeable electric shock).

○ Another man who was standing inside a cupboard when framing it up, pushed the nail gun into the frame by reaching around to the outside only for the nail to slide in and puncture his lung.

○ Investors (more than one) who have fallen through the roof or ceiling, or off it completely. Often it's when painting two-storey houses on a single ladder and reaching out to get to spots that should have the ladder moved and a person holding it at the very least, or otherwise scaffolding erected.

You are a long time dead, yet many investors have injured themselves and a few investors have died in the pursuit of their financial dreams. This is often because basic safety precautions weren't observed, which is often just stubbornness or stupidity.

Don't let your ego get in the way

I often attend the busy Wednesday auctions of Barfoot & Thompson, Auckland's largest real estate agency, as well as a healthy diet of property auctions around the wider Auckland region. I have seen some ridiculous purchases that would have to really challenge the concept of fair market value. Why does anyone pay over the odds for a property? Because the property market runs on emotion more often than logic.

That was particularly the case with one immaculately presented property in the upmarket Auckland suburb of Epsom. The agent suggested that the property would probably sell for around $900,000 to $950,000. It had a council valuation of $860,000, so the price guide already seemed generous. When the bidding reached $1.05 million, the property was 'on the market', having met the vendor's reserve. There were only two bidders in it, both hell-bent on getting the property — rather than an auction, you would have thought it was a competition. There was very little hesitation for either bidder as they raised the price by $20,000 or $50,000 with each nod of the head or flick of the hand.

The property finally sold for an amazing $1.315 million. The house was in a 'double grammar zone' (zoned for prestigious schools Auckland Grammar School and Epsom Girls Grammar School), was in close proximity into the CBD, and was a perfectly presented and well-marketed house. These factors really gave this property extra value — but $400,000 above the likely buy price? $455,000 over CV? I think that's more than a little bit extreme in a property downturn.

I definitely don't recommend that you engage yourself in ridiculous bidding wars for investment properties — it doesn't make commercial sense. The yield on that four-bedroom, two-and-a-half bathroom property (no tennis court, no swimming pool, no spa pool) would be an underwhelming 3.2% gross. However I really doubt that this would have been an investment property. The 'winner' took his elegantly dressed wife, and their two girls and boy along to the auction.

But whether you're buying for yourself, for your portfolio or for someone else, don't get so caught up in the rush that you bid far too much for a property. Remember that it's not a contest. Even if it was, who wants to win a competition called 'Who can start with the least equity?' or 'Who can pay the most ridiculous price for this house?' The auction process is not a game, or a showdown, or a chance to put one over the other guy. If you start thinking like that you're well on your way to making a silly decision and paying far too much for your property.

A perfect example of this is when I lost out on a property — though it was a far less fancy address. I attended an auction in Mangere, South Auckland, a few years ago, to bid on an investment property I liked the look of. I had done my financial due diligence and assessed my top offer at that time to be $235,000. It came down to me and one another investor, whom I shall call Mr Ego. Bidding against one another at the business end of the auction, my bids were going up in $1,000 increments. Mr Ego, though, began with $4,000 increments and then got really overheated and pushed his last few bids up to $14,000 each!

So a third party bid $195,000, I bid $196,000 and Mr Ego bid $200,000. The third party bid $205,000; I could tell she was weakening. I have been to a truckload of auctions over the years and when the bidder's voice gets softer and the bid time gets slower that's usually a giveaway that the certainty is ebbing out of the bidder and he or she is on the verge of abandoning the bidding. Mr Ego bid $219,000(!), and I bid $220,000 straight away in my usual assertive and loud voice with no emotion or flinching. That usually helps to scare off the nervous types like the third party at this auction. Sure enough, she was out — I could tell from her body language, the little head shakes and the husband who was accompanying her staring at me and Mr Ego with a look of 'damn you for beating us' (again, it's really not personal, and if you start thinking like that you can't make any money in this game!). I don't care for those looks; it was a good deal with true value of around $265,000 and potential to add value from a renovation. Plus, Mangere is one of the few suburbs in South Auckland that I believe has above-average potential for both capital and rental gain.

Mr Ego bid $234,000, I hit him with $235,000 straight away in my usual assertive and loud voice with no emotion or flinching again, and of course that was me out because I had reached my pre-determined limit. Mr Ego then bid $249,000! He had bid $14,000 more than I was prepared to pay. $236,000 would have won it, as would $235,500, so why he didn't bid lower was beyond me. It is not a smart auction strategy — especially on lower-value homes with just two bidders bidding — to bid so much more. I had to laugh to myself at the fact that he paid $13,500 more than was necessary. I couldn't help but ask him, 'Why did you bid so much at the end?' He said he wanted to beat the (then) vice president of the Auckland Property Investors' Association! Well, I hope he enjoyed the sensation, as it came at rather a high price. I told him I had hit my cap, and he just stared up at me. I wished him well on the renovations and walked away to focus on the next deal.

27 | Don't derail your own success

Too often investors are their own worst enemies. They make great money from property, having worked so hard to create positive cash flow in self-sustaining portfolios with great amounts of equity. Then they fritter some, or in some cases all, of the returns away by investing in a Gold Coast apartment, a subdivision in the wop-wops, an ill-thought-through purchase of tax liens or deeds in the USA, a network marketing thing or the latest get-rich-quick-scheme.

This really saddens me; if you have done really well in building up a performing long-term asset, you need to stick with it. As a property mentor I have too often seen clients derail their progress by changing horses mid-stream, so to speak. The reason they do this is because they think they have found a better investment. Greed and fear are two extremely powerful emotions. Desperate to know more, investors throw away the careful research they usually undertake, which has worked to help them build their property portfolio. A few charming salespeople who have their own needs at heart, not the needs of their investors, sell the investors a package that sounds irresistibly appealing. But you know the old saying; 'Anything that sounds too good to be true, probably is.'

US tax deeds and liens

An example of derailing your success is when you get distracted and invest in an overseas property-related product like US tax deeds or liens.

How it works: some states of the USA are tax deed states, others are tax lien states. States are divided up into counties for administrative reasons and each county levies property taxes for things like roads, streetlights, schools, policing, internal governance and administration and community services. If you don't or can't pay your property taxes a lien may by statute be put on your property in favour of the county, which takes priority over a lender's mortgage. Counties sell these liens from time to time (usually by auction) to investors, to help with revenue collection. The returns on both deeds and liens, in Texas for instance, which is one of the most common offerings, are portrayed at levels of 15% to 50%.

There were seminars held in New Zealand in 2010 that sold the potential benefits of US tax deeds and liens. However, it is what the salespeople don't mention that is important:

○ US accountancy fees, nor state and federal tax compliance — which all will cost the Kiwi investor money

○ New Zealand tax consequences (including the accrual regime) on the US tax liens

○ US initial structure (company/trust formation) costs

○ The minimum US$1,000 balance in the US bank account that apparently has to be opened by Kiwi tax lien/deed investors

○ exchange rate risks

○ legal costs to foreclose on a lien

○ the risk of buying a lemon property — you could purchase a piece of swampland, a landlocked property, a road, a tiny section with a tree on it, a footpath, who knows what it could be if you don't do your due diligence properly?

○ there is mention of being able to buy tax liens for as cheap as US$1, yet one person who went through tax lien training looked at deals every week for nearly 18 months and never found a lien anywhere near that cheap

○ the risk of not buying anything at all and blowing US$5,995. Investors who had purchased a tax lien course have said they have been trying to buy tax liens and deeds for months on eBay by following the techniques they were taught. Eight months of genuine trying later and they told me: 'Still no tax liens!' Other investors I spoke to at a property event said that they tried every couple of days for three months and had not been able to secure any deals either.

○ if it were so good why aren't more of the 310 million Americans purchasing tax liens? Why would they get the 4.4 million New Zealanders to purchase them?

○ why would an investor want to become a debt collector for US counties? Many counties collect the easy debts themselves, and pass on the hard ones to investors

○ If you were a lender owed US$250,000, would you rather pay out a US$1,200 tax lien to protect your security in the event legal foreclosure notice is served by the lien holder?

I believe that for the overwhelming majority of New Zealanders tax liens and tax deeds are a no-go zone. They may work if you are in the USA and can commit time and knowledge to becoming a tax lien and deed expert. It is my honest opinion that they will make the majority of New Zealanders investors poorer than when they started. Still not convinced? Or still thinking it sounds great? If so, my advice is to read a great article on tax liens and tax deeds by Rob Stock, who is one of New Zealand's finest and most respected finance journalists, in the widely circulated *Sunday Star Times*: http://www.stuff.co.nz/business/personal-finance/1762855/Beware-of-lien-returns.

28 | How to prepare an offer

If you have extra information at your fingertips when it comes to agreements for sale and purchase, you will feel far more confident when preparing offers. So I'd like to increase your level of technical knowledge and add in a touch of land law, just to help you have a leg-up on the competition.

To start with, it is important to familiarise yourself with agreements for sale and purchase — these documents form the basis of negotiations. In addition you simply cannot afford to assume that real estate agents know what they are doing. I have seen even experienced real estate agents make some horrendous mistakes in filling out agreements for sale and purchase.

One prime example: a very experienced agent failed to get the vendors' signature on what my clients and the agent thought was an agreement. In the time it took our agent to chase up those vital signatures, another agent — from the same office — came in with his buyer and a slightly higher offer to secure what would still have been an excellent deal for my clients. So don't miss out because you haven't checked the agreement yourself.

Since 1981 there has been a precedent or standard form agreement, developed by both the Auckland District Law Society and the Real Estate Institute of New Zealand. Currently we are up to the eighth edition. These agreements are used by every real estate agent and agency that I know, and by most lawyers (a few larger firms have their own agreements for higher-value properties — and higher fees to match!). So before I give you an overview of them and teach you the bare minimum I need to take you back to basics in terms of contract law.

What constitutes an agreement?

In a nutshell an agreement for sale and purchase is contract law in its purest form. There are three requirements for a contract:

- offer
- acceptance, and
- consideration.

The parties to the contract are:

- you (the purchaser) as the person buying or proposing to buy the property
- the vendor, who is the legal owner of the property.

By property I mean the land and improvements (buildings and fixed structures) on the land, which is technically called real property and informally called real estate.

So, you are making the vendor an offer to purchase his or her property, which meets the first requirement, the offer. If the vendor accepts your offer, then that is the second requirement, acceptance, achieved. The third requirement, consideration, is both the price and terms of the agreement.

If the vendor crosses out your offer, this is a counter-offer, which you in turn may accept. This can happen many times, particularly when a purchaser offers a very low price and the vendor counter-offers (or 'counters') at or very near their listing price. Then lots of gradual counter-movements may take place, which can then result in a somewhat messy agreement. This can be redrawn cleanly if both parties are happy for this to be done, but lenders and lawyers are actually quite used to messy agreements. The most important elements are to see the parties, the property being sold (legal description and street address) and the final price agreed upon.

The standard form ADLS/REINZ agreement

The first page of the standard form agreement is included overleaf. My notes on the various terms are listed opposite the agreement.

Feel free to be a bit creative; this is your offer, and the vendors don't have to accept it. Even if you can't get to a price the vendors want, it may still be worth negotiating with them. Consider negotiating on terms: short or long due diligence, quick or long settlement, keeping tenants on, renting the property back to them for a certain rate and time.

Date — only once an agreement is reached

Vendor — legal name of the vendor as per the certificate of title

Purchaser — your chosen purchasing entity's name (your name or your company name, for instance)

Property — the street address

Estate — strikethrough to eliminate the non-relevant descriptors

Description — enter details from certificate of title

Purchase price — in numbers only (make it including GST)

Deposit — in writing and pay to a trust account not to the vendors directly

Interest rate — as low as possible

Possession date – choose a date that suits

Conditions — you can strike out this box to make the deal appear as clean as possible (your conditions must then be covered by the further terms of sale).

Tenancies — if you want it empty, write vacant possession; if you want to keep tenants on you need to record all the relevant details.

Sale by — ignore this or let any agent involved put his or her details down.

Initial this page at the bottom (both vendor and purchaser).

Then the standard form wording is covered in the substantive part in fine print of clauses 1–18 (this includes the addendum for the compulsory zero-rating GST rules, which are covered in clauses 17 and 18). These are important clauses; although you will not have to understand them your lawyer definitely should! The definitions and interpretations have been litigated over three decades. You don't want to change them willy nilly either.

To complete the agreement you need to draft the further terms of sale — this comes after clauses 1–18. If you don't include this and have

Eighth Edition 2006 (4)

AGREEMENT FOR SALE AND PURCHASE OF REAL ESTATE

This form is approved by the Real Estate Institute of New Zealand Incorporated and by Auckland District Law Society Incorporated.

DATE:

VENDOR:

PURCHASER:

PROPERTY
Address:

Estate:	FEE SIMPLE	LEASEHOLD	CROSSLEASE (FEE SIMPLE)	CROSSLEASE (LEASEHOLD)
	STRATUM IN FREEHOLD		STRATUM IN LEASEHOLD	(if none is deleted fee simple)

Legal Description:
Area (more or less):   *Lot/Flat/Unit:*   *DP:*   *Unique Identifier or CT:*

PAYMENT OF PURCHASE PRICE
Purchase price: $ **Plus GST (if any) OR Inclusive of GST (if any).**
If neither is deleted the purchase price includes GST (if any).

GST date (refer clause 13.0):

Deposit (clause 2.0): $

Balance of purchase price to be paid or satisfied as follows:
    (1) By payment in cleared funds on the settlement date which is
OR
    (2) In the manner described in the Further Terms of Sale.   Interest rate for late settlement: % p.a.

POSSESSION
Possession date (clause 3.0):

CONDITIONS (clause 9.0)
Finance condition   LIM required: Yes/No
Lender:

Amount required: OIA Consent required: Yes/No

Finance date: Land Act/OIA date:

TENANCIES (if any)
Name of tenant:

Bond: Rent: Term: Right of renewal:

SALE BY:

Licensed Real Estate Agent

It is agreed that the vendor sells and the purchaser purchases the property, and the chattels listed in Schedule 1, on the terms set out above and in the General Terms of Sale and any Further Terms of Sale.

crossed out the finance and LIM clauses on the front page, you are buying a property unconditionally. Buying a property unconditionally is absolutely fine, but only if you have done your due diligence prior. For example, if you win a property at an auction you will be unconditionally committed to purchasing it.

Having your financial pre-approval in place does put you in the best position. (Usually this comes in the form of an email from your lender stating your pre-approval amount and any conditions imposed.) Even if you have this, though, you may want to go through the Land Information Memorandum (LIM) that the relevant council or territorial authority has on the property. Since perception is an important tool in real estate negotiations, I make my offers look as good as possible by crossing out the finance and LIM clauses on page 1, and using the following due diligence clause which makes the investigations sensitive on the financial aspects of the transaction.

My due diligence clause

A skilled conveyancing lawyer prepared this clause for me and I use it a lot:

> 19.0 This agreement is conditional on the Purchaser completing a due diligence investigation and being satisfied the property is entirely suitable for their requirements, within ten working days from the date of this agreement. The Purchaser must notify the Vendor in writing by 5 pm on the above date that this condition has been satisfied or the agreement will be at an end. This condition is inserted for the sole benefit of the Purchaser. The Purchaser shall not be obliged to provide to the Vendor any reason in the event this clause is not satisfied.

As a result I have the ability to tell real estate agents or private sellers the truth: that I am a pre-approved purchaser (this is very important as a significant number of conditional agreements do fall over, mostly because they are subject to finance). Then, since I am a professional property investor, I tell the agent or vendor up front exactly what the situation is in terms of the agreement. I explain the importance of a good return for me, in terms of the three pillars of property investment, cash flow, equity and growth. I also explain that the purchase price is critical to me. If I pay too much I will not get sufficient instant equity from buying below value, or enough cash flow because the loan I need to help fund the purchase price would be too high — I need ways to escape.

I can then use my expertise as an area expert, get a registered valuer's opinion, or even use the QV eValuer tool for a 'guesstimate', or talk to agents and colleagues actively operating in the area to find out how much of a bargain I am really getting. I look at school zones and rental levels to see what competitors in the area with similar sized and type properties are charging. I review the LIM and check for issues between the property as it is presented and the council's property file. If it is not good enough, I cancel the agreement.

Similarly, if you are proposing to do a minor dwelling, granny flat or subdivision, have a talk with the council's planning and building teams. If the costs are too high for your project, you can cancel the agreement on this clause too. I ask that all of my mentoring clients have current financial pre-approvals. Sometimes they only have room to do one deal, yet they can put offers on multiple properties because they have smart clauses in their agreements. These properties have ranged in price from small units in Waikato country towns to glamorous mansions in Kohimarama and Mission Bay in central Auckland's eastern beaches. Over the years, they — like me — have made offers on collectively thousands of properties across New Zealand, using this due diligence clause and cancelling or renegotiating price and terms for all sorts of reasons.

Protection from this due diligence clause

This clause offers excellent protection from the fact that if the purchaser (or their lawyer) doesn't advise the vendor about the exercise of the due diligence condition by a certain time, then the agreement is at an end. This is particularly useful when you have lots of offers on the go and cannot possibly satisfy them all — you wouldn't want to have to face getting finance for them all if you forgot about an agreement and had the clause the other way around! It is a condition 'inserted for the sole benefit of the purchaser', so it is crystal clear that the clause is designed as the purchaser's due diligence condition. Then it goes on to state that 'the vendor understands and agrees that they shall not be entitled to enquire on the purchaser's exercise of their discretion', which means that if the offer hasn't been declared unconditional then the vendor or more pertinently their lawyer is not entitled to ask the reasons why the purchaser has turned down the offer.

Some vendors don't understand, or refuse to sign the last limb of this due diligence clause. In this case I simply take that part out. My property lawyers all agree that there is enough protection in this clause in any event, and that it is exceedingly unlikely for a vendor to sue a purchaser for failure to complete purchase for cancelling due diligence on most investment properties, as it is notoriously hard to prove.

However, some vendors have tried to sue purchasers using differing due diligence clauses for cancelling due to invalid reasons. For instance, when the property market exited the boom and entered the downturn phase and the bite of the downturn kicked in, vendors weren't happy when purchasers cancelled agreements because the vendors could only on-sell their properties for 10 to 15% lower than the agreed price they thought they had in writing. In a recovering market or a boom, a vendor is highly unlikely to sue you. Instead they will in all likelihood sell their house at a higher price to another purchaser. Seek expert legal advice if ever you are in any doubt.

Other uses of due diligence clauses

You can use due diligence clauses to secure a property under a conditional contract, and to set the number of days for you to do your research. Please try to get your solicitor in the right frame of mind so they don't list a multitude of due diligence clauses. Remember that when you are presenting an offer, you are trying to 'sell' your offer to the vendor so it will be accepted. If the offer has too many clauses in it, it will appear unwieldy and you will be far less likely to get the agreement. This is where solicitors can get in the way.

Remember solicitors are your servants, and they are there to provide a service to you. If, as a purchaser, your lawyer writes an agreement which requires extra pages for due diligence clauses in the further terms of sale, this is highly unlikely to get acceptance from a vendor and will just incur a significant amount of legal fees. Put yourself in the vendor's shoes: would you want to accept an offer with the finance and LIM clauses circled in page 1 and then a towering clause line-up? It might look like this:

19.0 Subject to builder's inspection report
20.0 Subject to registered valuation report
21.0 Subject to title search
22.0 Subject to sale of another property (too many homeowners use this as a clause and it is weak as it relies on third parties — i.e. someone else to purchase the potential purchaser's own home)
23.0 Subject to business partner's approval
24.0 Subject to geotechnical report
25.0 Subject to surveyor's report

26.0   Subject to council file inspections

27.0   Vendor's warranty to paint the underfloor hatch door on the
         back side of the property in a matching colour to the rest of
         the base cladding, and to clean the wall and ceiling above
         the free-standing oven.

If you were a vendor, you would think the purchaser is probably either a lawyer, or someone so conservative that you would probably not want to go ahead with the purchase — knowing that any one of these nine aspects could go wrong. I have seen lengthy lists of due diligence conditions prepared by lawyers, and I love it; it means that my clean offers get accepted despite the fact that I have offered a much lower price. Some vastly experienced real estate agents believe that conveyancing lawyers would rather insert all the conditions to protect themselves, because nowadays they are just so risk-averse and afraid of making a mistake, or being the subject of yet another time-consuming complaint to the New Zealand Law Society. Unfortunately this may not be of best service to you.

These clauses I mentioned above are based on a story from a real estate agent colleague and are an excellent example of 'solicitor over-exuberance'. The offer gave the agent an almighty laugh, and the purchasers then questioned their own offer too. Sadly, agents are (no surprises) better at selling property than lawyers. When an offer has to be 'sold' to a vendor to get them to accept it, the fewer and simpler conditions the better. The price wasn't bad and the potential purchasers didn't want to go against their lawyer's advice as they had just paid over $500 extra for these due diligence clauses.

The vendor didn't laugh — he just ripped up the agreement, and said 'Bring me a serious offer.' Fortunately this is where I stepped in. My trust came in with the page 1 conditions all crossed out and the due diligence clause listed above (without the last limb whereby the vendor is not able to enquire about the purchaser's discretion, as the agent had told me all about this pedantic solicitor stuffing up the deal). I was $20,000 lower and I secured the property the next day. I should thank the solicitor who six years ago drafted the monster-sized conditions, as that property is an outstanding performer in my portfolio. For the record, it passed its geotechnical report and, while not subdivisible, it has a three-bedroom minor dwelling of 65m² on it, producing over $12,000 in actual cash flow for me each year and $125,000 in increased equity. I also painted the baseboard hatch, and my painter's wife cleaned the grime off the ceiling above the oven with bathroom cleaner. While she was at it, she cleaned the wall behind it. Long may 'special condition' solicitors and the fear-driven and pessimistic-looking property law profession remain!

There are a number of other clauses that you can use for varying situations, for instance:

○ vendor finance

○ early access before settlement

○ subject to resource consent being granted (eg. if performing a subdivision)

○ vendor warranty clauses — where the vendors warrant that they will perform some task prior to settlement, for instance, erect a new garage, remove the car wrecks from the property, paint the house, put in a working oven (watch that these aren't too unpopular with the vendor, as it is standard practice to just adjust the purchase price a bit lower).

Evolution of the legal profession

The legal profession is evolving and the general public's perception that many lawyers are self-serving is harsh. For a start the Lawyers and Conveyancers Act 2006 broke down the statutory monopoly lawyers had on conveyancing to permit conveyancers (often legal executives and land registrars) to do conveyancing work with effect from 1 August 2008. The system is becoming more customer focused with lawyers increasingly accepting their role as your servant. We now have mobile lawyers that will come to see you in the evening and weekend, and this is proving popular. There will be even greater numbers of mobile lawyers in future years as technology continues its rapid advancement.

Our system of conveyancing is world renowned for its integrity and speed of doing transactions. We have a great e-dealing system with Landonline, where properties can be bought and sold with mortgages placed on them quickly and inexpensively. The costs of a conveyance have moved little in the past 25 years, which is great for consumers.

In addition New Zealand does not permit gazumping like in the UK and various other jurisdictions. Gazumping is where the vendor accepts a new higher offer to purchase from someone else, where they have already accepted a lower offer from another potential buyer. Under English law, the vendor is not legally committed to go ahead with the sale until the point at which contracts are exchanged. So what happens is that a buyer with ready cash will often be in position to 'gazump' a purchaser who has to get a loan to complete settlement.

I don't mean to be dismissive of conveyancers and conveyancing lawyers as many have amassed an absolute wealth of knowledge and a very high level of training. It is just that often they are not skilled property investors themselves and they can innocently and accidentally put barriers in your path that can prevent you from getting a very good property. As you gain experience you may need to rein them in a little, and align them to your goals. Remember that not all conveyancers and property lawyers are created equal. It is important to have a skilled conveyancer or conveyancing lawyer in your team.

29 | Due diligence

Due diligence is not just a fancy phrase developed by lawyers to try to sound smarter than we really are. The dictionary defines it as 'such diligence as a reasonable person under the same circumstances would use: use of reasonable but not necessarily exhaustive efforts'.

Due diligence allows you to do your research on a property that you are interested in purchasing. You can check for any defects or issues with the property before you decide to buy it. Due diligence is not for properties that you don't want to buy because they are against your buying rules. What do I mean? I know some people that refuse to buy houses with flat roofs and with internal gutters. They simply walk away and don't offer on these properties. There's no point in researching a property which doesn't meet your criteria.

If you have found a property and you are happy with the price you have offered and the terms stated, you will probably want to do some checks to ensure you are happy to become the legal owner of the property.

There are a number of things that you would want to check prior to purchasing a property:

○ condition of the buildings on it — building inspection report

○ title search

○ council-held information

○ value of the property

○ rental levels of the property.

On certain other properties you may wish to add value to them. In these cases you would want to check with all or some of the following: an architect, planning consultant, engineer, surveyor and the council. They would be able to give you a clearer picture of whether or not you could subdivide, for instance, and build a new four-bedroom home, build a minor dwelling, self-contained flat or perhaps a double carport.

Building inspection reports

It is important to inspect a property for any defects. If you know what to look for you could do this by yourself, and if not then seriously consider getting a building inspection report.

I am a big systems fan so have detailed inspection sheets for site visits. I firstly divide the property into the exterior and interior. Then I further partition the list to cover exterior areas like:

- foundations
- drains
- walls
- exterior door
- windows
- roof
- fencing and letterbox
- porches, conservatories (sunrooms) and outbuildings
- garden, paths and driveway

Next I cover the interior areas like:

- walls and ceilings
- kitchens
- bathrooms
- plumbing
- heating and fireplaces
- stairs

○ electricity

○ floors

○ basement

○ attic

I have lists within lists to further detail things to look for, which I share with my mentoring clients.

Title search

The last thing you want is a property that has issues with the title. It could be that the property is subject to a Treaty of Waitangi claim, or it's a property that is on leasehold land where the ground lease payment is reviewed every seven years with no rights of objection. You probably don't want to tackle either of these situations, but either way it's better to know in advance; forewarned is forearmed.

Title searches can be obtained very cheaply as the Land Transfer Office is now totally online. As a result, football fields of filing cabinets fully loaded with paperwork about property titles have moved into the digital era. All documents have been scanned and imaged and are available to the public for download. You can do a basic title search through a product like www.terranet.co.nz, but your lawyer (or conveyancer) will include a title search as part of a conveyance anyway, and it is best practice to get a professionally trained expert to read through the title just in case it is one of the rare properties with which there is an issue.

Your lawyer will be able to get any relevant information for you if your property is on a cross-lease or leasehold title — such as the lease agreements, including covenants and easements (right of ways). These are important to check as you may be able to freehold a leasehold property. Also, if you were contemplating an extension or subdivision, the covenant registered on the title may prevent you from blocking a certain property's views by having tough rules on boundary set-backs and height in relation to boundary. Typically easements are for access issues like drainage easements for council's public drains, and right of ways for allowing the rear section(s) access via a driveway.

Council-held information

There is a lot of information held by councils. This information is able to be extracted by:

○ getting a LIM report

○ getting a property file

○ contacting the council.

Each of these options can give you a lot of information about a property, but contacting the council gives you the most information and it is free. Councils hold information on all sorts of things which is freely available to you — it is public information and not protected by the Privacy Act.

A LIM report includes information on:

○ the designated zoning of a particular property

○ whether there are any rates arrears (both land rates and water rates)

○ consents and permits that have been applied for and issued

○ any swimming and spa pools recorded

○ other issues or actions recorded

○ planning

○ special land features

○ attachments (code of compliance certificates, consent conditions, private drainage plans, public drainage and water services map, district plan map and a special features map are often attached).

I personally rebel against my legal training on this and don't usually bother to pay for LIM reports. If they are given to me, great, but I don't go out of my way to get a LIM report, unless it appears to be a leaky building. Then it becomes an insurance policy — you need to prove you have obtained a LIM report as a subsequent purchaser of a leaky building to be able to sue your council for negligence in that they have breached their duty of care, following the North Shore City Council decision by the Supreme Court in December 2010.

However, I usually get a property file, and I always contact the council. You can go to your local council's website (if they are efficient) and download or order a property file for a fraction of the cost of a LIM (usually under $30 and it can often be emailed to you within a few hours). These property files contain information about works on the property, including building consents, to show what building structures are permitted, the floor plan of these structures, the as-built drainage plan, which shows the location of the stormwater (for example, rainwater collected by the roof, or in cesspits on concrete driveways) and wastewater/sewer drains (which include collecting all of the material in the wastepipes from the kitchen, bathroom and laundry).

In addition you should check to see if the property is marked as being on a flood plain, particularly if it is in a 1-in-50-year flood plain or a similar lower frequency. Councils can assist you with information about coastal erosion, such as properties on sandstone cliffs where your backyard can be lost in a random slip, or storms erode your lawn on a beachfront property. Councils also have information on previous uses of properties, so if you don't want to have a house on a former petrol station, landfill or market garden (that used organo-pesticides which are in your soil), you can find this out. Many councils have aerial maps going back many decades; these are often worth a look and of interest to see the development intensification as time goes on.

There's no substitute for your own eyes

Physical inspections are vital to compare the actual situation with the theoretical. This involves noting the physical structures on the property and the layout of the house, as from time to time you will have unpermitted structures, which could easily mean that there is an illegal structure. You need to compare what you see with what in theory should be there. While usually they are the same, there are all sorts of interesting things that can crop up.

For example, in January 2011 I visited a property in Wairau Valley, on Auckland's North Shore, with a couple that I was mentoring. On the property file this was permitted as a four-bedroom house with a double garage and a bathroom downstairs. Upstairs, all was fine with the four-bedroom house, but downstairs there were six bedrooms and a kitchenette, all totally illegal when I compared this to the property file. The North Shore City Council (before they were abolished on 1 November 2010 to become part of the Auckland Council) had issued a property investor register notice (PIR) on this property.

On clarifying this in person at the Auckland Council's North Shore branch, I was told that the next step is for the Auckland Council's enforcement team to issue a requisition order or notice to fix, giving a certain number of days to remedy the defect or face a fine and prosecution for illegal works. Now if you are doing your due diligence properly you should be budgeting on a four-bedroom home with a double garage and not a four-bedroom and six-bedroom home-and-income property. The numbers will be quite different too, as a double garage with a bathroom doesn't rent as well as a six-bedroom flat!

Other examples of issues I have picked up under due diligence from property files or calling council and asking whether certain structures I have seen on the property are legal include:

○ a carport erected on a property without a permit

○ a double garage that had been converted into a studio, complete with laundry, bathroom and small kitchenette

○ a pool-house converted into a two-bedroom luxury home

○ an area of around 200m², close to a third of the approximately 600m² site, which had been filled in with concrete, despite being specified as a grassed or permeable surface area

○ an illegal add-on to get another bedroom and laundry, by extending the roof-line and building outwards towards the rear of the section

○ an ensuite bathroom with no consent

○ building in the downstairs of a property (a pool-house) with no building consent.

These things may all be fine if you don't get caught, but you must think about the potential risk. If you had a fire would your insurance company pay out? Not if it found you hadn't adequately disclosed the risk. Is a $30,000 (or much higher) fine smart property investing? How about if that fine is also combined with a requisition order to revert the buildings to what they should be on the permit plans, at your own cost? It takes a lot of extra rent in savings to pay for something like that.

Some older houses didn't need building consents

I have seen houses with no building consents in old established areas of central Auckland like Epsom, Remuera, Mt Eden and Parnell, but these have been villas that are often over 100 years old, in which case owners didn't have to file anything with the council, so they might only have an aerial photograph on the file. So don't worry about these older houses quite so much in terms of the council not having floor plans and as comprehensive information as on newer properties. Ensure that you talk to council about the property and what you have seen when visiting, to ensure the council is happy with this situation.

Works completed without council approval

There are many thousands of properties that have had works completed without council approval. I have seen dozens of them, with the highest concentration of them being in the cheapest parts of South Auckland, most of which I saw when I started investing in 2002. Garages would have carpet put down, a kitchenette installed and sometimes things like a toilet connected into a stormwater drain. Others were more temporary in terms of just putting up tarpaulins on the sides of a carport to make a bedroom. In one house a living room had been divided into three bedrooms with partitions made from large wool blankets held by clothes pegs on a wire about 20 cm below the ceiling running only roughly parallel to the walls. Other properties were simply overcrowded with three sets of bunk beds in a bedroom. Some houses would have a downstairs garage and basement storage area converted into a three-bedroom self-contained flat with a kitchen and bathroom.

All areas of New Zealand have these unpermitted works, in both rural and urban areas. I am told by property traders and investors that it is not as bad as it used to be but there are still plenty of unpermitted properties.

Anyone who puts up an unpermitted structure runs a high risk of being caught when the council is called. If it's not the tenants, or the neighbours, or someone he or she mentioned it to in passing, then it would almost certainly occur when the vendor of a property with illegal works advertises to sell the property.

Council enforcement

Here's an example: an Auckland-based property trader and investor got fined $30,000 in June 2008 by the District Court at Manukau for unconsented building works.

His company was granted a building consent based on plans to extend an existing house. The company submitted a plan to build an upstairs bedroom with ensuite and a four-car garage. Instead five bedrooms were built upstairs and part of the garage was turned into a living area, leaving room for only two cars. Despite many warnings and a number of opportunities to remedy this situation before it went to court, the trader did not act. As a result, Manukau City Council compliance and enforcement manager Kevin Jackson was left with no alternative but to uphold the law, as councils have to ensure safety for occupiers and potential future homeowners and ensure minimum safety and construction standards are met.

'People can't put in one set of plans to the council then do something completely different and hope to get away with it,' said Jackson. 'I am disappointed that this was an experienced property developer who knew the rules but chose to break them.'

Getting a $30,000 fine is not smart, and it can get council's back up for future dealings with them. It's certainly not going to make it easier when that investor next wants to develop a property, and his future developments will be carefully scrutinised.

Options with unconsented works

Even if you see a deal at a great price, don't be afraid to walk away if the problem is too big. You don't want to get a 'notice to fix' or requisition order as this could be costly. In some cases there are demolition orders given for works that have a major safety risk. Typically though, the requisition orders and notices to fix are to bring the property back to what is consented, so the council will specify that you must remove this bedroom, remove this kitchen, or whatever needs to be done.

I advise that if you see a property with unconsented works or a building consent that is not completed, that you do your numbers based on what is legal, including allowing for the costs to make it so. If the numbers still work for you on this basis then do it. Otherwise, strongly consider walking away.

Remember that if you are selling a property prospective purchasers will usually look at the property file and/or LIM report, and they will note that the buildings on the property differ to the approved plans held by council, or that there are insufficient inspections recorded against a building consent of permit (that is, no code of compliance certificate or certificate of acceptance).

How to fix works completed without council sign-off

Since the government, including local government (councils), know a number of properties have not been signed off, there are procedures and legislation to deal with them. Some properties with illegal works will never have consent granted. For instance, a house built with untreated external timber, flat roof, internal gutters with no eaves, and stucco cladding with no cavity system, will never be granted consent. However, for many other cases you can remedy the problem.

Works carried out after 1 July 1992 without council approval

You need to apply for a certificate of acceptance (CoA), which includes complete plans and details of the works. Note that this application is based on the building code at the time of the application being made, not the time the works were carried out. Once the council has approved the application a CoA is issued. Then the certificate and processed application is put on the relevant property file and LIM report. A CoA may exclude any works not able to be assessed (such as in-ground foundations, insulation, pipework in the walls).

Approved works carried out after 1 July 1992 that had no final inspections and no code of compliance certificate

You should call your council to book in a final inspection. The council will, upon payment of the inspection fees, schedule an inspection with you. The council's building inspector will check the works and issue a code of compliance certificate (CCC) or a letter of acceptance. Councils across New Zealand have different policies on whether to issue a CCC or letter of acceptance. Some will happily issue a CCC for works that have a building consent and all of the inspections previously passed apart from the final building and final plumbing and drainage inspection, even if more than 10 years has passed since the final inspections. Other councils are tougher and only issue a CCC for building consents issued within the last five years.

I know some investors like to purchase houses with no CCC at a significant discount to true valuation. I personally prefer to make the CCC the vendors' problem by putting in a warranty in the agreement for sale and purchase in the further terms of sale, along the lines of 'The Vendor warrants that they will obtain a CCC in respect of all building improvements on the Property'.

There are examples where it can be difficult to get a building consent. I know of a case where a house was declined consent as it had a flat corrugated iron-roof, which was acceptable at the time of the building consent. The minimum pitch is now eight degrees so the trusses, outriggers, fascia, guttering, part of the exterior cladding and so forth needed to be removed or changed.

I will give a mention about the many thousands of monolithic cladding systems (with no cavity) where a CCC has not been issued. You should get a report from an approved weathertightness assessor like Citywide Building Consultants or Step Up Group. If this report indicates a problem, you may have to reclad the property under a new and compliant building consent (for instance, recladding the whole house in treated timber weatherboards, linea or similar). It is beyond the scope of this book to go into further detail.

If you have a suspected leaky building, you need to engage competent professional advice. If you are thinking of purchasing a suspected leaky building you need to ensure that you offer the right price, and ensure that you do your due diligence just in case you are left with an unexpected nightmare, such as having to replace the exterior framing, all the windows, the front door jambs, the French doors, plus change the roofline and trusses, remove the internal guttering, and reclad the entire exterior of the house. That is a hideously expensive exercise.

Works carried out prior to 1 July 1992 without council approval

You can do one of the following:

○ apply for a building consent to demolish the unauthorised structure and rebuild to comply with the relevant acts; or

○ apply for an unauthorised works application.

To apply for an unauthorised works application, you need to provide a certificate of title, two A3-sized scale copies of the property (you generally need to engage an architect) with an outline of the buildings, contours (you need to engage a surveyor), relative ground and floor levels, all drainage work, permeable area and site coverage, scale floor plan, elevation plan and cross-section information. Suitably qualified professionals acceptable to council then need to declare the unauthorised work to be safe and not unsanitary. If any part of the works is not safe or sanitary, a building consent application will be needed to upgrade the works to safe and sanitary status. There is usually a set form to complete and a set fee to pay.

Where the application has been processed, the council will send you a letter to confirm that the works remain in a safe and sanitary condition, and that no further action will be taken. A copy of this letter and the processed application will be placed on the property file and LIM. Councils do not accept responsibility or liability for the findings in the report for these works, and having a letter confirming the works remain in a safe and sanitary condition doesn't imply clearance for the work undertaken.

Permitted works carried out prior to 1 July 1992 but with no final inspection recorded

You can arrange for a qualified professional's report to be placed on the property file. Council will view this report and if acceptable place it on the file for the benefit of current or future owners. They charge a fee to put this on the property file. Again councils do not accept responsibility or liability for the findings in the report for these works, and having a letter confirming the works remain in a safe and sanitary condition doesn't imply clearance for the work undertaken.

Be aware that it is not unheard of for there to be issues in processing an application for a certificate of acceptance or unauthorised works permit — these issues can sometimes result in a notice to fix being issued, or requiring the application to be amended to address the issues.

Valuations

It is really important to know what your property is worth from a market value perspective. You may be paying too much for it. In some rare cases that could result in you having your lending scaled back; remember, the banks lend on the lesser of registered valuation and purchase price.

As a result you need to ensure you don't go unconditional on a property if you have no realistic idea of what its value is. For example, Ann purchased a house for $112,000 in a negotiation situation in Tokoroa. She got a registered valuer to look at the house and after looking at comparable sales the valuer initially said he could only put $100,000 on the property, and that was being generous. Ann had a loan offer from her bank at 80% of the lesser of purchase price or valuation. As a result the bank lent her only $80,000 towards the $112,000 purchase price. She had thought she would get a bank loan for $89,600 (80% of $112,000). Therefore Ann had to come up with the additional $32,000 herself, and she didn't have this much money, so she had to get a bank loan from her sister and brother-in-law and short-term finance from a consumer finance company. This isn't a smart investment at all. It is one of my golden rules that you should never purchase a property for above registered valuation.

Registered valuations are exceptionally useful. They don't just prove to a bank that the price you have offered or paid is fair or a good deal. They are also very useful in telling you whether you have got a bargain or not by showing you that the price you've offered is below its real value. A good registered valuer will also be able to tell you what the potential value would be after improvements. You can explain to the valuer the ways you would add value to the property, like renovating the kitchen and bathroom to a medium standard with new fittings, or adding a sleepout, or subdividing, or adding a four-bedroom, two-bathroom brick-and-tile home built to a high specification. The valuer can then give you some estimates on what the property would be worth after the improvements, which can help you to set budgets for the work you're considering undertaking.

For more in-depth uses of registered valuations, see Chapter 23.

Rental appraisals

It is really important to know what your property is worth from a rental perspective. As a condition of giving you finance, your lender will want to know that you meet its debt-servicing criteria. To check on this, the lender will usually expect an estimate of the weekly rental figure, provided by a professional property manager on company letterhead. Choose a property manager experienced in letting properties in the area.

You will want to know what income you would likely get now with the property in its current condition. In addition, I recommend talking your property manager through any proposed renovation works and requesting an appraisal of the estimated weekly rental per week on completion of these works.

30 | Education

Education is the key

If you don't have the right financial mindset and wonder why you are not as good at attracting money as you would like to be, you will need to change the way you think. You need to begin with the right mindset, so read books and consult websites which inspire you and make you feel optimistic for the future. Look for success stories of ordinary people achieving extraordinary results; not just in the financial sphere but also in their sports or careers, from Lance Armstrong to Oprah Winfrey.

If you don't have the technical skills or confidence to succeed in the wonderful world of property investment, then you will need to get others with excellent communication and teaching skills to educate you. Choose people who practise what they preach. I am talking about financial education, which is not taught in school or universities. To learn more about the financial tenets that make you successful, try books and websites which give practical advice for everyday people. *The Millionaire Next Door* and *Rich Dad, Poor Dad* are two books which can help you have a better understanding of how you can change your financial know-how. *Rich Dad, Poor Dad* is one of the books which is most often cited by investors as having inspired them to get started on the track to success.

What separates many property investors is the level of property education they have. I have known cleaners and florists that have more wealth and passive cash flow than doctors and lawyers of a similar age. You can definitely do property investment the wrong way, buying property above its true value in a poorly located area, going massively over budget in your renovations, choosing a poor loan product that costs you thousands of extra dollars, and managing your property poorly. When it comes to being smart about property, you can read books and websites, but ensure they are up to date. Subscribe to newsletters and statistical updates so you are always informed of the latest numbers — this helps you to make the best decisions at the right time. More free tools are available online at this book's website, www.investandprosper.co.nz, and also at www.positivepropertyinvestment.co.nz.

While this book provides some excellent technical knowledge it is by no means an exhaustive guide or guarantee on how to grow a multi-million-dollar portfolio. My mentoring clients use some of the teachings in this book, but they also need a skilled property mentor in a one-on-one situation to tease the information out of them that they don't know. If you want to transform your property knowledge into practical skills and get help choosing the right properties and negotiating the best deal, contact me.

The essential aspect when it comes to education is this: it never stops. If you think that you can be successful by learning what you need to know about your market and then leaving it alone, you're not going to make the most of your investment. You need to become a 'lifelong learner', which sounds pretty geeky, but it turns you into someone who knows what your money is doing, how, why and what the outcomes are likely to be.

Learn all you can, get started, and keep learning as you go. Invest and prosper. Good luck!

31 | Useful websites

There are so many websites that are helpful as you grow and improve your property investment portfolio. These include:

Interest rates

www.mortgagerates.co.nz

www.interest.co.nz/borrowing

www.bnz.co.nz

Property educators (events and mentoring)

www.nzwealthmentor.com

www.davidwhitburn.com

Real estate

www.realestate.co.nz

www.trademeproperty.co.nz

www.investandprosper.co.nz

www.positivepropertyinvestment.
  co.nz

Rental information

www.dbh.govt.nz/landlords-index

www.dbh.govt.nz/market-rent

www.tenancy.govt.nz

Other information

www.tinz.net.nz

www.hnzc.govt.nz

www.statistics.govt.nz

www.rbnz.govt.nz

www.treasury.govt.nz

www.interest.co.nz/calculators

www.kevingreen.co.uk

Glossary

Assignment — a method of transferring an agreement or mortgage from one person to another.

Associated person — natural persons, companies, trusts or partnerships that are associated under the Income Tax Act 2007, or other tax laws.

Beneficiary — a person who is entitled to benefit from a trust, annuity or insurance contract.

Bond — the amount a tenant agrees to pay to their landlord after agreeing to rent a property. This is typically three weeks' rent, but can be up to a maximum of four weeks' rent under the Residential Tenancies Act 1986. The landlord must lodge the bond money with the Department of Building and Housing's Tenancy Services within 23 working days of receiving it. When the tenant leaves the property, the bond is either returned to the tenant, or used to cover unpaid rent or any damage to the property done by the tenant.

Capital expenditure — expenditure that improves a property and is not tax-deductible, eg. replacing a dilapidated concrete tile roof with a brand new longrun steel roof.

Capitalisation rate (cap rate) — the rate commonly used in a commercial property context that measures the ratio between the net operating income produced by an asset and the original price paid to buy the asset (or alternatively its current market value).

Certificate of title (CT) — a record of who owns or has an interest in land in New Zealand. This is held by Land Information New Zealand (LINZ), a Government Department. There are four main categories of title: freehold; leasehold; cross-lease or unit-title; or company share structures (very rare).

Code of compliance certificate — a certificate issued by the local council to state that the property complies with the Building Act.

Conditional agreement — a conditional agreement is a legally binding contract, but the property is not bought or sold until the condition(s) stated in the agreement have been satisfied. These conditions are usually the purchaser's conditions, eg. subject to a due diligence investigation.

Compound interest — when interest earned on a deposit is added to the principal, resulting in the added interest then earning interest itself.

Cross-lease — a form of title where a certain number of persons own a share of the freehold title. The homes built on the land are technically leased from the other landowners, eg. if person A purchased a house in a two-lot development that is a cross-lease title, person A would be the registered proprietor of a long-term lease from both of the owners of the two houses, and an undivided half share in the land and buildings.

Deed of assignment — a formal document in which a person (the assignor) transfers their rights in relation to an agreement to a third party (the assignee). If the assignee doesn't meet their obligations, the original contracting party can sue the assignor to perform these obligations. You don't need to obtain consent to enter into a deed of assignment from the original contracting party.

Deed of nomination — a formal document in which a person nominates another entity they control to complete the obligations under the agreement, eg. you enter into an agreement in your own name and then you nominate your company to be the purchaser and be named on the certificate of title.

Department of Building and Housing (DBH) — a department of the New Zealand government that is responsible for a number of building- and housing-related areas, including Tenancy Services and the Weathertight Homes Resolution Service. Their website is currently located at http://www.dbh.govt.nz

Depreciation — an allowance for the wear and tear over the useful life of items of depreciable property costing over $500, like curtains, appliances and carpets.

Due diligence — the process of doing research on a property to ensure it meets the purchaser's requirements.

Equity — the value of your investments measured by assets less liabilities. In reference to a particular property, the equity you have in it is its value less the loans on it.

Fee simple — a common form of freehold legal title where the owner owns and has unrestricted enjoyment of both the land and buildings. It is the maximum interest a person can have in real estate in New Zealand.

Freehold — a type of title, which has three subsets: fee simple; life estate; and stratum estate. Freehold can also be used as a term to describe when you have fully repaid a loan on a property.

Gearing — the amount of lending on a property or portfolio, often measured as a percentage of debt to assets, ie. an investor with $300,000 of lending on a $400,000 property has 75% gearing.

Gross yield — a rough measure to assist in calculating the return on a property, which is measured by the weekly rental multiplied by the number of weeks per year, divided by the purchase price. Some investors also like to measure their gross yield on their (current) valuation, in which case the calculation is weekly rental x 52/current valuation.

Guarantee — a legal promise to make payment if the borrower defaults on the terms of the loan, usually secured in writing.

Guarantor — the person who promises to make payment in the event the borrower cannot fulfil their obligations under an agreement.

Interest-only loan — a loan agreement where the borrower makes no repayments of principal during the entire loan, but they must repay the whole of the principal on loan maturity. Regular payments of interest accruing on the loan principal will usually be required.

Leasehold — a form of title where one person purchases the right to occupy land for a certain period of time at a specific rent (ground rent). Any improvements (buildings) on the land legally belong to the occupant, but this ownership is subject to the terms of the lease. You can also have leasehold apartments (the land tenure would then be termed stratum in leasehold).

Land Information Memorandum (LIM) report — this is a comprehensive report containing all relevant information that a council or territorial authority knows about a property or section. Councils charge a fee and take some time to send you this information.

Limited liability partnership (LLP) — this is a legal ownership entity that is a special type of partnership with a separate legal personality to its partners. An LLP has one general partner and one limited partner at all times (they cannot be the same person). The general partner is responsible for operations and management of the LLP and the limited liability partner is a passive investor who contributes capital to the LLP and is *only liable to the extent of their capital contributions.*

Look-through company (LTC) — this is a special tax structure for companies that took effect on 1 April 2011. The owners of an LTC are regarded as holding the LTC's assets directly and carrying on the activities of the LTC personally, and can offset tax losses from rental properties against their salaried/waged income subject to compliance with the loss limitation rule. LTCs file IR7 annual income tax returns like partnerships.

Loss attributing qualifying company (LAQC) — a company with very special tax features that permitted tax losses to be attributed against the personal income earned by the company's shareholders, which resulted in paying less tax for most LAQC owners. LAQCs ceased to exist on 31 March 2011.

Low equity fee (LEF) — when borrowing more than a certain percentage of a property's valuation (commonly 80%), a low equity fee is usually payable to the mortgage provider/lender.

LVR (loan to value ratio) — the amount of the loan compared to the value of the property, usually expressed as a percentage, eg. if the property value is $250,000 and you borrow $200,000 then your LVR is 80%. The greater the LVR then the more likely you are to incur the additional costs of an LEF or mortgage repayment insurance.

Market value — the fair market price, or price a willing buyer would pay a willing seller for the property.

Negative gearing — a term used to describe the situation where the income from the property does not cover the interest on the loan.

Net lease — a term used in commercial property to mean that the tenants pay for the outgoings (eg. rates and insurance) on the property, not the landlord.

Net yield — the rate of return an investor gets after subtracting ownership costs (eg. rates, insurance, provision for repairs and maintenance, property management fees and any body corporate fees and levies), divided by the purchase price.

Option — a right to purchase, eg. a lease option which gives the prospective buyer the right to purchase the property before a certain predetermined time, at a predetermined price.

Rating valuation — this is the valuation done by your council or territorial authority. It is generally done on the basis of computer data modelling and does not involve a visit to the property or even a drive-by visit outside the property. Also known as a goverment valuation (GV), council valuation (CV) and occasionally as a rateable valuation. RVs are performed in New Zealand by Quotable Value, the government valuation agency. They contain all the key information for a property, including the capital value, floor area and property age. All properties in a council or territorial local authority area have their RVs done at the same time to calculate the rates levy against each property. This usually happens every three years. These are widely considered to be less accurate than a registered valuation, but nonetheless can provide a comparison between properties in the same area.

Refinancing — the term used when you replace an existing loan with another loan that has different terms.

Registered valuation — this is the professional opinion of the value of property given in a report by a registered valuer.

Sole trader — a term given to classify the structure of a property investor buying property in their own name. They would do accounts in their own name, and have to file an IR3 tax return.

Table loan — when the repayments on a loan are the same for the term of the loan.

Tenancy Services — the area in which the government's Department of Building and Housing administers tenancies, including having a bond centre, 0800 TENANCY phone line, online resource centre for both landlords and tenants, and the tenancy tribunal and phone mediators to resolve tenancy disputes.

Tender — a way of selling and establishing the sale price, whereby the buyers make their best offer in writing for that property by a specified date. The vendor then chooses the best offer.

Title — See certificate of title.

Title search — a process usually conducted by your conveyancer or lawyer when you are doing your due diligence on a property to check:

- that the vendor on the agreement for sale and purchase is legally entitled to sell the property (eg. husband and wife are both on the title, but only one of them has signed the agreement),

- the restrictions or allowances as to the use of the property (covenants, easements etc), and

- any caveats or liens on the title, which will need to be removed before settlement.

Trust — an arrangement whether express (written) or implied that has an equitable obligation binding the trustee to deal with property they have control over in the best interests of other persons, the Beneficiaries.

Unconditional agreement — a legal contract that binds both the purchaser and the vendor to settle on the agreed date at the agreed price. It is either not subject to any conditions being satisfied or those conditions have already been satisfied.

Unit title — a form of ownership of apartments, flats and home units whereby each owner obtains full freehold ownership of his/her particular dwelling and the ancillary units attached to it (such as garage, parking space) as defined by the unit plan, referred to as a strata title. Each unit owner usually becomes a member of a body corporate in respect to administration of all units shown on a particular unit plan.

Yield — the income return of an investment. Yield is usually expressed annually as a percentage based on the investment's cost, or sometimes its current market value. See also Net yield and Gross yield.

Zero-rating — where GST applies to a transaction but it is at the rate of 0%.

Zoning — classification of areas by local government with various rules and regulations relating to building and development in these zones.

Index

accelerated-repayment loans 164–5, 166, 171
accountability for reaching outcomes 70
accounting systems 172–3
accounts
    balance sheet 173
    preparing for year end 178–9
    profit and loss statement 173–8
affirmations 66–7
affordability 59
AMP NZ Office Trust 51
apartments 75, 77, 81, 194, 200, 239–40
    financing 240
    leasehold 135, 138, 198, 240–1
    small 55, 68, 135, 138, 198
arbitrage 35
area – see location
asset protection 117, 118, 119, 120
assets 15, 16–17, 20–1 – see also depreciation
associated persons rules 128–31
Auckland District Law Society (ADLS) 113, 248, 249–52
Auckland Railway Station 240–1
Auckland Trotting Club (Inc) v CIR 177
auctions 242–4
automatic investment 23–4

back-to-back settling 78–9, 80
Bank of New Zealand, TotalMoney loan facility 146–7, 159
banks
    see also term deposit accounts; loans
    analysis of loan applications 138–9
    contributions towards fees 158
    credit checks 137–8
    cross-collateralisation 141

    fees 143, 154, 157, 158
bankruptcy 22
boarding houses 237–8
bonds, tenancy 219, 233–4, 237
Bonus Bonds 34
break fees 158
    tax deductibility 175–6
building 81–2, 84, 85 – see also minor dwellings
Building Act 2004 60, 81, 84
Building Code 81, 84
building consents 60–1, 82, 262
    enforcement 264–5
    fixing works completed without council sign-off 265–6
    older houses 263–4
    options with unconsented works 265–268
building inspection reports 259–60
business interruption insurance 208
buy and hold strategy 13, 67, 68–9, 73–4, 76, 129, 130, 131
buy, build and hold strategy 79, 81
    example 81–2
buying property
    checking it out 113–15
    criteria 105–6
    finding good deals 110–12
    looking for properties 105–12
    ownership structures 116–22
    process (the funnel) 111
    property below value 91, 93, 94–104
    selection process 105, 108–10

capital appreciation 17
capital gain 13, 34, 38–9, 40–1, 48, 73, 76, 252
    look-through companies 117

capital gains tax (CGT) 124, 179, 180–1
capitalisation (cap) rates 54–5
capitalism 16–17
car finance 24, 25, 26
cash flow 13, 16, 34, 37, 63, 71, 73, 87,
    92, 125, 134–5, 211, 240, 252–3
        see also passive income
        positive 12, 38, 42
cash unconditional offers 136
certificate of acceptance (CoA) 266, 268
chattels appraisals 185–6
CIA Debt Recovery Group Limited (CIA)
    219
code of compliance certificates (CCC)
    81, 84, 92, 207, 261, 265, 266
commercial property 51
        compared to residential property
            53, 55–6
        depreciation 191
        financing 53, 54–6
        five types 51–2
        insurance 208
        rent reviews 54
        tenants 52–6
commodities 33, 34, 35, 36
Companies Act 1993 117, 118, 126
compound interest 17–18
conditional contracts 113–14, 136, 252
    – see also sale and purchase agreements
consumer finance 22
Consumer Price Index (CPI) 54
conveyancing 115, 116, 117, 256–7
councils
        see also building consents
        information held by 261–4
        leaky buildings 261
        letter of acceptance 266
        works completed without consent
            263, 264–8
credit cards 15, 22, 24, 25, 144–5
        balance transfers 25–6
credit checks 137–8
        tenants 218, 219
Credit Contracts and Consumer Finance
    Act 2003 (CCCFA) 24, 88, 89

creditor protection 120
cross-collateralisation 141

death duties 180
debt, serviceability/indebtedness 59–60
debt management 14
debt reduction 23, 24–5, 34, 46–7, 59, 60
deed of assignment 79, 80
Department of Building and Housing
    (DBH) 176, 211–12
        bonds 219, 233–4, 237
        disputes between tenant and
            landlord 225–6
        market rental information 222
        mediation service 226–8
        tenancy statistics 109
depreciation 178
        building fit-out and chattel items
            189, 191
        building structure items 189
        building structures 47, 124, 125,
            127–8, 179, 186–90
        chattels appraisals 185–6
        claiming for a part-year 184
        commercial property 191
        depreciable property 182–3, 189,
            191
        disposal of fixed assets 184–5
        loading on economic depreciation
            rates 190
        methods 183
        pooling assets 190–1
development – see property development
diminishing value depreciation method
    183
disposable income 14, 15, 59, 60
dividends 16, 49
divorce
        sales 99
        trust property treated as
            individual 121
due diligence 78, 80, 91, 113–15, 258–69
        clause in sale and purchase
            agreements 252–6
        tenants 211, 218–19

earthquakes, claiming insurance after
207–9
economic cycles 19, 33, 34, 45, 50, 52, 54,
89, 138, 148, 156–7, 200
education, financial 22–3, 270–1
employer superannuation contribution tax
(ESCT) 27
equity 13, 20, 34, 37, 42–3, 44, 50, 71,
106, 110, 134–5, 136, 240, 252–3
buying below value 94
in own home 43, 140–1
investment strategies 73, 74, 75,
79, 83, 84, 85, 86, 87, 90,
91, 92, 93
estate duties 180
estate sales 100
expenses, tax-deductible 174–8

family home 15, 16, 34–5
family trusts 35
fees
break, contribution towards 158
legal and valuation, contribution
towards 158
paying less 157
rollover 154
waivers 143
finance companies 18–19, 24–5, 45
financial education 22–3, 270–1
financial planners and advisors 19
fixed rate loans 142, 149–51, 152
fees 157
interest-averaging strategy 153–5,
156
pros and cons 151
fixed-term tenancies 215–16, 229, 230,
236
terminating 231, 233, 237
floating rate loans 123, 142, 148–9, 150,
152, 160
interest-averaging strategy 153–5,
156
pros and cons 151
forestry investment 33, 42

gazumping 256–7
goal setting – see outcome design
global influences on New Zealand
property market 62
goods and services tax (GST) 46, 86,
124, 181, 250
grand-slamming 90–3
green investment housing 85

home loans – see loans
home office 167
hospitality industry property 52
house prices 63, 180–1
and credit growth 61–2
housing sales volumes 62–3
hyper-inflation 156

iAdvise service 107, 114
income
see also disposable income; passive
income; rental income;
retirement income
recording 174
target 67–8
Income Tax Act 2007 117, 128, 129,
175, 182
industrial property
inflation 11, 16, 33, 34, 48, 156
Inland Revenue Department 172–3, 175,
176, 177, 185, 186–7, 191
insurance 19, 115, 138, 204–5
business interruption 208
claiming after an earthquake
207–9
contents 206, 207
duties of disclosure and good faith
204, 205, 263
importance of 206–7
mortgage 42, 157
reasons for claims being denied
209
structures without consents 263
tips for 109
interest, compound 17–18
interest-only loans 47, 163–4, 171

compared to principal-and-
interest loans 168–70
interest-rate averaging strategy 152,
153–7
interest rates
see also fixed-rate loans; floating
rate loans
calculating 114
charged by finance companies
24–5
credit cards 24, 25
debts 24
indicator for property cycle
58–9
information on 156–7
investments 16
negotiating 142–3
websites 109
internal rate of return (IRR) 43–4
internet 108–10, 217, 272
investment options 32, 49

KiwiSaver 23–4, 26–31
2011 Budget changes 27–8
age of contributors 30–1
first home subsidy 28–9

Land Information Memorandum (LIM)
report 114, 115, 252, 253, 254, 261,
26, 266, 268
land tax 124, 129, 131
land values 19, 47
landlords
see also tenants
agents 236
insurance 207
obligations 212, 236–7
property inspections 222–3,
233–4
selling a tenanted property
229–30
Landonline 256
lawyers 114, 115, 256–7
conveyancing 115, 116, 117,
256–7

fees 55, 80, 101, 116, 117, 121,
158
mobile 256
Lawyers and Conveyancers Act 2006 256
leaky buildings 240, 261, 266–7
perception of 84
lease options 87–90
leasehold properties 55, 260
apartments 135, 138, 198,
240–1
leases 67
5 + 5 + 5 54
legal fees 55, 80, 101, 116, 117, 121, 158
letter drops 112
leverage 33, 40–6, 132, 134, 152
liabilities 20–1
LIM (Land Information Memorandum)
report 114, 115, 252, 253, 254, 261,
26, 266, 268
limited liability companies 118, 128
limited liability partnerships (LLP) 119
liquidity 61–2
loan fees 24, 25, 42
loan-to-value ratio (LVR) 43, 45, 132,
135, 141
loans 35, 41, 132–4
see also consumer finance; fixed
rate loans; floating rate loans;
interest rates; leverage
applications 138–9, 157
borrowing strategy 134–5
commercial property 53, 54–5
defaulting on payments 239
expiry statistics 150
length 167–8
margin loan accounts 42, 45
own home 26, 30, 32, 167, 170
paying off v saving 26, 30
personal 22
pre-approval 135–6, 137
residential property 53, 56, 132
rollover fees 154
spreading borrowings among
different lenders 141–3
structure 167–71

TotalMoney loans 146–7
types 159–66
location 106–7
becoming an area specialist 110
commercial property 52, 54
helpful software 107
important factors 107–8
property investment strategy 68
look-through companies (LTC) 117–18,
124, 126–7, 128, 130
example 128
loss limitation rule 127, 180
loss attributing qualifying companies
122, 123, 124, 126, 127–8

managed funds 26, 33, 36, 49
margin loan accounts 42, 45
measurement, achievement of outcomes
69
mediation, landlord and tenant 226–8
mentoring 14, 49, 70, 271
mileage allowance 175
minor dwellings 38, 46, 75, 77, 81,
86–7, 91, 92, 93, 253
money 50
mortgage brokers 142
mortgage insurance 42, 157
mortgagee sales 100, 134, 230
mortgages – see loans
multi-income property 35, 46, 67, 74,
75, 76–7, 81, 85
insurance 210

needs, distinguished from wants 22
neighbours 115
net worth 20–2
New Zealand Property Investors'
Federation 124, 125, 176, 219

offices, investment in 51
official cash rate (OCR) 148–9
offsetting accounts/loans 146–7, 159–60,
166
offshore property ownership structures
122

option to purchase agreements 87, 103–4
outcome design 65, 66–9, 71–2
assistance in setting 71
successful implementation 69–70
ownership structures 116–22

partnerships 118–19, 128
passive income 14, 16, 48–50, 67, 71,
92, 211
periodic tenancies 214, 215, 229, 236
terminating 230–1, 233, 237
pooling (offsetting) accounts/loans
146–7, 159–60, 166
population
ageing 19–20
growth/migration 58, 61, 181
positive cash flow 12, 38, 42
presentation of properties for sale 97–8
principal-and-interest loans 46–7, 161–2,
166, 171
compared to interest-only loans
168–70
private sales 96–7, 111–12
private sector credit (PSC) 61–2
property cycles 19, 45–6, 58, 59, 62–3,
128, 131, 141, 179, 180–1, 200, 240
property development 13, 35–6, 73,
74–5, 76, 79, 85–7 – see also building;
property investment; renovations;
subdivision development
property files, council 261–2, 266, 268
property inspection reports, rental
property 213–14, 223, 233
property inspections, rental property
222–3, 233–4
Property Institute of New Zealand 198
property investment
see also buying property;
commercial property; loans;
multi-income property;
ownership structures;
property market; risks of
investment
advantages 33–4
managing 36

websites 110
property investment strategies 73, 93
    see also buy and hold strategy;
        buy, build and hold strategy;
        property trading
    classic long-term 73–4
    residential 76–93
    to achieve target income 67–8
property investor register notice (PIR)
    262–3
property investors 13
Property IQ iAdvise service 107, 114
Property Law Act 2007 134
property management
    boarding houses 237–8
    bonds 219, 233–4
    commercial property 52–4
    Department of Building and
        Housing statistics 109
    good 220
    impact of capital gains tax 181
    impact of ring-fencing of tax
        losses 179–80
    rent arrears 223–5, 228
    rent payments 219–20
    residential property 19, 24, 36,
        56, 61, 69, 74, 106, 107,
        211–38
    retaliatory notice 231
    selling a tenanted property
        229–30
    and valuations 201–2
    viewings of property 218
property market 34–5, 38–9, 40, 96
    see also leverage; property values
    factors influencing 57–64
property managers, rental property
    216–17, 220–1
property trading 13, 33, 46, 67, 74–6,
    78–9, 129
    see also buy, build and hold
        strategy
    diagram 80
property trusts – *see* trusts
property values – *see* land values; property
    market
PropertyGuru 107
purchase agreements – *see* sale and
    purchase agreements

Quotable Value 59, 277
    eValuer tool 140, 253

rating information 109
real estate agents 79, 110, 248, 255
    buyer-friendly 102–3
Real Estate Agents Act 2008 74, 80, 103
Real Estate Institute of New Zealand
    (REINZ) 79
        standard agreement form 113,
            248, 249–52
Real Estate Investar software 107
reducing-balance loans 165–6, 171
regenerating properties – *see* property
    development
renovations 78, 79, 80, 82–4, 91, 93
    best areas to focus on 194–5
    budgeting and project planning
        193
    overcapitalisation 193–4, 196,
        203
    risks 194, 241
    types of 192
    and valuations 203
rent
    14-consecutive-day letter 223–5,
        228
    arrears 223–4, 228
    increasing 222, 234–5
    market rents 211, 215, 216, 217,
        221–2
    payments 219–20
    reviews 54, 234–5
rent-to-buy home ownership 87–90
rental accommodation, supply 60, 180,
    181
rental income 13, 16–17, 33, 35, 36,
    37–8, 48, 49
    analysis, loan applications 138
    appraisal before buying property

114, 269
growth in 61, 63, 73–4, 76
impact of capital gains tax 181
impact of depreciation changes
128
losses 117
minor dwellings 81, 87
new buildings 79
recording 174
ring-fencing of tax losses 179–80
repairs and maintenance
buying property in need of 98–9
rental properties 36, 232
tax deductibility 176–7
residential property, compared to
commercial property 53, 55–6
Residential Tenancies Act 1986 212,
215–16, 222, 223, 225, 228, 229,
232
Residential Tenancies Amendment Act
2010 212, 215, 236–8
Resource Management Act 1991 60
retail property 52
retirement income 15–16, 19–20, 50
see also KiwiSaver; superannuation
revolving credit accounts/loans 144–5,
152, 160–1, 166
how to use effectively 145–6
pros and cons 146
rewards, on achieving milestones 70
risks of investment
finance companies 18–19
high risk 33
impact of natural and financial
disasters 34
low risk 33
medium to high risk 33
minimising 239–44
property investment 19, 75, 78
special-risk properties 135, 138,
198, 239–41
RPNZ 107, 112, 198
rule of 72 39–40
rural property 52

sale and purchase agreements 248
conditional 113–14, 136, 252
due diligence clause 252–6
requirements 249
special clauses 256
standard form 113, 249–52
saving 16–20, 22, 48, 50
automatic 23–4
compared to debt reduction
24–5
compared to paying off home
loan 26, 30
selecting property 105, 108–10
serviceability/indebtedness 59–60
settlements
back-to-back 78–9, 80
long-term 103
shares 16, 27, 33, 34, 35, 36, 42, 49
leverage on 45
sole traders 117, 128
spending habits 21, 22, 48
straight line depreciation method 183
subdividing land and building on it 74
subdivision development 75, 76, 85
succession planning 120
superannuation 15, 19–20
SWIFT telephone mediation 226, 227

table loans – *see* principal-and-interest
loans
tax
see also depreciation
associated persons rules 128–31
break fees 175–6
deductible expenses 174–8
employer superannuation
contribution tax (ESCT) 27
goods and services tax (GST) 46,
86, 124, 181, 250
interest 175
interest on own home 167
land 124, 129, 131
long-term strategies 74
look-through companies 117,
118, 124, 126–7, 128, 130

loss attributing qualifying
    companies 122, 123, 124,
    126, 127–8, 130
property trading 75
selling property 86
trusts 120, 121–2
tax deeds and liens, United States 245–7
tax losses, ring-fencing 179–80
tax rebates 47, 71
Tax Working Group 123–5, 182–3
tenancy agreements 87, 212–16
    'address for service' 214, 236
    boarding houses 237–8
    property inspection reports
        213–14
Tenancy Information New Zealand
    (TINZ) 219
Tenancy Tribunal 222, 223, 226, 228,
    231, 234, 238
tenancy types
    fixed-term 215–16, 229, 230,
        231, 233, 236, 237
    periodic 214, 215, 229, 230–1,
        233, 236, 237
    service 215
tenants
    see also landlords; property
        management; vacancy rates
    credit checks 218, 219
    disputes with 225–6
    ending tenancy 229–35
    finding 216–19
    obligations 212, 232–3, 236–7
term deposit accounts 11, 17, 33, 34, 35,
    36, 49, 77
title searches 260
TradeMe
    property sales 108–9
    rentals 217, 221, 222
trusts 36, 119–22, 127, 129, 130

unauthorised works applications 267–8
United States tax deeds and liens 245–7

vacancy rates
    commercial property 51, 52, 54
    residential property 53, 56, 60,
        69, 106, 176, 240
valuations 197
    commercial property 51, 54–5
    council 199
    fees 158
    historical abuse of 200
    QV eValuer tool 140, 253
    registered 197–8, 199, 200, 253,
        268, 269–70
    top 10 ways to achieve a high
        valuation 201–3
    use of 199–200
Valuers' Registration Board (VRB) 198
Valuit Asset Appraisals 185–6
vendor warranty clauses 256
vendors
    circumstances leading to property
        sale below value 100–1
    overly emotional 101–2
vision boards 66

wealth 20–3, 45, 48–50
websites 108–10, 217, 272
wraps 89

Acknowledgements

Compiling this book has taken me a long time. I have very much enjoyed writing it as I love to share knowledge. However, I acknowledge that this has been a team effort and has come at a cost to several people, so I would like to thank my wonderful wife Bridget for her patience, understanding, property renovation skills and proof-reading. Thanks to my baby girl Emily and my little boy Liam, who have been amazing in 'helping' me type this book on my laptop. They motivated and inspired me. I have lost countless hours of quality time with them due to my writing, a situation which has changed now this book has been completed.

I would like to thank Rene McLean for his assistance in compiling the valuations chapter, as well as Stuart Shutt of Investor Homes for his permission to use one of his company's floor plans, and the Forms and Precedents Committee of the Auckland District Law Society who have kindly allowed me to use and dissect their standard form Agreement for Sale and Purchase 8th edition (4) for residential property sales. Thank you to Troy Churton and the team at the Department of Building and Housing for reviewing the property management chapter and letting me use DBH information and resources; I value the relationship we have in my capacity as president of the Auckland Property Investors' Association.

Special thanks need to be reserved for a number of people in the BNZ, particularly to Sandy Richardson and Briar Douglas for the enormous amount of time and commitment they have spent with their review, comments and edits of this book, especially in relation to the finance chapters. Thank you to Kaine Lasenby and Maryana Sydoruk for their excellent assistance in compiling the source data that has contributed to most of the graphs and charts in this book. I appreciate all of BNZ's support.

A massive thank you to Amy Hamilton-Chadwick for her editing and rewriting of the first cut of this book, David Leon for writing the goal-setting chapter, my mother Alison Whitburn for her thorough proof-reading and edits, and thanks to Tracey Wogan, Margaret Sinclair and the team at Random House for their dedication and professionalism in achieving what I hope will be a great resource to New Zealand property investors.

Meet Anna and James

Since buying their first home more than a decade ago, they've seen the New Zealand real estate market go through some ups and downs.

Last year the youngest of their two boys started high school and Anna returned to full time work. The extra income from her salary has got them thinking about investment options.

Like many New Zealanders, Anna and James are looking for a consistent source of income to give them some freedom in the future. When they eventually retire, they'd like something over and above what their weekly superannuation payments will provide.

Since they already have some experience with the real estate market, Anna and James are keen to investigate property investment. Their banker at BNZ suggests they speak with a specialist from the Residential Property Investment team.

Taking the first step

Anna and James are put in touch with the team and speak to John[1]. They soon discover that not only can he help with the financial aspects of buying an investment property, he's also got a few investment properties of his own.

John explains that predicted levels of immigration growth mean around 236,000 additional rental homes will be needed before 2016[2]. In Auckland alone it's anticipated that almost 10,000 extra rental properties will be needed each year for the next 10 years – a rate far above the demand for the past 10 years.

After discussing Anna and James' financial goals, John offers a couple of options. The first is an interest only home loan, allowing up to ten years with no payment on the principal. This will allow Anna and James to focus on repaying the remaining balance on their own home. An interest only loan could be combined with BNZ's award winning TotalMoney home loan. This home loan will allow them to reduce their interest costs using the funds in their TotalMoney accounts.

The only bank with a dedicated Residential Property Investment Team.[3]

Any bank in the country may have a home loan expert, but only at BNZ will you find a dedicated Residential Property Investment team. This is a group of specialists who live and breathe residential investment property. They're on call Monday – Friday from 8.30am – 7pm to help you with any residential investment decisions. They offer:

> Loans up to $1 million, approvals within 24 hours
> Up to ten years interest only
> Tailored solutions to suit your portfolio

Because having the right support is so important, our specialists can guide you in structuring your portfolio finances, securing a competitive home loan, getting to grips with current market activity, as well as insuring your property.

Our Residential Property Investment team works with every type of residential investor. So whether you're thinking about investing in property for the first time, or the sixth, start by giving us a call on 0800 269 009.

The right home loan

Something Anna and James hadn't even considered was the possibility of an offset home loan like BNZ TotalMoney.

While their boys were growing up, they tried to put a little away each fortnight in an account called Rainy Days & Education. In the next few years, these savings will provide for the boys' university fees. They also have their combined salaries going through their everyday account.

After comparing home loan options, John recommends TotalMoney. This will allow them to have a separate account for their new rental property, then combine this with their TotalMoney everyday and savings accounts, so all of their funds are working together to offset their loan amount to reduce the interest they pay on their home loan.

Get mortgage-free faster with TotalMoney.[4]

With this type of floating home loan, you can offset the balances of your transaction and savings accounts against your home loan balance, reducing the interest you pay on your home loan. This option is more likely to appeal to investors with a focus on debt-reduction.

Many BNZ customers have reduced their effective interest rate this way. For example, you might have a loan of $150,000 and $5,000 in your TotalMoney transaction and savings accounts. For the purposes of calculating interest, the total in these accounts would be subtracted from the total amount owing, and the remaining balance is what you pay interest on.

So if the home loan interest rate in this example was 5.59% per annum, the effective interest rate would actually be 5.40% per annum. If the total amount in your combined TotalMoney accounts was the sames as the amount owing, you wouldn't pay any interest on your home loan, for as long as it remains like this.

To find out more about BNZ TotalMoney, call us on 0800 269 009 or visit us at bnz.co.nz/totalmoney

4. Account opening and lending criteria apply. Establishment or redocumentation fees apply. A Low Equity or Low Doc interest rate may apply. Not for business purposes. Full details, TotalMoney terms and conditions and BNZ's current Disclosure Statement and Qualifying Financial Entity Disclosure Statement may be obtained free of charge from any store or www.bnz.co.nz. All information current as at 7/07/11.

The proper insurance

Quite a few years ago Anna and James were tenants themselves. Remembering their flatting days (and some of the more unpredictable individuals they've lived with) has made them apprehensive about the security of their investment.

John introduces them to PremierCare with landlord benefits, a type of insurance cover designed to provide special benefits to rental property owners. He explains to them it includes cover for intentional damage caused by tenants, and even provides cover against loss of rent if a tenant moves out unexpectedly.

As it happens, it's the very same insurance cover John chooses for the properties in his own investment portfolio.

Home Insurance with landlord benefits.[5]

There are plenty of things that might happen, but with the right insurance product, you can be confident your investment will be protected.

PremierCare home insurance with landlord benefits has been created for property investors such as loss of rent if your property is tenanted but it can't be lived in due to an accidental event such as a fire or even an earthquake.

By purchasing additional cover you'll also be protected against any deliberate damage or vandalism to your property or possessions. In most cases, your chattels are covered for actual value if they're lost, stolen or broken. Should a tenant be evicted, or suddenly leave without paying rent, your rental income may also be protected.

To find out more about BNZ PremierCare with landlord benefits, call us on 0800 269 009.

Bank of New Zealand

Ready to take the first step?

The hardest thing can be making the decision to get started. So if like Anna and James, you're ready to take the first step, here is a quick list of things to think about before our first meeting.

What do you hope to achieve through property investment?

_____

_____

_____

How does property investment fit in with your other life goals?

_____

_____

_____

	Y	N
Do you want to partly replace your household income through property investment?	☐	☐
Are you familiar with the current property market?	☐	☐
Are you looking for a property that's ready to rent out right now?	☐	☐
Do you like the idea of buying properties and renovating them to create profit?	☐	☐

...PTO

Bank of New Zealand

		Y	N
Are you interested in creating income by buying, doing up and selling properties in a short period of time?		☐	☐
Would you like to develop or build properties?		☐	☐

Do you have:

	Y	N
Equity in existing property?	☐	☐
Cash deposit?	☐	☐

Are you interested in investing in a property in the next?

3 months ☐   6 months ☐   12 months ☐

	Y	N
Would you like access to a team of residential property investment banking specialists who can support you through all of the financial steps when buying an investment property?	☐	☐
Would you like to speak with a property investment mentor who can help accelerate the process and have one-on-one support in the location you choose to invest in?	☐	☐

If property investment appeals to you, you can find more information and additional resources, including an online version of this checklist at www.bnz.co.nz/rentalproperty.

To discuss your options, talk with BNZ's Residential Property Investment team today on 0800 269 009, visit your nearest BNZ store, or to speak directly with a Property Investment Mentor call (09) 302 2799.

NZ Wealth Mentor
nzwealthmentor.com